THE ART OF
PREACHING
OLD TESTAMENT
NARRATIVE

THE ART OF
PREACHING
OLD TESTAMENT
NARRATIVE

Steven D. Mathewson

Baker Academic
A Division of Baker Book House Co
Grand Rapids, Michigan 49516

paternoster

© 2002 by Steven D. Mathewson

Published by Baker Academic
a division of Baker Book House Company
P.O. Box 6287, Grand Rapids, MI 49516–6287

and

Paternoster Press, an imprint of Paternoster Publishing
P.O. Box 300, Carlisle, Cumbria, CA3 0QS, UK
www.paternoster-publishing.com

Printed in the United States of America

Library of Congress Cataloging-in-Publication Data

Mathewson, Steven D., 1961–
  The art of preaching Old Testament narrative / Steven D. Mathewson.
      p.   cm.
  Includes bibliographical references and indexes.
  ISBN 0-8010-2296-7
  1. Bible. O.T.—Homiletical use. 2. Bible. O.T.—Sermons. I. Title.
BS1191.5 .M38   2002
251—dc21   2001035942

British Library Cataloguing in Publication Data
A catalogue record for this book is available from the British Library

ISBN 1-84227-138-5

For information about Baker Academic, visit our web site:
www.bakeracademic.com

To my wife,
Priscilla,
whose love for Jesus has stirred my own devotion to him
and whose love for me still fills up my senses

And to my parents,
Maynard and Ruth Mathewson,
whose insistence that "God is still good"
during their respective struggles with cancer
has strengthened my trust in him

Contents

❀ ❀ ❀ ❀ ❀

Figures and Tables

✵ ✵ ✵ ✵ ✵

Figures

Tables

FOREWORD

❋ ❋ ❋ ❋ ❋

My grandmother lived in Northern Ireland, and I visited her once when I was a lad about eight years old. When I met her, she was wrinkled, had snowy white hair, and stooped a bit under the weight of her years. I felt I knew my grandmother. She was that thin old lady who gave me cookies and told me how much I resembled my grandfather who had died many years ago.

Recently, I visited Ireland again and talked with cousins who knew my grandmother far better than I. They pulled out faded yellow photographs of grandma when she was a girl and later when she was first married. They shared their memories based on knowing her much longer than I did. I came away from that second visit wondering if I ever really knew my grandmother at all.

For many modern readers, the Old Testament narratives resemble my memories of my grandmother. We know them, but then again we hardly know them at all. Some of us grew up hearing these stories, and they form part of our memory bank. We listened to them at home curled up in a parent's lap, or we saw them pasted on flannelgraph boards in Sunday school, our short legs dangling from the big chairs. We identified with David, the brash teenager with slingshot in hand, taking on Goliath, who resembled the bully at our grade school. We smirked at the neighbors who mocked Noah and his boys for building a boat miles from the nearest lake because we knew how the story came out, and we decided the moral was not to laugh at someone doing something strange because you might need them later on if you were drowning in a flood. We pictured Moses and Aaron battling Pharaoh much like the Lone Ranger and Tonto standing up against the bad guys, or we admired Daniel taming the lions in their den at the zoo. We knew these stories well, but we may not have known them at all! Because we thought of them as simple little stories, we missed how thick they were with meaning.

In recent years, many literary critics, both Christian and Jewish, have also read the stories again for the first time. Instead of regarding the narratives as cadavers to be dissected and "demythologized," they began to approach them for what they were—sophisticated literature of great significance and splendid power.

Because narrative makes up the dominant genre of the Old Testament, biblical preachers need to revisit those narratives. As adults, we can look at the stories with fresh eyes, and we can develop an appreciation for the skill of the authors who composed them. They were not only corking good storytellers, but they were also brilliant theologians who taught their readers about God through stories. We can read these old, old stories in a new way and sense how much they speak to the condition of modern hearers. More than that, we can see God through them.

One of the strongest reasons for a serious and fresh study of Old Testament narratives is reflected in the sad history of what happens when we misread them, read them poorly, or read them to prove a point outside the purpose of the biblical storyteller. In fact, the more committed we are to the authority of Scripture, the more dangerous it is to read the narratives incorrectly. There is no greater abuse of the Bible than to proclaim in God's name what God is not saying. God commands us not to bear false witness.

In this book, Steve Mathewson helps us to read Old Testament narratives perceptively. As you study them, you will realize they are not quaint tales crafted to teach children simple moral lessons. They are great literature, every bit as powerful as Homer, Milton, Shakespeare, or Hemingway. And as God-breathed literature, they speak to the entire person. I commend Steve Mathewson as a thoughtful guide to help us get a handle on the great stories of the Bible. I also commend him as a preacher who provides some very workable leads on how to effectively communicate these stories to modern listeners.

Haddon W. Robinson

PREFACE

I remember my fledgling attempt to preach through an Old Testament narrative book. In 1988, my second year of pastoral ministry, I decided to take my congregation (read: victims) through 1 and 2 Samuel. Coincidentally, I was reading John Steinbeck's novel *East of Eden*. A scene in *East of Eden* forced me to admit my ineptness at preaching the stories of the Old Testament. Three men are sitting at a table and discussing the Cain-Abel story in Genesis 4. Lee, Adam Trask's pig-tailed Chinese cook, pinpoints the genius of Hebrew narrative during the exchange with Adam and a neighbor, Samuel Hamilton. Lee argues, "No story has power, nor will it last, unless we feel in ourselves that it is true and true of us."[1] He concludes, "A great and lasting story is about everyone or it will not last. The strange and foreign is not interesting—only the deeply personal and familiar."[2]

I thought about the sermon I preached the previous Sunday from 1 Samuel 7. Did people leave with a sense that the story was about them? I had to admit they probably did not. A lady approached me after the worship service and asked for point number three. She didn't get it all written down when she took notes. "Uh, point number three was 'The Resulting Prosperity of God's People' from verses twelve through seventeen," I said.

I had preached a sermon chock-full of exegetical insights and laced with historical-cultural data. I even pressed it into a neat analytical outline. But my sermon did not do justice to the purpose of Old Testament stories: to lure people into real-life dramas where they run smack into God's agenda and his assessment of their lives.

---

1. John Steinbeck, *East of Eden* (New York: Viking, 1952), 268.
2. Ibid., 270.

This experience triggered the quest to raise my level of preaching in Old Testament narrative texts. At this point in my quest I want to assist others. In this volume, my purpose is to help preachers excel at preaching Old Testament narrative texts. It's time for preachers to raise the bar and clear a higher standard when they preach stories from Genesis or 1 Samuel. For preachers whose preaching diet does not yet include Old Testament stories, this volume may encourage them to take a leap of faith over the bar.

You deserve to know a little bit about my journey in studying and preaching Old Testament stories. This will help you decide if you want me to serve as a mentor. My journey began in the spring of 1986 when I served as a teaching assistant in Hebrew grammar and exegesis to Dr. Ronald B. Allen at Western Conservative Baptist Seminary. My esteemed professor asked me to fill in for him in his introductory Hebrew exegesis class and teach the lecture on "Exegesis in Hebrew Narrative Literature." This opportunity forced me to start thinking through a methodology for interpreting Old Testament narrative literature. I devoured Robert Alter's book *The Art of Biblical Narrative*, and the journey gained momentum. That same spring I completed a master's thesis on an Old Testament narrative text—Genesis 38.

Two years later, my first stab at preaching through an Old Testament narrative took place as I described it above. My struggles in preaching 1 Samuel propelled me further in my quest to learn how to preach Old Testament narratives effectively. I listened to masters like Haddon Robinson, Donald Sunukjian, and Paul Borden. I ordered their tapes and traveled to listen to them in person. I even had the nerve to write, e-mail, and phone them for input. I cringe when I remember the sermon manuscripts from my 1 Samuel series that I sent to Paul Borden to solicit his input.

In recent years, I've devoured every article and book I could find on interpreting and preaching Old Testament narratives. I've also devoted a large chunk of my doctoral studies at Gordon-Conwell Theological Seminary to preaching Old Testament narrative literature. Furthermore, as a tape screener for the *Preaching Today* audiotape series, I've listened to and evaluated several sermons from Old Testament narrative texts.

Most important, I've tried to practice what I preach. Or to be more precise, I've tried to preach what I practice. Over the last thirteen years of pastoral ministry, I've preached through Genesis, Exodus, 1 and 2 Samuel, Joshua, Judges, Ruth, Esther, and Nehemiah. I've also prepared sermons from individual texts in every other narrative book in the Old Testament.

Of course, I still have much to learn. I am confident I will be learning how to preach Old Testament stories until the day I die. But I have reached a point in my journey where I feel compelled to help other preachers who struggle with the proclamation of Old Testament narrative texts. I am attempting to write the book I needed when I first started. I have often wished that someone else would write the book I need, for though I work hard in the Hebrew Bible, I do not feel worthy to carry the armor of first-class Hebrew scholars. Likewise, I do not envision myself in the starting lineup with the Michael Jordans of modern preaching—both preachers and teachers of preachers. But in the sovereignty of God, he has given me abilities and interests in two fields: Old Testament exegesis and homiletics. With a foot in both disciplines and armed with the experiences I have described, I am ready to begin my task.

This volume consists of three parts. Part 1 will take you from text to concept—what we call the *hermeneutical* side of the task. It will teach you a method for studying Old Testament narrative texts. You can apply this method whether or not you can read biblical Hebrew. Then, part 2 will take you from concept to sermon—what we call the *homiletical* side of the task. This part of the book will help you take the raw exegetical material and craft a sermon that bristles with accuracy, clarity, interest, and relevance. Part 3 offers some model sermon manuscripts from the masters of the craft: Paul Borden, Alice Matthews, Don Sunukjian, and Haddon Robinson. I have also included a sermon manuscript of my own. These manuscripts on Old Testament narrative texts will show you how to apply the concepts described in this volume. An analysis of the sermon and an interview with the preacher accompanies each manuscript.

Finally, here's a personal word to my readers. I write as an evangelical pastor to other evangelical pastors who have the amazing privilege and awesome responsibility of proclaiming the Word of God to their congregations week after week. You are my heroes. We're in the trenches together, and I pray that I can help you. This means that I also write to pastors-in-training who are learning to preach. What a privilege to help shape a new generation of preachers. I hope I can help you get your hermeneutical and homiletical acts together in Old Testament stories a lot more quickly than I did. I also write with appreciation to those readers—men and women—who communicate the Word of God in a variety of settings, including Sunday School classes, small group Bible studies, and men's and women's retreats. The church needs you to exercise your teaching gift well. I hope this volume helps you communicate Old Testament stories effectively.

Above all, I write for the glory of God, the central character in the grand story of redemption. I am amazed at what he has provided for me through Jesus Christ. To God be the glory forever and ever.

ACKNOWLEDGMENTS

❁ ❁ ❁ ❁ ❁

A section of acknowledgments resembles the credits that roll at the end of a movie and don't seem terribly important to the viewer. As the reader, you can afford to skip these acknowledgments. As the writer, I cannot. I deeply appreciate the people who helped me turn my vision for this book into a reality.

It's easy to know where to start. I thank my remarkable wife, Priscilla, for her encouragement, support, and sacrifice. She never once complained to me about my preoccupation with this project. She has impacted my life with her love for Jesus Christ as well as her love for me. Priscilla is the love of my life and the joy of my heart. I also thank my dear children, Erin, Anna, Benjamin, and Luke, for their love, patience, and support. I hope my growth in proclaiming the stories of the Old Testament will contribute to their growth in the faith.

I am grateful to Haddon Robinson for his interest in this project, as well as his input. Doing doctoral work in preaching under Haddon will rank as one of the greatest privileges of my life. I am a better man for God because of the time spent with such a brilliant, godly mentor.

I thank Paul Borden, Don Sunukjian, Alice Mathews, and Haddon Robinson for graciously consenting to share their sermon manuscripts with me. God's Spirit used each sermon to impact me personally as well as professionally.

The elders and congregation of Dry Creek Bible Church have been wonderful. No one has ever complained to me about the time I have devoted to this project. The elders have provided me with time to research and write, and they shared my vision of how this endeavor might enrich other pastors. It's an honor to serve with elders like Bryan Brucks, Curt Halvorson, and Bill Skinner.

I deeply appreciate the labor of love performed by my secretary, Jan Halvorson, in transcribing sermon tapes, typing other data, making reams of photocopies, and helping at every turn in the process.

Several people went out of their way to help me track down hard-to-find sources: Claudia Glover, a librarian at Denver Seminary; Meredith Kline and his staff at the Goddard Library at Gordon-Conwell Theological Seminary; and Robert Stanbery, a student at Dallas Theological Seminary.

John Sailhamer provided helpful insight regarding the textlinguistic sections of this book. Also, Warren Wiersbe offered valuable suggestions as well as enthusiastic support. In addition to reading the manuscript, David Wyrtzen has prayed for me and encouraged me to keep writing in this field.

I also thank my friend Jerry Vreeland for his exacting comments on an earlier paper I published on preaching Old Testament narrative literature. Jerry introduced me to the field of textlinguistic studies in Hebrew narrative.

Also, Brian Larson of *Preaching Today* took an interest in this project and dialogued several times about the concepts I have presented in the book. He steered me to a couple of excellent sources.

I am grateful to Knute Larson for inviting me to The Chapel in Akron, Ohio, to share this material at a pastors' seminar. One of the attendees, Tim Walton, turned out to be a doctoral student from the Free University in Amsterdam—an important center for textlinguistic studies in the Hebrew Bible. He affirmed my work and introduced me to a couple of helpful new Hebrew grammars. Thanks, Tim.

Each of my brothers supplied input. David Mathewson and Mark Mathewson both recommended key books and interacted with ideas in this book. Kevin Mathewson shared with me the fine work he has done in preaching first-person sermons from Old Testament narrative texts.

The older I get, the more I value the close friends God has given to me. Several contributed significantly to my efforts. David Hansen has supported this project from its outset. We often discussed its contents while fly-fishing together or plodding through the Hebrew text of Judges. Dave Goetz and I forged a friendship in college that has flourished to this day. He interacted with me on several ideas in the thesis, and he has helped me grow as a writer and as a man of God. Eric and Lisa Pierson have shown a real interest in this project, have prayed faithfully, and most of all, have enriched my wife and me with their incredible friendship.

Furthermore, I thank Amy Nemecek and Brian Bolger of Baker Academic for their fine editorial work, and I am grateful to Paula Gibson for the care she took in designing the cover.

Last, but hardly least, I thank my parents, Maynard and Ruth Mathewson, for modeling faithful and effective service of Christ through the thick and thin of pastoral ministry. The preacher who has had the greatest impact on my life is my father. This book has its roots in his commitment to preach the Word of God "in season and out of season."

1

❀ ❀ ❀ ❀ ❀

THE CHALLENGE
OF PREACHING
OLD TESTAMENT NARRATIVES

❀ ❀ ❀ ❀ ❀

People crave stories. Just watch people sitting in an airline terminal waiting to catch a flight. Several are reading novels by Tom Clancy, John Grisham, or Mary Higgins Clark. Some are devouring the latest scoop in *People* magazine or *Sports Illustrated*. Many who are not reading stories are telling them or listening to them.

A thirty-something mom tells two friends about a run-in with her daughter's fifth-grade teacher. A grandpa tells his grandson about the time he fooled a three-pound rainbow trout with a size 16 Royal Wulff dry fly. A cluster of business professionals listen to three CEOs describe how their engineering firms survived the mid-1990s bust in the semiconductor industry. Others give animated accounts of a particular scene in *Star Wars*. Several pairs of eyes are glued to the television monitor mounted on the terminal wall. CNN is running a story about the latest developments on the war against terrorism.

When preachers open up the text of Scripture each Sunday morning, they face twenty-first century audiences who are programmed to think in stories. They speak to people who unknowingly get their theology from stories they've watched on HBO or MTV. How does a preacher address Builders or Boomers shaped by the "sermons" conveyed via news stories on *60 Minutes* or *20/20?* How does a Bible expositor communicate to the Busters who come to church with scenes from NBC's latest sitcom dancing in their heads? How does a minister of the Gospel relate God's truth to the fourteen-year-old who has fed on the sermons projected on the big screens at the movie multiplex?

The sheer number of stories in the Old Testament seems to give preachers an edge. According to the most conservative estimates, stories account for 30 to 40 percent of the Old Testament. Preachers can cash in on the stories of David, Ruth, Samson, and Jezebel when they stand before their video-saturated, story-driven congregations.[1] R. C. Sproul says, "I'm big on preaching from narratives because people will listen ten times as hard to a story as they will to an abstract lesson."[2]

Unfortunately, it's not as simple as it seems. Preachers often neglect Old Testament narratives or, like beginners playing the saxophone, preach them poorly. Neither problem says much about our reverence for God's Word, let alone about our love for the people to whom God has called us to preach. As journalist Terry Mattingly observes, "Most people hear academic lectures at church, then turn to mass media to find inspiring tales of heroes and villains, triumph and tragedy, sin and redemption, heaven and hell."[3]

It's time to take the stories of the Old Testament seriously. Veteran preaching professor Haddon Robinson argues,

> Anyone who loves the Bible must value the story, for whatever else the Bible is, it is a storybook. Old Testament theology comes packaged in narratives of men and women who go running off to set up their handmade gods, and of others who take God seriously enough to bet their lives on Him.[4]

As evangelicals, we've taken Old Testament stories seriously enough to defend their historicity. Now it's time to learn to preach them effectively. While this volume focuses on Old Testament stories, readers can apply much of it to the stories in the Gospels and Acts.

1. Preacher David L. Larsen argues, "This is the milieu and matrix for the explosive rebirth and renewal of interest in the story, a rekindling that has reached and powerfully shaken the world of Christian communication as well. Good storytellers are gurus in our society" (*Telling the Old, Old Story: The Art of Narrative Preaching* [Wheaton: Crossway, 1995], 14–15).

2. Michael Duduit, "Theology and Preaching in the 90s: An Interview with R. C. Sproul," *Preaching* 9 (March-April 1994): 23.

3. Terry Mattingly, "Star Wars—The Only Parable in Town," *Scripps Howard News Service,* 2 June 1999.

4. Haddon W. Robinson, *Biblical Preaching: The Development and Delivery of Expository Messages,* 2d ed. (Grand Rapids: Baker, 2001), 130.

A Commitment to Expository Preaching

I am writing primarily for preachers who are committed to expository preaching. I want to help them do exposition in Old Testament narrative literature. By "expository preaching," I refer to preaching that exposes the meaning of a text of Scripture and applies that meaning to the lives of the hearers. Two well-known preaching professors supply helpful definitions.

> The technical definition of an expository sermon requires that it expounds Scripture by deriving from a specific text main points and subpoints that disclose the thought of the author, cover the scope of the passage, and are applied to the lives of the listeners. (Bryan Chapell)[5]

> Expository preaching is the communication of a biblical concept, derived from and transmitted through a historical, grammatical, and literary study of a passage in its context, which the Holy Spirit first applies to the personality and experience of the preacher, then through him to his hearers. (Haddon Robinson)[6]

When people finish listening to an expository sermon, they should understand the author's meaning and should even be able to track the development of the author's thought in the text. They should also have some idea of what the truth will look like fleshed out in their lives. Listeners who hear expository preaching week after week will get to think through books and major blocks of text. While a series of expository sermons may cover assorted passages on a particular theme, expositors generally work through individual books of the Bible or major sections in those books. The payoffs are tremendous. As John MacArthur Jr. notes, expository preaching promotes biblical literacy and leads to transformed preachers and congregations.[7]

At its core, expository preaching is more of a philosophy than a method. That is, it amounts to a set of commitments or convictions rather than a particular method. Let me share a couple of convictions that expositors must bring to the task. Without these convictions, they are likely to pursue methods that sell short their efforts. While these convictions apply to preaching from any literary genre in the Bible, they are especially critical to preaching from Old Testament narratives.

1. Exposition is more than an exegetical lecture. A few expositors to whom I listen seem to equate exposition with backing up the exegetical dump truck and unloading on their congregations. They basically offer a running commentary on the text without any sense of unity. Hearers who exalt this style

5. Bryan Chapell, *Christ-Centered Preaching: Redeeming the Expository Sermon* (Grand Rapids: Baker, 1994), 129.

6. Robinson, *Biblical Preaching,* 21.

7. John MacArthur Jr., introduction to *Rediscovering Expository Preaching,* ed. John MacArthur Jr. (Dallas: Word, 1992), xv.

frequently describe it as "verse-by-verse teaching." Usually, these folks come from preaching-deficient backgrounds. They are so starved for God's Word that they are willing to receive raw data. They love baskets of exegetical nuggets, and they want preaching that squeezes every ounce of insight out of a Greek or Hebrew term. With this style of preaching, preachers can go until time runs out. It doesn't matter if they quit at verse 4, verse 7, or verse 16. There is no development of a flow of thought—simply a litany of exegetical goodies.

Richard Mayhue clarifies that expository preaching "is not a commentary running from word to word and verse to verse without unity, outline, and pervasive drive." Furthermore, "it is not pure exegesis, no matter how scholarly, if it lacks a theme, thesis, outline, and development."[8]

While this approach hampers effective preaching of any literary genre in Scripture, it especially damns the preaching of Old Testament narratives. Stories unfold. Their ideas take time to develop and gel. Furthermore, their ideas may not be as highly concentrated as in other types of literature. In Old Testament narrative, it may take an entire chapter before the author's intended principle emerges. In an epistle like Colossians, particularly in its latter two chapters, author-intended principles crop up in almost every verse. Working through verses 1–11 in Colossians 3 will produce several biblical principles that people can live out—even if these principles are not tied together or applied. Working through verses 1–11 of Genesis 38, however, will only produce the background necessary for understanding the story. Attempts to preach principles solely from Genesis 38:1–11 will result in principles that are imported into the text and miss the author's intent.

In exposition of Old Testament narratives, it's better to concentrate on preaching scene by scene or paragraph by paragraph than verse by verse. Take Genesis 38 as an example. While preachers will work through the entire narrative, they may quickly summarize the events in verses 1–11 without pausing for extended analysis.

2. There is no form inherent in expository preaching. Richard Mayhue is on target when he writes, "Exposition is not so much defined by the form of the message as it is by the source and process through which the message was formed."[9] To put it another way, there is no such thing as an expository sermon form. Ideally, the form should come from the text. As Sidney Greidanus argues, an expository sermon should impart a Bible-shaped word in a Bible-like way.[10]

---

8. Richard L. Mayhue, "Rediscovering Expository Preaching," in *Rediscovering Expository Preaching,* ed. John MacArthur Jr. (Dallas: Word, 1992), 10.

9. Ibid., 11.

10. Sidney Greidanus, *The Modern Preacher and the Ancient Text* (Grand Rapids: Eerdmans, 1988), 18–20.

Thus, expositors who work in Old Testament narratives will have to adjust their style and even discard the captioned survey approach (e.g., I. Abraham's Test, II. Abraham's Obedience, III. Abraham's Reward). We often pan this as the "three points and a poem" method. This style ends up working against rather than for the preacher who employs it when preaching a Bible story. We will return to this problem later in the chapter.

Why We Struggle with Old Testament Stories

Evangelical pastors who may shine in Ephesians often preach poorly in Nehemiah. Why? Why do evangelical pastors committed to expository preaching struggle with preaching Old Testament stories? Answering this question will help us get back on track. It will reveal areas that need adjustment. Several factors contribute to our poor performance in the pulpit when we open Scripture to an Old Testament narrative.

1. We view stories as fluff. One problem is our tendency to view stories as fluff. Wesley Kort explains why we often sell them short:

Generally we hold narrative to be optional, to be a matter of taste rather than of necessity. We may even disdain narrative as a form of discourse more suited for children than for adults or more for ancient and otherwise underdeveloped people than for the educated and sophisticated. As modern and enlightened adults we have the strength to view our world as it is without the illusions and comforts of narrative wholes. We have little patience for narrative and are tempted to press for an enumeration of facts or a set of clearly and sharply formulated ideas.[11]

As a result, many churches teach Bible stories to children downstairs in the basement while the adults study Paul's epistles upstairs in the auditorium.[12] Eugene Peterson challenges pastors who look down on stories:

Why is the story so often dismissed as not quite adult? Why, among earnest pastors, is the story looked down upon as not quite serious? It is ignorance, mostly. The story is the most adult form of language, the most serious form into which language can be put. Among pastors, who have particular responsibilities for keeping the words of Scripture active in the mind and memory of the faith communities, an appreciation for the story in which Scripture comes to us is imperative.[13]

---

11. Wesley A. Kort, *Story, Text, and Scripture: Literary Interests in Biblical Narrative* (University Park: Pennsylvania State University Press, 1988), 12–13.

12. For a discussion of this problem, see T. L. Thomas, "The OT 'Folk Canon' and Christian Education," *Asbury Theological Journal* 42 (1987): 45–62.

13. Eugene H. Peterson, *Working the Angles: The Shape of Pastoral Integrity* (Grand Rapids: Eerdmans, 1987), 119.

2. We minimize the role of Old Testament stories in the canon. Another reason why evangelicals struggle with preaching Old Testament stories is a faulty view of their role in the canon. Even in the preaching of some premier Bible expositors, Old Testament stories rarely make it into the starting lineup. Instead, they ride the bench. For example, a respected preacher like John MacArthur calls them into the game only when he needs illustrative material or variety from a steady diet of New Testament sermons. In his popular volume *Rediscovering Expository Preaching,* MacArthur explains that he preaches predominately from New Testament literature because of his responsibility to herald the new covenant.[14] However, David C. Deuel, writing in the same volume as MacArthur, offers a needed corrective:

> Using Old Testament narrative *only* to illustrate New Testament teaching, however, results in ignoring much Old Testament instruction that may serve as background for New Testament theology, or else as teaching not repeated in the New Testament. Creation, law, and covenant are in Old Testament narrative which, if ignored or used for illustrations only, will create many problems of biblical imbalance. An adequate theological framework must include the whole Old Testament (cf. 2 Timothy 3:16, "All Scripture . . .").[15]

3. We get intimidated by the language and literature of the Old Testament. A third reason evangelicals struggle with preaching Old Testament stories is more practical: the language and literature of the New Testament seem more manageable. Choosing New Testament studies over Old Testament studies resembles specializing in United States history instead of the history of Western civilization. With United States history, there's a smaller body of material to learn, and it's more familiar. A college Greek professor explained to me that he pursued graduate studies in New Testament language and exegesis because there was too much to master in Old Testament studies. The sheer size of the Old Testament, the length of Old Testament history, and his difficulty in learning Hebrew steered him towards the New Testament. Evangelical seminaries reinforce this problem when they require less hours in Hebrew grammar and exegesis courses than in Greek grammar and exegesis courses. Fortunately, the easiest reading in the Hebrew Bible is found in narrative literature. That's why first-year Hebrew students often begin reading the book of Ruth within a few weeks. Appendix A will help preachers ease back into the world of Biblical Hebrew and use it with profit.

4. We get enslaved to a particular style of exposition. A final reason why preachers struggle with Old Testament stories is enslavement to a particular

---

14. John MacArthur Jr., "Frequently Asked Questions about Expository Preaching," in *Rediscovering Expository Preaching,* ed. John MacArthur Jr. (Dallas: Word, 1992), 341–42.

15. David C. Deuel, "Expository Preaching from Old Testament Narrative," in *Rediscovering Expository Preaching,* ed. John MacArthur Jr. (Dallas: Word, 1992), 283.

homiletical method. Don Wardlaw argues, "When preachers feel they have not preached a passage of Scripture unless they have dissected and rearranged that Word into a lawyer's brief, they in reality make the Word of God subservient to one particular, technical kind of reason."[16] Similarly, Fred Craddock encourages preachers who want to stand at the threshold of new pulpit power to ask "why the Gospel should always be impaled upon the frame of Aristotelian logic."[17]

As previously noted, some evangelicals preach through an Old Testament narrative text by using the "captioned survey" form. Basically, this sermon develops through the points of an analytical outline. Usually, the preacher will state these points clearly so the listeners leave the sermon with an outline in their minds or at least on paper. For example, the sermon I preached several years ago on 1 Samuel 7 chewed its way through the following outline:

I. The Repentance of God's People (7:2–6)
   A. The determination to seek the Lord (v. 2)
   B. The decree to put away idols (vv. 3–4)
   C. The decision to offer confession (vv. 5–6)
II. The Victory of God's People (7:7–11)
   A. The Philistine advance toward Israel was frightening (v. 7)
   B. The Israelite cry to the Lord was compelling (vv. 8–9)
   C. The Divine thunder against the Philistines was overwhelming (vv. 10–11)
III. The Resulting Prosperity of God's People (7:12–17)
   A. God was worshiped (v. 12)
   B. The enemy was subdued (v. 13a)
   C. The land was at peace (vv. 13b–17)

The recipe for such a sermon is simple: (1) divide text into units; (2) summarize each unit; (3) mash the summary into an analytical outline; (4) season the points of this analytical outline with parallelism; (5) sprinkle the points with alliteration; and (6) serve for 30–45 minutes on a fill-in-the-blank outline sheet in the bulletin. Is this an overblown caricature? No. I recently checked out the web site of a prominent midwestern evangelical church. Their senior pastor, a leader in his particular denomination, made his sermons available in sermon notes and in an audio format. He had been preaching through 1 Samuel, so I clicked on some of his outlines. Presto! He had certainly mastered the analytical outline approach. One of his sermons broke down the text according to three Vs: "the *vilification* of the Lord's glory," "the *vindication* of the Lord's glory," and "the *vengeance* by the Lord's glory."

16. Don M. Wardlaw, "Introduction: The Need for New Shapes," in *Preaching Biblically*, ed. Don M. Wardlaw (Philadelphia: Westminster, 1983), 16.
17. Fred B. Craddock, *As One without Authority* (Nashville: Abingdon, 1971), 45.

When I listened to the sermon on audio, the preacher made each of his points prominent with statements like, "In verses 1–2, we find the vilification of the Lord's glory," or "Verses 3–5 describe the vindication of the Lord's glory."

The problem is, good storytellers do not convey their stories through analytical outlines. Veteran expositor Warren Wiersbe reminds preachers that a sermon must present biblical truth "in a manner that is reasonable, imaginative, and intrinsic to the text."[18] He adds, "To preach biblically means much more than to preach the truth of the Bible accurately. It also means to present that truth the way the biblical writers and speakers presented it."[19] When Stephen preached a Bible story in Acts 7, he did not organize his material in an analytical outline. This does not mean that an analytical outline sermon is categorically unbiblical. But it does suggest that an expositor is not bound to this type of sermon form even though it remains popular today in evangelical circles. The analytical outline approach presses the story into a mold that often works against it, especially when the outline points are alliterated or parallel.

A Learning Strategy

We're ready to start the process of building or remodeling a method for preaching Old Testament narratives. This volume will build on the methodology presented in Haddon Robinson's classic textbook *Biblical Preaching*. Robinson breaks the task of sermon preparation into ten stages (see table 1.1). The present volume will follow the same strategy. Please don't let this deter you if you slice the pie differently. You may follow a slightly different approach. That's fine. You should be able to fit the principles I suggest into your own process of sermon development.

Table 1.1
Robinson's Stages of Sermon Preparation

1. Selecting the Passage
2. Studying the Passage
3. Discovering the Exegetical Idea
4. Analyzing the Exegetical Idea
5. Formulating the Homiletical Idea
6. Determining the Sermon's Purpose
7. Deciding How to Accomplish this Purpose
8. Outlining the Sermon
9. Filling in the Sermon Outline
10. Preparing the Introduction and Conclusion

18. Warren W. Wiersbe, *Preaching and Teaching with Imagination: The Quest for Biblical Ministry* (Wheaton: Victor, 1994), 304–5.
19. Ibid., 36.

Let me add another clarification. The process of developing an expository message from an Old Testament narrative text should be fluid and artistic. You must develop a feel for it. However, to learn the process you must break it down into its component parts. Years ago when I learned how to drive, my driver's education manual broke down a left-hand turn into twelve steps. I thought it was ridiculous then. But breaking the process down helped me learn the fundamentals correctly. Learning to preach an Old Testament narrative works the same way. We have to break the process down into mechanical steps so that we can reassemble them into a fluid, artistic motion.

Now, here's a word about the three major sections of this volume. The first section will help you move from *text to concept*. This phase of the process consists of exegesis. If you know Biblical Hebrew or can learn it, it will give you an edge. Thankfully, the easiest type of literature to read in the Hebrew Bible is narrative. So you might want to resurrect your Hebrew or take the plunge and learn it. However, if you don't know Hebrew, don't panic. Perhaps your ministry circumstances are not conducive to investing the time needed to learn the language. You can still do quality exegesis and arrive at the author's intended meaning. The second section will help you move from *concept to sermon*. Here you take your exegetical conclusions and craft a sermon that exposes the meaning of the text and applies it to your hearers. The third section offers some good models of sermon manuscripts from Old Testament narrative texts. When I learned to hunt whitetail deer, I devoured copies of *Outdoor Life* and read several good books. These materials helped, but ultimately I learned more about hunting whitetail deer by watching my father and grandfather. While these manuscripts do not allow you to hear or see the communicators present their sermons, the manuscripts provide models that will help you see theory put into practice.

PART 1

❀❀❀❀❀❀

From Text
to Concept

❀❀❀❀❀❀

2

✤✤✤✤✤

CRITERIA AND CAUTIONS

✤✤✤✤✤

Before preparing a meal for a dinner party, a chef must determine what food to prepare. Should she go with sauteed shrimp and pasta or London Broil and baked potatoes? Similarly, preparing an expository sermon from an Old Testament narrative requires selecting a text. While this step is obvious, it is often difficult because it requires you to choose from dozens of options.

Basically, you can choose from any of the books in your English Bible from Genesis through Esther. These books form collections of narratives. Of course, books like Exodus, Leviticus, Numbers, and Deuteronomy contain a significant amount of legal literature. But they also contain narratives, and their overall framework is narrative. Narrative sections sometimes appear in prophetic books such as Isaiah and Jonah.

If you have never before ventured into Old Testament narratives, spend some time reading through the narrative books and note the stories that seem to grab you. Start with a single sermon on one of these stories. You can always select a familiar story such as God's test of Abraham (Gen. 22:1–19), Esau's sale of his birthright (Gen. 25:19–34), Deborah's victory (Judg. 4), David and Goliath (1 Sam. 17), or Elijah and the prophets of Baal (1 Kings 18). But beware. Though more familiar stories may appear easier, sometimes they are more difficult. If you start with stories like David and Bathsheba (2 Sam. 11–12) or Elijah and the prophets of Baal (1 Kings 18), you will be preaching texts that require more creativity and thought because of their familiarity. On the other hand, your congregation may not be as familiar with some stories as you might assume. They have heard constant references to Samson and Delilah in popular love ballads, but they may know little of the details. The key is to select a story that will not intimidate you with its size or its content.

Planning a sermon series from a narrative book is the next challenge to tackle. A series on stories in Genesis or Samuel makes sense because some of the best commentaries and studies have been written on these books. The sheer length of Genesis and Samuel, however, may require you to take smaller narrative units such as the Abraham cycle (Gen. 12–25) or David's wilderness years (1 Sam. 16–31). While it's natural to base text selection on personalities such as Abraham or David or Elijah, remember that the writer intended to do more than give a life of Abraham. Besides, some of the most potent stories in 1 Samuel come in chapters 4–7, before David is even introduced in the story.

The rule of thumb in text selection is to choose a text that constitutes a unit of biblical thought. Preachers who are used to working with one paragraph in the Epistles may be surprised when they have to select several paragraphs, a whole chapter, or possibly two chapters in order to assemble a preaching unit. For example, Haddon Robinson observes,

> When exploring an episode such as David's adultery with Bathsheba, we would violate the story were we to preach it a paragraph at a time. Instead we would probably base the sermon on the entire eleventh chapter of 2 Samuel and at least part of the twelfth, because this entire section of 2 Samuel records David's sin and its devastating consequences.[1]

What constitutes a unit of thought in narrative text? A whole story. The limits of a story (where it begins and ends) are determined primarily by analyzing the plot. Stories typically contain an exposition, a crisis, a resolution, and sometimes a conclusion. Additionally, if the narrator uses a chiastic structure, the beginning and final items in a chiasm will mark off the boundaries of a story. Chapter 3 and appendix A will help you do plot analysis and identify chiastic structure.

Paying attention to changes in *place*, *time*, and *persons* will also help you see breaks in a narrative.[2] Sometimes these changes work in concert. For example, Genesis 18:33 signals closure of a narrative by reporting a change of place: "When the LORD had finished speaking with Abraham, he left, and Abraham returned home." In the next statement, Genesis 19:1, a change of persons in-

---

1. Haddon W. Robinson, *Biblical Preaching: The Development and Delivery of Expository Messages*, 2d ed. (Grand Rapids: Baker, 2001), 55.
2. John H. Sailhamer, "A Database Approach to the Analysis of Hebrew Narrative," *MAARAV: A Journal for the Study of the Northwest Semitic Languages and Literatures* 5–6 (spring 1990): 327–33.

dicates the beginning of a new unit. The shift is from the LORD and Abraham to the two angels and Lot. A change of place in Genesis 19:30 begins a new narrative as Lot and his two daughters leave Zoar and settle in the mountains. Then, in Genesis 20:1, a change of both place and persons introduces a new unit as Abraham takes the stage again and moves into the region of the Negev.

Changes of time also signal breaks in a narrative. For example, the narrator introduces a new story in Genesis 22:1 by saying, "Some time later . . ." Similarly, he begins a new story in Genesis 15:1 with the words, "After these things." In Genesis 16–17, the narrator uses Abram's age to indicate a break between two stories. The first story concludes by noting that "Abram was eighty-six years old when Hagar bore him Ishmael" (Gen. 16:16). A new story opens in Genesis 17:1 with the words, "When Abram was ninety-nine years old, the LORD appeared to him."

Sometimes a shift from prose to poetry brings a narrative to a close. Stephen Weitzman argues that early Jews expected their biblical heroes to break into song whenever they were delivered by miracles.[3] He argues that the narrative role of the songs in Exodus 15 and Judges 5 parallels a technique of closure often used in ancient Egyptian battle accounts.[4]

The bottom line is, make sure you select an entire story. You may even choose to group stories together if they develop a similar theme, such as the three stories in 1 Samuel 24–26 that revolve around revenge or the three stories in Exodus 15:22–17:7 that center on complaining.

Nailing down a story to preach is a significant step. But the journey has just begun. Now the work really starts!

Mastering the Mechanics

Successfully studying a text requires a grasp of some fundamentals or mechanics. In this respect, exegesis resembles golf. The more you master the fundamentals, the more the fundamentals will make a master out of you. My friend Steve Jones is a prime example.

Watching Steve drive a golf ball is an astonishing sight. He creams the ball with the force of a freight train, yet his motion is as smooth and fluid as a figure skater's. In the 1996 U.S. Open, Steve stood on the eighteenth tee tied for the lead with his friend Tom Lehman. As a *Sports Illustrated* writer later wrote, Steve stepped up to the ball with his driver and "lasered it down the right side, over some bunkers and into the fairway." Several minutes later, he tapped in the winning putt to clinch his first major tournament win.

Developing a lightning-quick swing with such power and grace took years

---

3. Steven Weitzman, *Song and Story in Biblical Narrative: The History of a Literary Convention in Ancient Israel,* Indiana Studies in Biblical Literature (Bloomington: Indiana University Press, 1997), 125, 131.

4. Ibid., 125.

of breaking it down and working on its component parts. Steve had to master the mechanics: grip, stance, shoulder position, arms, backswing, and follow-through. Similarly, interpreting Old Testament narratives requires mastering a set of mechanics. The goal is for interpretation to become a fluid process. Skilled interpreters possess a feel for the text. There is an art to their reading, not just the mechanical performance of a list of steps. Like skilled golfers, however, skilled interpreters take time to master the fundamentals.

In the next chapters you will have the opportunity to develop a method of exegesis that will capture the story writer's intended meaning. You will acquire the necessary skills to equip you for a lifetime of study in Old Testament narrative literature.

Perspectives That Make the Mechanics Work

Before turning to the mechanics, let's pause to consider some perspectives that must accompany the mechanics if the exegetical process is going to work. Like golf, exegesis requires more than executing the mechanics or fundamentals. Golfers must bring to the course a vision of what they're trying to accomplish as well as an eye for the hazards on the course and a sense of dependence on a personal coach who can provide input. Preachers who hope to do effective exegesis in Old Testament narrative texts must bring a similar package of perspectives to the process. Let's examine four crucial perspectives from which preachers must operate when they practice the fundamentals of their craft.

1. Exegesis Must Zero in on the Author's Intended Meaning

Stephen Covey counsels leaders to begin with the end in mind. He claims, "The extent to which you begin with the end in mind often determines whether or not you are able to create a successful enterprise."[5] Golfers begin a course's first hole with the goal of finishing all eighteen holes in the fewest possible strokes. Likewise, preachers need to begin with the end in mind when they set out to study an Old Testament narrative text. So ask yourself, What am I trying to accomplish through my study of the passage? What am I aiming to accomplish when I finish my study of the story? The basic goal of studying the text is to determine the author's intent and to describe this intent in a single sentence, referred to in this volume as the story's *big idea*.

In our evangelical neighborhood, the existence of an author-intended meaning is a given. However, when we venture outside our neighborhood we run smack into a bully. Years ago the bully was historical criticism. Evangelicals expended their energy defending the historicity of the biblical text.[6] To-

5. Stephen R. Covey, *The Seven Habits of Highly Effective People* (New York: Simon and Schuster, 1989), 99.

6. For a superb defense of the historicity of Old Testament narratives, consult V. Philips Long, "The Art of Biblical History," in *Foundations of Contemporary Interpretation,* ed. Moisés

day evangelicals encounter a bully known as postmodernism. Egged on by its older brother deconstructionism, postmodernism scoffs at the notion of authorial intent. Like a virus on your computer's hard drive, it lurks in the thought processes of your listeners. Without realizing it, they get exposed to the postmodern bug every time they watch television or listen to a pop song.

Let's invest a couple of minutes figuring out this virus. As its name suggests, postmodernism is a reaction to modernism, a cultural outlook that banked on optimism, progress, the pursuit of objective knowledge, and science. Modernism dominated the cultural landscape in America from roughly the early 1700s to the 1950s. More than a hundred years ago, German philosopher Friedrich Nietzsche introduced a postmodern perspective when he suggested that what we think we know we really do not know.[7] As a result, James Sire notes, "no longer is there a single story, a metanarrative (in our terms a worldview), that holds Western culture together. . . . All stories are equally valid."[8] David Henderson assesses postmodernism in these terms: "At bedrock, postmodernism is the affirmation that there are no absolutes. Postmodernism is not so much a new worldview as it is the death of any coherent worldview."[9]

Postmodernism has especially infected the generation we label "Baby Busters" or "Generation X." Theologian Stanley Grenz has identified four assumptions of postmodernism that characterize Xers:[10]

1. *Emotionalism*—Feelings and relationships supersede logic and reason.
2. *Pessimism*—The demise of the environment is inevitable.
3. *Holism*—Community must replace individualism.
4. *Relativism*—There is no objective truth. Truth is relative and possibly nonexistent.

Behind postmodernism stands an older brother we know as deconstruction or deconstructionism. Deconstruction, as its name suggests, refers to dismantling or taking apart the notion that a text can be limited to one meaning. Deconstructionists resist closure. They prefer to keep texts open since they

Silva (Grand Rapids: Zondervan, 1996). For a similar but more concise discussion, see Sidney Greidanus, *The Modern Preacher and the Ancient Text* (Grand Rapids: Eerdmans, 1988), 24–47. Also see the conclusions in K. A. Kitchen, *The Bible in Its World: The Bible and Archaeology Today* (Downers Grove, Ill.: InterVarsity, 1977), 61–64.

7. James W. Sire, *The Universe Next Door,* 3d ed. (Downers Grove, Ill.: InterVarsity, 1997), 177.

8. Ibid., 174.

9. David W. Henderson, *Culture Shift: Communicating God's Truth to Our Changing World* (Grand Rapids: Baker, 1998), 192. See pages 189–218 for the complete discussion.

10. These observations, shared at the 1994 Charlotte symposium on Generation X, are listed in Kevin Graham Ford, *Jesus for a New Generation: Putting the Gospel in the Language of Xers* (Downers Grove, Ill.: InterVarsity, 1995), 115–18.

claim there are several ways to put them together. Ultimately, the reader determines meaning.

Preachers must be aware of these bullies because the denial of authorial intent creeps into the study and preaching of Old Testament narratives. For example, David M. Gunn and Danna Nolan Fewell make this comment about their 1993 work *Narrative in the Hebrew Bible:* "Our book understands interpretation to hinge crucially upon the reader, and not just in terms of a reader's 'competence.' Meaning is not something out there in the text waiting to be discovered. Meaning is always, in the last analysis, the reader's creation, and readers, like texts, come in an infinite variety."[11] Similarly, mainline preacher Richard Jensen contends that the stories of the Bible "invite us to participate in their reality, not to understand that reality."[12] Jensen adds, "I have sought to make it crystal clear that I do not believe that the Bible is primarily a book of ideas."[13]

Do evangelical exegetes follow the correct path when they insist on authorial intent? My answer is a confident yes. While this volume is not the place to construct a full-blown answer, let's briefly reflect on why the answer is yes. After all, we preach to people who get hit with a heavy dose of postmodern thought during their weekly routines of listening to the radio, watching television, and interacting with peers.

Is authorial intent a valid concept? Kevin Vanhoozer, an evangelical theologian, provides one of the most in-depth affirmative answers in his book, *Is There a Meaning in This Text?*[14] He writes, "The present work sets out to affirm that there *is* a meaning in the text, that it can be known, and that readers should strive to do so. Postmodern appearances to the contrary, we can continue to defend, and to promote, the possibility of understanding."[15] Vanhoozer asks,

> How can we account for a poem moving us to tears, a promise that evokes a firm hope, or a parable that prompts us to sell all our goods and give the profits to the poor? How can we account for the hundreds of daily transactions, punctuated by simple phrases ("Come in"; "Please be quiet"; "That will be $4.99, please"; "I love you"), that shape our lives? Does deconstruction adequately account for what is, after all, an everyday occurrence, namely, communication?[16]

11. David M. Gunn and Danna Nolan Fewell, *Narrative in the Hebrew Bible* (Oxford: Oxford University Press, 1993), xi.

12. Richard A. Jensen, *Thinking in Story: Preaching in a Post-Literate Age* (Lima, Ohio: CSS, 1993), 62.

13. Ibid., 109.

14. Kevin J. Vanhoozer notes that his title alludes to the work by Stanley Fish, *Is There a Text in This Class?* Fish argues that there is no such thing as a meaning in the text outside the reader. Meaning is not prior to, but rather a product of, the reader's activity (*Is There a Meaning in This Text?* [Grand Rapids: Zondervan, 1998], 24).

15. Ibid.

16. Ibid., 202.

He continues, "Why is there something rather than nothing in texts? Because someone has said something about something to someone. Not just *anything*, but *something*."[17] A text, then, is "a communicative act of a communicative agent fixed by writing."[18] As such, the reader's responsibility is to grasp what the author has done in, with, and through the text.[19]

Philosopher Nicholas Wolterstorff reaches similar conclusions in his work *Divine Discourse: Philosophical Reflections on the Claim That God Speaks*. Wolterstorff takes on Jacques Derrida, the French philosopher often recognized as the father of deconstruction. Wolterstorff counters Derrida's argument that authorial discourse interpretation is untenable because authorial discourse is untenable. Wolterstorff observes, "Paradoxical as it may seem, he [Derrida] wants us to apply to his own texts that very mode of interpretation against which he launches a general attack; he wants us to interpret his texts for what he was saying and to get that right."[20]

In other words, the very act of making claims about the lack of meaning is contradictory. Let's return for a moment to Richard Jensen's skepticism about the Bible being primarily a book of ideas. Despite his skepticism about meaning in Bible texts, Jensen makes statement after statement that presupposes a commitment to meaning. For example, in his discussion of the psychodynamics of oral culture he observes, "Oral communities tell their stories in such a way that particular stories are the way to grasp more abstract or universal concepts."[21] Later he speaks of "the theme" of the Nebuchadnezzar story in Daniel 4.[22] He even says, "The gospel message which we hope to communicate is the word of God's gift of love for sinful humanity." Jensen also encourages preachers to "fill peoples' heads with biblical people. The people of the Bible can live in our heads helping us sort through a maze of images and information that assaults us."[23] To be sure, as Jensen notes, "stories work by indirection."[24] But indirection does not negate meaning or intention. As literary critic Erich Auerbach claims in his classic *Mimesis*, "The Scripture stories do not, like Homer's, court our favour, they do not flatter us that they may please us and enchant us—they seek to subject us, and if we refuse to be subjected we are rebels."[25]

17. Ibid., 218.
18. Ibid., 225.
19. Ibid., 218.
20. Nicholas Wolterstorff, *Divine Discourse: Philosophical Reflections on the Claim That God Speaks* (Cambridge: Cambridge University Press, 1995), 153.
21. Jensen, *Thinking in Story*, 22.
22. Ibid., 86.
23. Ibid., 63.
24. Ibid., 62.
25. Erich Auerbach, *Mimesis*, trans. Willard Trask (New York: Doubleday, 1953), 12.

Meaning is an unavoidable result of communicating. Turning to Old Testament experts themselves, we find scholars from a variety of persuasions recognizing that Old Testament narratives convey meaning. Take a few moments to ponder their conclusions.

The Bible's main form of exposition, the narrative, is most appropriately characterized as primary rhetoric, its primary objective being to persuade its audience. (Dale Patrick and Allen Scult)[26]

The aim of the intrinsic study of literature is to understand the text from inside, guided by the obvious and quite natural question: "What do you mean? What are you actually saying?" This question is simultaneously the most essential question which we could ask of the text or, more generally, of any work of art or, even more generally, of any partner in conversation. (J. P. Fokkelman)[27]

The biblical authors are of course constantly, urgently conscious of telling a story in order to reveal the imperative truth of God's works in history and of Israel's hopes and failings. Close attention to the literary strategies through which that truth was expressed may actually help us to understand it better, enable us to see the minute elements of complicating design in the Bible's sacred history. (Robert Alter)[28]

Rather than seeking to let the literature of ancient Israel address us on its own terms—however remote from ours, and however we may finally judge them— it too easily makes of biblical literature a reflection of our own concerns at the end of the twentieth century, whether secular or theological. . . . Narrative rhetoric, like any other rhetoric, is designed to create a certain impression on the hearer or reader, and that impression is lessened or confused by a reader's ignorance of the presuppositions of the texts. (Simon B. Parker)[29]

Custodians of narrative texts should not compromise the fundamental characteristics of the material. Required is the recognition that the religious meaning of the material is generated first of all because of features constitutive to its fundamental nature as narrative and text. The religious meaning and significance of biblical material and its literary and textual form are inseparable. (Wesley Kort)[30]

---

26. Dale Patrick and Allen Scult, *Rhetoric and Biblical Interpretation* (Sheffield: Almond, 1990), 29.

27. J. P. Fokkelman, *Narrative Art and Poetry in the Books of Samuel: A Full Interpretation Based on Stylistic and Structural Analyses,* vol. 1: *King David (II Sam. 9–20 and I Kings 1–2)* (Assen, The Netherlands: Van Gorcum, 1981), 1.

28. Robert Alter, *The Art of Biblical Narrative* (New York: Basic, 1981), 46.

29. Simon B. Parker, *Stories in Scripture and Inscriptions: Comparative Studies on Narratives in Northwest Semitic Inscriptions and the Hebrew Bible* (Oxford: Oxford University Press, 1997), 4.

30. Wesley A. Kort, *Story, Text, and Scripture,* x–xi. He argues that narrative is "articulated belief structure" (20).

It is through the [literary] techniques [in Hebrew narrative] that the meaning of the facts of the narrative is determined. (Shimon Bar-Efrat)[31]

Communication presupposes a speaker who resorts to certain linguistic and structural tools in order to produce certain effects on the addressee; the discourse accordingly supplies a network of clues to the speaker's intention. In this respect, the Bible does not vary from any other literary or ordinary message except in the ends and the rules that govern the forms of communication. (Meir Sternberg)[32]

To summarize, evangelical Old Testament scholar John Sailhamer reminds interpreters, "A text is . . . an embodiment of an author's intention, that is a strategy designed to carry out that intention."[33] As an interpreter studies the text, he or she must ask, What did the author intend to communicate with this set of facts? Nicholas Wolterstorff claims, "The issue is not whether one's interpretation is valuable in one way or another—exciting, original, imaginative, provocative, beneficial—but whether it is true."[34]

2. The Search for the Author's Intent Leads to a Big Idea

Golfers who begin with the end in mind understand that they want to finish a round or a tournament with the fewest possible strokes. However, this goal may take an even more specific form. A golfer may shoot for finishing at par or at ten under par. Similarly, while preachers shoot for the author-intended meaning of a story, their goal must take an even more specific form.

In their quest for truth, some preachers comb an Old Testament story for a list of moral principles they can preach. They may find three strategies for finding God's will or four keys to a healthy marriage. However, no research suggests that Old Testament authors used narratives as a vehicle for communicating lists. Obviously, biblical writers sometimes compile lists. The writer of Proverbs signals a list by saying, "There are six things the LORD hates, seven that are detestable to him" (Prov. 6:16). In Hebrews 10:19–25, the writer draws three conclusions from the access to the Father provided by Jesus. Each item is introduced by the exhortation "let us."[35] In 1 Peter 4:7–11, the apostle Peter offers a list of implications for believers who live in the end times. Yet

31. Shimon Bar-Efrat, *Narrative Art in the Bible* (Sheffield: Almond, 1989), 10.

32. Meir Sternberg, *The Poetics of Biblical Narrative: Ideological Literature and the Drama of Reading*, Indiana Studies in Biblical Literature (Bloomington: Indiana University Press, 1985), 9.

33. John H. Sailhamer, *Introduction to Old Testament Theology* (Grand Rapids: Zondervan, 1995), 46–47.

34. Wolterstorff, *Divine Discourse*, 181.

35. In the Greek text, verses 22–24 each begin with a hortatory subjunctive. While the NIV includes two more "let us" statements in verse 25, these statements consist of two participial phrases that describe strategies for carrying out the "let us" statement (hortatory subjunctive) in verse 24.

Old Testament narratives seem to work like other stories and focus more on a single idea. Stories tend to fire bullets rather than buckshot.

Listeners recognize this feature of stories when they ask, What's the moral of the story? Recently, a writer in *U.S. News & World Report* observed that mothers who first told a story like Cinderella to their children told it to communicate a message.[36] The idea they were conveying ran something like this: "Remember, my dears, that the worst thing imaginable would be for me to disappear and for your father to replace me with another woman." Even Robert May's entertaining story-poem about Rudolph the Red-nosed Reindeer contains a message: Given the opportunity, you can turn a liability into an asset.

I am not saying that every Old Testament text contains only one concept or idea. I am saying that the concepts and ideas embedded in a text form a unified whole. Haddon Robinson, the dean of big idea preaching, clarifies it like this: "Sermons seldom fail because they have too many ideas; more often they fail because they deal with unrelated ideas."[37] Multiple ideas work in concert to form a larger, overarching idea. The interpreter sets out on a quest to find the overarching idea that subsumes all the others. When an interpreter finds the idea that accounts for the most data in the story, he or she has discovered what we'll call the big idea. Chapter 7 will explore in detail the process of expressing the author's intended meaning as a big idea.

3. Keep Shop Talk in Its Place

When a golfer prepares to tee off, he or she must be aware of the hazards that line the fairway. For example, a bunker may lurk along the right side of the fairway about 250 yards away. Similarly, a preacher preparing a sermon from an Old Testament narrative must be alert to a hazard called "shop talk." Interpreters of Old Testament narratives have developed an extensive vocabulary to refer to the features found in stories. While you can't avoid labels and technical terms, they do present a couple of dangers. One danger is that interpreters will reduce the hermeneutical process to slapping labels on elements in the text. The goal of exegetical analysis is not a mere pile of analytical data and labels. Rather, exegetical analysis should produce understanding of a text. Alter argues,

> Reading any body of literature involves a specialized mode of perception in which every culture trains its members from childhood. As modern readers of the Bible, we need to relearn something of this mode of perception that was second nature to the original audiences.[38]

36. Wray Herbert, "The Uses and Abuses of Cinderella," *U.S. News & World Report*, 29 November 1999, 62.
37. Robinson, *Biblical Preaching*, 35.
38. Alter, *The Art of Biblical Narrative*, 62.

Simply labeling the plot type as a comedy or classifying a character as a protagonist does not guarantee understanding. Nor does it cause you to experience the story in the way the author intended. As Jean Louis Ska observes, "The object of analysis is the movement of a living being, not the autopsy of a corpse."[39] He further explains, "Analysis should make the text more understandable. If it produces the opposite effect as, for instance, when it atomizes the text into very short segments . . . there is something wrong either in the theory or in its application."[40]

A more grave danger is contaminating your sermon with these technical terms. Your listeners need to hear you use terms like *archetype* and *back-grounded clause* about as much as you need to hear your dentist tell you that you have a mesio-occlusal distal carious lesion on number 14. All you need to hear is that you have a cavity on your first upper left molar. Shop talk may impress a few listeners, but throwing around expressions like *chiastic structure* and *protagonist* will confuse and frustrate most of them. As one of my seminary professors joked, "We use terms like this so we can justify the high tuition we charge!"

So why bother with labels and technical terms if we shouldn't use them on others? Fair question. Using the labels and technical terms employed by Old Testament scholars and commentators will help you interact more quickly with important concepts. Ska explains,

> All these [literary] categories are indicators of the way to proceed when one enters into a narrative. They are never pigeon-holes to arrange neatly and permanently the texts proposed for analysis which is more often a question of nuance and degree than of mere classification. They are rather a compass and maps that a traveller uses for a journey through the Biblical narratives.[41]

Shop talk is necessary. It works for you when you interact with the writings of Old Testament scholars and commentators. It works against your interpretation when you become enamored with the labels and not the story. It works against your preaching when you slip it into your sermon and cause a higher level of confusion.

4. Saturate Your Exegesis with Prayer

Professional golfers look to others for input. Sometimes they burn up the phone lines, calling a personal coach who has watched them on television and can detect a flaw in their swing that no one else notices.

---

39. Jean Louis Ska, *"Our Fathers Have Told Us": Introduction to the Analysis of Hebrew Narratives* (Roma: Editrice Pontificio Instituto Biblico, 1990), 36.

40. Ibid., 67.

41. Ibid., 94.

Successful preachers burn up the phone lines, too—specifically the phone lines to the throne of God. Preaching lacks power when it lacks prayer. The need to saturate sermon preparation with prayer starts with the exegesis phase.

In *Preaching with Freshness*, Bruce Mawhinney's novel about preaching, retired seminary professor Dr. William Vickerson coaches former student and struggling preacher Paul Andrews. In one of their conversations, Dr. Vickerson warns Paul about preaching sermons devoid of the Spirit of God: "Often, we spend so much time gathering information in our studies that we never stop to pray over it. We plunge headlong into our sermon outlines without seeking the Lord's guidance on how to handle the materials before us."[42]

Preachers who hope to preach Old Testament stories with accuracy and power must saturate their study of the text with prayer. When I sit down to study a narrative text, I begin with a time of prayer. I ask God to help me concentrate and work diligently in the text. At various points in my exegetical study, I rise from my desk and walk down the hall from my office into our worship center. As I wander through the aisles, I pray that God will help me work through a particular gap in my understanding of the story I'm studying. Sometimes I even take my notes and pray through them as I kneel near the place where I'll stand on Sunday to deliver my sermon. Later in the sermon preparation process, I'll pray about applying the story to my life and to the congregation I serve. For now, I simply ask God to grant me understanding.

I try to follow the example of commentator William Lane. In the preface to his commentary on the Gospel of Mark, he shares,

> When a critical or theological decision has been demanded by the text before I was prepared to commit myself, I have adopted the practice of the Puritan commentators in laying the material before the Lord and asking for his guidance.[43]

Well, are you ready? Do you have the right perspectives in mind to accompany the text you have in hand? Take a quick inventory before proceeding. Are you committed to finding the author's intended meaning? Are you willing to look for a big idea that ties together all the other ideas? Do you agree to keep shop talk in its place? Will you commit to saturating your exegesis with prayer? If so, let the journey begin. Like hiking to the top of a 14,000-foot peak in the Rocky Mountains, the challenges of exegesis are terrific, but so are the rewards.

---

42. Bruce Mawhinney, *Preaching with Freshness* (Eugene, Ore.: Harvest House, 1991), 137.

43. William L. Lane, *The Gospel according to Mark*, New International Commentary on the New Testament (Grand Rapids: Eerdmans, 1974), xii.

3

❀ ❀ ❀ ❀ ❀

THE SHAPE OF STORIES

❀ ❀ ❀ ❀ ❀

The quest for the meaning of an Old Testament narrative text revolves around four key elements found in all stories: plot, characters, setting, and point of view.[1] Preachers who do exegesis in Old Testament narrative texts need to look at the text through the lens of each element.

Like you, I am a busy pastor. My ministry plate is full, so I have limited time I can spend on exegesis. I've tried to develop an exegetical process that is as lean as possible yet substantial enough to help me determine the author's intent. You can usually do the work in three to eight hours, depending on your exegetical skill level, whether or not you study the text in Hebrew, and the complexity and size of the story you select.

To begin, you need your Bible, a pencil, and a legal pad or word processor for recording some notes. Writing down observations, questions, summaries, and conclusions will force you to think at a higher level.

Initially, don't run to the commentaries. If you study the text in Hebrew, you will need tools such as a lexicon and a grammar. Otherwise, save the reference tools for later. The idea is to think through the passage on your own before diving into commentaries, theological wordbooks, and the like. I'll say

---

1. Tremper Longman III, "Biblical Narrative," in *A Complete Literary Guide to the Bible*, ed. Leland Ryken and Tremper Longman III (Grand Rapids: Zondervan, 1993), 71.

more about commentaries in appendix B. Suffice it here to say that many of them do not provide the kind of literary and linguistic analysis you need for Old Testament narratives anyway. Even the best ones should be saved for later so that you can interact with them once you've done your own thinking.

Plot

The place to start your analysis is the plot, since Old Testament stories focus more on action than on the development of particular characters.[2] Basically, plot refers to action. It consists of a sequence of events that usually hinges on a conflict or crisis. The events in the story move through this conflict or crisis towards some kind of resolution. Why is tracking the plot so important? Israeli scholar Shimon Bar-Efrat observes, "The plot serves to organize events in such a way as to arouse the reader's interest and emotional involvement, while at the same time imbuing the events with meaning."[3]

Plot Shape

As I read a story the first time, I look closely at the shape of the plot. Plots in Old Testament narrative assume the same basic shape. Generally, they consist of four main stages or elements in the flow of action: exposition, crisis, resolution, and conclusion or denouement (see table 3.1).[4] Sometimes it's hard to tell where the shift from one element to another takes place. Interpreters do not have to agonize over exactly where each change occurs. Often the changes between plot elements reflect the almost imperceptible shift from first to second gear with an automatic transmission. You know the change has occurred, but it's difficult to pinpoint precisely where it occurred.

Table 3.1
Elements in the Plot

1. Exposition
2. Crisis
3. Resolution
4. Conclusion (denouement)

To see how these elements work, let's examine three Old Testament stories: Abraham's test (Gen. 22:1–19), the Judah-Tamar story (Gen. 38), and the

2. Jean Louis Ska, *"Our Fathers Have Told Us": Introduction to the Analysis of Hebrew Literature* (Roma: Editrice Pontificio Instituto Biblico, 1990), 17.

3. Shimon Bar-Efrat, *Narrative Art in the Bible* (Sheffield: Almond, 1989), 93.

4. Some exegetes use slightly different terms to speak of the same phenomenon. They refer to five elements in the flow of action: exposition, conflict, complication, climax, and denouement. While the four-stage scheme I have presented does not list complication as a separate step, it recognizes the presence of rising tension or further complication between the crisis and the resolution. The other items correspond exactly.

story of Esther. If you're not familiar with these stories, set this volume aside and read them in your Bible before going any further.

Exposition

The exposition provides the information that sets up the story. It introduces the characters, informing us of their names, traits, physical appearance, state in life, and relationships. It may also describe the geographical or historical setting. Ska comments, "In an exposition, the reader finds only short notices about the situation of the main characters. The information is often laconic, generic, and abstract, whereas the first scene is detailed, concrete, and unique."[5] Whatever the story writer includes, it will help the reader understand the action that follows.[6] For example, in Genesis 22:1–19, verse 1 contains the exposition. In this story, the exposition is relatively brief, informing the reader that what follows amounts to a God-given test.

In the Judah-Tamar story of Genesis 38, verses 1–6 function as exposition, introducing us to the geographical setting ("went down to . . . Adullam") and the characters who will play a part in the plot (Judah, his three sons, and Tamar). This information, which shows Judah making a break with his brothers and establishing relationships with the Canaanites, tips off the reader that Judah is not walking in fellowship with Yahweh.[7]

The book of Esther provides another example. Chapters 1 and 2 serve as the exposition. To understand the story of Esther, a reader must grasp King Xerxes' anger and compulsive behavior, Esther's secret nationality, and Mordecai's uncovering of an assassination plot. According to Esther 2:23, Mordecai's heroic deed was recorded in official court records. This information will become crucial in the events of chapter 6.

Crisis

From exposition, the plot moves into the crisis, variously described as the complication, the conflict, or the tension. Once the conflict appears, the tension rises as the story moves toward its resolution. For this reason, some scholars point to an inciting moment or occasioning incident when the problem appears for the first time. Subsequent development is described as complication or rising tension. Scholars describe the highest level of intensity in the conflict as the climax or peak moment.

Returning to the previous three narratives, readers can see examples of the crisis stage in the plot structure. In Genesis 22:1–19, the crisis runs from

---

5. Ska, *"Our Fathers Have Told Us,"* 23.
6. Bar-Efrat, *Narrative Art in the Bible,* 114.
7. For an analysis of Genesis 38, see Steven D. Mathewson, "An Exegetical Study of Genesis 38," *Bibliotheca Sacra* 146 (October–December 1989): 373–92. Again, it is hard to determine precisely where the exposition ends. Ska, for example, says the exposition runs through verse 11 (*"Our Fathers Have Told Us,"* 23–24).

verses 2–10. It first appears in verse 2, and the tension rises in verses 3–10. In Genesis 38, verses 7–24 form the crisis. There are actually two crises in this story. First, in verses 7–11 Yahweh puts two of Judah's sons, Er and Onan, to death. Tamar, Er's wife, is left as a childless widow when Judah refuses to give her his third son, Shelah, in keeping with the custom of levirate marriage.[8] Rather than moving quickly to a resolution, verses 12–24 build towards another crisis that flares up in verse 24.[9] There, Judah discovers Tamar's pregnancy and sentences her to be burned. In the book of Esther, the crisis occurs in chapters 3–4 where Haman plots to destroy the Jews.[10]

Resolution

Eventually, the story moves from crisis to resolution and the plot descends rapidly from its climax to a solution of the original conflict.[11] Ska comments,

> What matters most in the analysis of a narrative, we think, is to pinpoint the resolution of the plot. This moment, more than any other, is the one the reader is waiting for. It is also easier to uncover the resolution than the other moments. After this resolution, the dramatic tension drops and can even disappear completely.[12]

Resolution takes place in verses 11–14 of Genesis 22 as the angel of the LORD stops Abraham from sacrificing Isaac. Abraham then sees a ram caught by its horns in a thicket and understands it to be God's provision.

In Genesis 38, the resolution occurs in verses 25–26 when Tamar produces the objects that indict Judah as the man who impregnated her. This might be described as the climax peak. The tension quickly subsides into resolution as Judah then pronounces her more righteous than himself.

In the book of Esther, the resolution takes place in 5:1–9:19 as Mordecai receives the honor Haman intended for himself, Haman receives the hanging he intended for Mordecai, and the Jews triumph over their enemies.

---

8. Verses 7–11 could be classified as a "preparatory scene" that "prepares for a decisive meeting and creates the appropriate atmosphere of hope, fear, or curiosity" (Ska, *"Our Fathers Have Told Us,"* 26). Ska discusses this in conjunction with the complication stage or moment of a plot.

9. Bar-Efrat calls this type of plot structure an "illusory conclusion." He writes, "In contrast to . . . examples, where the storyline gradually rises to a climax and then descends rapidly to the serene conclusion, here the narrative does not end after the gradual ascent and the rapid decline, but rises once more to another pinnacle, only then descending to the genuine conclusion" (*Narrative Art in the Bible,* 124).

10. Once again, the fluid changes between plot elements make it difficult to determine if the crisis section ends with chapter 4 or extends into chapter 5 where two more mini-crises transpire: Esther has to approach the king, and Haman builds gallows on which to hang Mordecai.

11. Tremper Longman III, *Literary Approaches to Biblical Interpretation* (Grand Rapids: Zondervan, 1987), 92.

12. Ska, *"Our Fathers Have Told Us,"* 29.

Conclusion

Finally, stories end in a conclusion or denouement. The latter term refers to the tying up of loose ends.[13] The conclusion or denouement generally sums up the outcome of the story or the fate of the main characters in the wake of the resolution. Or the conclusion can offer a special message to the reader. Some narratives do not have a conclusion distinguishable from the resolution. Some narratives "are open-ended or contain elements that prepare for another plot (Joseph story, Jonah, Judges 8:28–35 [Gideon] . . .)."[14] Often the conclusion is marked by someone who returns home or leaves for another destination.[15]

Returning to our examples, the narrative in Genesis 22:1–19 has a definite conclusion in verses 15–19. The angel of the LORD calls to Abraham a second time and announces the positive consequences of Abraham's action. In Genesis 38, it is less certain whether verses 27–30 function separately from the resolution. However, Esther 9:20–10:3 certainly functions as a conclusion. It informs the reader that Mordecai and Queen Esther established the feast of Purim and that Mordecai rose to greatness in the Persian government and in his people's esteem.

Archetypes

Another way to analyze plot is to identify the archetypes that show up in a story. When applied to the plot, the term *archetype* refers to a repeated pattern. In Old Testament narratives, these repeated patterns occur at the level of overall plot *(plot motifs)* and at the level of episodes or scenes within the plot *(type scenes)*. Identifying them will help an interpreter see how a story develops in comparison to other Old Testament narratives or scenes of the same type.

Leland Ryken has produced an extensive list of plot motifs (see table 3.2).[16] Most notable are the comedy and the tragedy. A *comedy* is a "U-shaped story that begins in prosperity, descends into tragedy, and rises again to end happily."[17] The plots in Genesis 22:1–19, Genesis 38, and the book of Esther take a comic direction. A *tragedy*, on the other hand, is "the story of excep-

---

13. Leland Ryken, *Words of Delight: A Literary Introduction to the Bible* (Grand Rapids: Baker, 1987), 104.

14. Ska, *"Our Fathers Have Told Us,"* 29.

15. Bar-Efrat, *Narrative Art in the Bible,* 130–31. Cf. Robert Alter, *The Art of Biblical Narrative* (New York: Basic, 1981), 65.

16. Adapted from Ryken, *Words of Delight,* 49; and Ryken, *How to Read the Bible as Literature* (Grand Rapids: Zondervan, 1984), 53–54, 191–92.

17. Ryken, *How to Read the Bible as Literature,* 82. Ryken lists the following elements that have become virtually synonymous with literary comedy: disguise, mistaken identity, character transformation from bad to good, surprise, miracle, providential assistance to good characters, sudden reversal of misfortune, rescue from disaster, poetic justice, the motif of lost and found, reversal of conventional expectations such as the preference of the younger child over the older, and sudden release.

tional calamity. It portrays a movement from prosperity to catastrophe."[18] Tragedies in the Old Testament include the stories of Samson (Judg. 13–16), Saul (1 Sam. 8–31), and Esau (Gen. 25–27).[19]

Table 3.2
Ryken's List of Plot Motifs

1. *The quest [heroic narrative, hero story],* in which a hero struggles to reach a goal, undergoing obstacles and temporary defeat before achieving success. (Examples: Joseph, David, Ruth, Abraham)

2. *The death-rebirth motif [pathetic plot],* in which a hero endures death or danger and returns to life or security. (Examples: Hezekiah, Joseph)

3. *The initiation [admiration],* in which a character is thrust out of an existing, usually ideal, situation and undergoes a series of ordeals as he or she encounters various forms of evil or hardship for the first time. (Examples: Elisha, Daniel, Jacob)

4. *The journey,* in which the characters encounter danger and experience growth as they move from one place to another. (Example: Jacob)

5. *Tragedy,* or the more specific form of *the fall from innocence,* depicting a decline from bliss to woe. (Examples: Saul, Samson)

6. *Comedy,* a U-shaped story that begins in prosperity, decends into tragedy, but rises to a happy ending as obstacles to success are overcome. (Examples: Judah and Tamar, Ruth, Esther)

7. *Crime and punishment [punitive plot],* in which an unsympathetic or villainous character undergoes an adverse change of fortune as a punishment for misdeeds. (Examples: Gehazi, Jezebel, Ahab, Absalom)

8. *The temptation,* in which someone becomes the victim of an evil tempter or temptress. (Examples: Eve, Samson and Delilah)

9. *The rescue.* (Examples: Esther, Elisha at Dothan)

10. *The suffering servant motif,* in which a character undergoes undeserved suffering for the benefit of others. (Example: Joseph)

11. *The Cinderella or rags-to-riches motif,* in which a character overcomes the obstacles of ostracism and poverty. (Example: David, Gideon)

12. *The movement from ignorance to epiphany [revelation story],* in which a character progresses from ignorance to insight and illumination. (Example: Abraham)

Simon Parker opens up some additional categories in his comparative study of narratives in Northwest Semitic inscriptions and the Hebrew Bible. He identifies *petitionary narratives* (2 Sam. 12:1–7; 14:1–23; 1 Kings 3:16–27; 20:38–42; 2 Kings 4:1–7; 6:24–30; 8:1–6), *stories of military campaigns* (2 Kings 13–14; Josh. 10; 2 Sam. 8), and *stories of miraculous deliverance from a siege* (2 Kings 3:4–27; 6:24–7:20; 18:13–19:37). Parker's analysis of the petitionary narrative in 1 Kings 3:16–27 (Solomon and the two

18. Ibid., 83.

19. For a specialized study of the Old Testament tragedies of Saul, Jephthah, select members of Saul's house, and David, see J. Cheryl Exum, *Tragedy and Biblical Narrative: Arrows of the Almighty* (Cambridge: Cambridge University Press, 1992).

prostitutes who claim to be mother to the same baby) demonstrates the value of his study. He observes, "In all petitionary narratives, the reader's sympathies or interests are engaged on the side of the petitioner rather than the party against whom the petition is lodged."[20] In this story, "the narrator chose to quote fully the petition of the one woman, and the effect of that choice is to dispose the reader in her favor."[21] Thus, this petitionary narrative "engages us morally; we now have an emotional investment in the outcome, and we are not only intellectually satisfied but also emotionally relieved when Solomon exposes the truth."[22]

Within the overall framework of a plot, type scenes recur as well. Type scenes are repeated events or situations that occur in Bible stories. These scenes "are built around understood conventions about what should be included and in what order items should appear."[23] Ryken likens type scenes to a brief interview on the evening news. Such an interview typically starts with a shot of the interviewer in front of an appropriate background. Depending on the news story, the background might be the stands of a sports stadium or the wreckage of a disaster. Then the interviewer begins a question-and-answer dialogue with a point guard or a congressional leader or a biology teacher. Finally, the camera zooms in on the interviewer who looks into the camera and offers a summary or interpretation. Why does virtually every television news interview follow this format? According to Ryken, it is simply the established convention of the genre.[24]

Robert Alter lists some of the most commonly repeated biblical type scenes: the announcement of the birth of a hero to his barren mother, the encounter with one's future spouse at a well, the epiphany in the field, the initiatory trial, danger in the desert and discovery of a well or other source of sustenance, and the testament of a dying hero.[25] Robert Culley also identifies several types of "action sequences" on which plots may be built (see table 3.3). In each action sequence, something arouses an expectation, and then the expectation is fulfilled.[26] Most biblical stories contain more than one action sequence.

---

20. Simon B. Parker, *Stories in Scripture and Inscriptions: Comparative Studies on Narratives in Northwest Semitic Inscriptions and the Hebrew Bible* (Oxford: Oxford University Press, 1997), 23.

21. Ibid., 24.

22. Ibid.

23. Ryken, *Words of Delight*, 50.

24. Ibid.

25. Alter, *The Art of Biblical Narrative*, 51.

26. Robert C. Culley, *Themes and Variations: A Study of Action in Biblical Narrative*, Society of Biblical Literature Semeia Studies, ed. Edward L. Greenstein (Atlanta: Scholars Press, 1992), 50.

Table 3.3
Culley's List of Action Sequences

- Punishment Sequences
    1. *Wrong/punished* (Elijah's curse of boys; fate of Lot's wife)
    2. *Injury/avenged* (Amnon and Absalom; Dinah)

- Rescue Sequences
    3. *Difficulty/rescued* (Elisha and lost axhead; Elijah and widow's boy)
    4. *Difficulty/escaped* (Hebrew midwives; Michal's rescue of David)

- Achievement Sequences
    5. *Desire/achieved* (Ahab and Naboth's vineyard; Gehazi; Isaac's deceit)
    6. *Task/accomplished* (wife for Isaac; Abraham's test)

- Reward Sequences
    7. *Good deed/rewarded* (couple who hosts Elisha; Hebrew midwives)

- Announcement Sequences
    8. *Announcement/happened* (creation story; Abram's call; Micaiah)

- Prohibition Sequences
    9. *Prohibition/transgressed* (Lot's wife; Garden of Eden)

What is the payoff for identifying type scenes? Weston W. Fields argues, "In a word, a motif often carries the essential message of a story."[27] Alter explains what happens when a storyteller came, for example, to the moment of his hero's betrothal:

> Both he and his audience were aware that the scene had to unfold in particular circumstances, according to a fixed order. If some of those circumstances were altered or suppressed, or if the scene were actually omitted, that communicated something to the audience.[28]

We find an example in Genesis 38. Throughout Genesis, the motif of the elder serving the younger occurs frequently. Normally, the younger brother would serve the older brother. In Genesis 38, this motif is worked out in the birth of Tamar's twin sons, emphasizing God's sovereign plan of grace in which he accomplishes his purpose by using unexpected and even weaker means. God's blessing is extended to those who have no other claim to it.[29]

27. Weston W. Fields, *Sodom and Gomorrah: History and Motif in Biblical Narrative,* Journal for the Study of the Old Testament Supplement Series, 231, ed. David J. A. Clines and Philip R. Davies (Sheffield: Sheffield Academic Press, 1997), 20. "The function of motifs and submotifs, therefore, is *representational*: the intent is to communicate a message or a series of messages beyond the action, object, character, or situation portrayed, or to offer plastic illustrations which present all the options" (21).
28. Alter, *The Art of Biblical Narrative,* 52.
29. See John H. Sailhamer, "Genesis," in *The Expositor's Bible Commentary,* ed. Frank E. Gaebelein, vol. 2 (Grand Rapids: Zondervan, 1990), 182–83.

Repetition

When I took advanced composition in my junior year of high school, I always dreaded the red-ink symbol "R&R" on my writing assignments. "R&R" meant "redundant and repetitive." Mrs. Blair, my English teacher, frowned upon repeated statements. Her preference was to say it well one time. When it's necessary to refer to something twice, she told us to use a different term the second time. In English literature, repetition is a sin.

In Old Testament narratives, though, repetition is a virtue. It is a technique used by writers to accomplish what we accomplish today through larger font sizes, boldface type, or italics. Thus, plot analysis requires paying attention to repetition.

David M. Gunn and Danna Nolan Fewell comment on the technique of repetition employed in Old Testament narrative literature:

> Whereas English prose eschews repetition, so that we are constantly looking for synonyms as we write, ancient Hebrew prose enjoys it. The verbatim repetition of a word, phrase, sentence, or set of sentences, or even the recurrence of words falling into the same semantic range can function to structure the story, to create atmosphere, to construct a theme or character, to emphasize a certain point to the reader, or to build suspense.[30]

Where does repetition occur? Sometimes, a command or prophecy is cited at one point and then "closely followed by its verbatim fulfillment."[31] For example, Joshua 6:20 describes the Israelite conquest of Jericho by repeating the identical terms that God used in issuing the command in Joshua 6:5:

> Now it will happen when there is a blast of the ram's horn, when they *hear the voice of the shofar,* that *all the people will shout a great war-shout.* Then the city *wall will fall down to the ground, and the people will go up, each one straight ahead.* (Josh. 6:5)

> So the people shouted, and they blew the shofars. Now it happened as the people *heard the voice of the shofar,* that *the people shouted a great war-shout.* Then the *wall fell down to the ground, and the people went up* to the city, *each one straight ahead.* (Josh. 6:20)[32]

---

30. David M. Gunn and Danna Nolan Fewell, *Narrative in the Hebrew Bible* (Oxford: Oxford University Press, 1993), 148. Alter also attributes the use of repetition to the oral context in which the Bible was communicated since its audience generally listened to rather than read the text (*The Art of Biblical Narrative,* 90).

31. Alter, *The Art of Biblical Narrative,* 90–91. See also Bar-Efrat, *Narrative Art in the Bible,* 161.

32. Author's translation. The corresponding elements have been italicized.

This kind of repetition highlights the people's precise obedience, indicating "that everything happens exactly as God commanded."[33] On the other hand, Bar-Efrat suggests that "special attention should be paid to the differences which often exist between the first and second versions, such as addition, omission, expansion, summarization, changed order, and substitution."[34] For a classic example, compare the dialogue between the woman and the serpent in Genesis 3:1–3 where God's original command (Gen. 2:16–17) is distorted by the serpent and expanded by the woman.

Repetition may also occur in the recurrence of a key word (*leitwort*).[35] Alter cites David's response to Absalom's death as an example: "The poet-king, who elsewhere responds to the report of deaths with eloquent elegies, here simply sobs, 'Absalom, Absalom, my son, my son,' repeating 'my son' eight times in two verses (2 Sam. 19:1, 5)."[36] The narrative in 2 Samuel 9 provides another example in its repetition of the term *lovingkindness* (vv. 1, 3, and 7). J. P. Fokkelman argues that David's wish to show lovingkindness to Mephibosheth is the driving force of the action: "Not only are there three scenes and three protagonists but the passage II Sam. 9 has three paragraphs of text in which *ḥsd* [the Hebrew term translated "lovingkindness"] appears three times. Also, the manifestation of lovingkindness comes up three times."[37] Similarly, the variations in 1 Samuel 15 on the terms *listen, voice,* and *word* stress the theme. This repetition highlights Saul's failure to listen to God's word and instead to listen to the people's voice.[38]

Textlinguists have noted that the technique of "renominalizing" (the repetition of a proper name) may mark a climactic point in the text, such as in Genesis 37:28 where the name Joseph occurs three times (rather than being referenced after the first occurrence by pronouns).[39] Repetition of a proper name to refer to a participant when a pronoun is sufficient may also "indicate that what he says is important, surprising, or unexpected (e.g., Gen. 18:13; 42:14; 46:30; Judg. 6:13; 8:23)."[40] In order to mark a participant, unnecessary pronouns sometimes appear with verb forms. Pastors who can read their

33. Bar-Efrat, *Narrative Art in the Bible,* 162.

34. Ibid.

35. Alter, *The Art of Biblical Narrative,* 92.

36. Ibid. In English Bibles, the references would be 2 Samuel 18:33 and 19:4. For comments on the slight inversion in the wording between the two laments, see Adele Berlin, *Poetics and Interpretation of Biblical Narrative* (Sheffield: Almond, 1983), 75.

37. J. P. Fokkelman, *Narrative Art and Poetry in the Books of Samuel: A Full Interpretation Based on Stylistic and Structural Analyses,* vol. 1: *King David (II Sam. 9–20 and I Kings 1–2)* (Assen, The Netherlands: Van Gorcum, 1981), 26.

38. Alter, *The Art of Biblical Narrative,* 93.

39. Christo H. J. van der Merwe, "Discourse Linguistics and Biblical Hebrew Grammar," in *Biblical Hebrew and Discourse Linguistics,* ed. Robert D. Bergen (Dallas: Summer Institute of Linguistics; Winona Lake, Ind.: Eisenbrauns, 1994), 35.

40. Ibid.

Hebrew Bibles understand that Hebrew verb forms are already inflected to indicate whether the subject is "he," "she," "you," "I," "they," or "we." Adding an extra pronoun adds emphasis.

וְאַתֵּנָה יְדַעְתֶּן

And you *yourself* know (Gen. 31:6)

וַתָּקָם הִיא וְכַלֹּתֶיהָ

And she stood up, *she* and her daughter-in-law (Ruth 1:6)

Time and Pace

While tracking the plot, an interpreter must observe the pace at which a narrative unfolds. Literary scholars differentiate between *narrated time* (or *narrative time*) and *narration time* (see table 3.4). Narrated time consists of the time within a narrative. It describes the length of the actions in the story and is thus measured in "real" units, such as days or years.[41] Narrated time is subject to gaps, delays, acceleration, and even movement in different directions.[42] Bar-Efrat comments on some of the functions of narrated time:

> Apart from its role within the narrative itself, such as providing emphases or implying connections between separate incidents, narrated time can fulfil direct functions for the reader, such as creating suspense or determining attitudes. . . . Since the decision as to what to include and what to omit, what to convey rapidly and on what to dwell at length, is closely bound up with the importance of the various subjects, the character of time as it is shaped within the narrative will be of great value in any attempt to analyze and interpret the narrative.[43]

Narration time refers to the time required for telling or reading the narrative.[44] To put it another way, narration time equals the length of material, that is, how many words or sentences or paragraphs it takes to tell or read the story.[45]

Table 3.4

Narrated Time	vs.	Narration Time
Time of actual events		Time needed to tell events
Measured in days/weeks		Measured in story's length

What is the value of comparing narrative time (length of actual events) with narration time (length of material needed to relate actual events)? Ska

41. Ska, *"Our Fathers Have Told Us,"* 7.
42. Bar-Efrat, *Narrative Art in the Bible*, 142.
43. Ibid., 142–43.
44. Ibid., 143.
45. Ska, *"Our Fathers Have Told Us,"* 8.

answers, "The ratio between the two makes it possible for the reader to detect the necessary choices of the narrator and the effects he wanted to produce."[46] Bar-Efrat elaborates on this idea:

> By studying the relation between narration time and narrated time the relative weight of the various sections of the narrative will be clarified, as well as their proportions with regard to one another and the narrative as a whole, thereby disclosing the focal points of the narrative. By elucidating the relationship between the two systems we will be able to see in how much detail matters are presented within the narrative, enabling us to draw conclusions about the meaning of the narrative, its central theme, etc.[47]

For example, the narration in Genesis 38:1–11 moves at a rapid pace to lay the groundwork for the subsequent events in the story.[48] Alter explains,

> Genesis 38 begins with Judah fathering three sons, one after another, recorded in breathless pace. Here, as at other points in the episode, nothing is allowed to detract our focused attention from the primary, problematic subject of the proper channel for the seed. . . . In a triad of verbs that admits nothing adventitious, Judah sees, takes, lies with a woman; and she, responding appropriately, conceived, bears and . . . gives the son a name. Then, with no narrative indication of any events at all in the intervening time, we move ahead an entire generation to the inexplicable death . . . of Er, Judah's firstborn, after his marriage to Tamar.[49]

After Genesis 38:12 signals a sizable time-gap (וַיִּרְבּוּ הַיָּמִים "Now after the days became many"), the action slows down as it enters the heart of the story. Verses 12–23 linger on Judah's sexual liaison with the disguised Tamar and his unsuccessful attempt to make payment. The action accelerates again in verse 24. While the quick pace in verses 1–11 served to cover background information, the return to a quick pace in verse 24 enables the narrative to proceed "quickly to its dramatic climax."[50]

To summarize, while the narrated time in Genesis 38:1–11 amounts to approximately eighteen to twenty years,[51] the narration time amounts to about

---

46. Ibid.

47. Bar-Efrat, *Narrative Art in the Bible*, 143.

48. Steven D. Mathewson, "An Exegetical Study of Genesis 38," 376–81. Gerhard von Rad writes, "The real action in the Judah-Tamar story begins at vs. 12ff. But for the reader to understand this extremely odd occurrence the narrator must first acquaint him with a few conditions . . ." (*Genesis*, trans. John H. Marks [London: SCM, 1961], 352).

49. Alter, *The Art of Biblical Narrative*, 6.

50. von Rad, *Genesis*, 355.

51. For the chronology of the events in Genesis 38:1–11, see Mathewson, "An Exegetical Study of Genesis 38," 382–83.

32 percent of the narrative.[52] In Genesis 38:12–30, the narrated time amounts to approximately nine months, while the narration time amounts to about 68 percent of the narrative.

Genesis 22 provides another good example. In verses 9–10, a string of seven verbs rapidly advances the main storyline, forcing the reader to agonize with Abraham as he reaches the place, builds the altar, arranges the wood, ties up his son Isaac, lays him on the altar, reaches out his hand, and takes the knife.[53] Alter argues that "sudden dense concentrations or unbroken chains of verbs, usually attached to a single subject, . . . indicate some particular intensity, rapidity, or a single-minded purposefulness of activity."[54] By contrast, earlier in the story (v. 2) the narrator suspends the action as he relates God's instructions to Abraham. Four phrases slow down the narrated time, creating suspense. With each phrase, the tension builds as the specificity increases. God said, "Take your son . . . the only son you have . . . the one you love . . . Isaac."[55]

Creating an Exegetical Outline

Your analysis of a story's plot should culminate with the creation of an exegetical outline. You will not preach from this outline, so you don't have to polish it excessively. The best way to create an outline is to organize the story along the lines of its plot elements. If more than two or three scenes or episodes make up a plot element, then list them as subpoints in the outline. Finally, write out your outline points as sentences. This will force you to think more accurately. Again, this is not a sermon outline; it is an exegetical outline. You will return to it later when you prepare a sermon outline. The following is an example of an exegetical outline from Genesis 22:1–19.

    I. *Exposition:* The narrator explains God's intent to test Abraham (v. 1)
    II. *Crisis:* God commands Abraham to sacrifice his son Isaac (v. 2)
    III. *Rising Tension:* Abraham responds to God's command with obedience (vv. 3–10)
        A. Abraham travels to the mountain of sacrifice to worship God (vv. 3–6)
        B. Abraham replies to Isaac's question about the lamb by asserting that God will provide (vv. 7–8)

52. This percentage is based on the number of lines in the Hebrew text (*Biblia Hebraica Stuttgartensia*) of Genesis 38. It is also confirmed by a word count.

53. These are all *wayyiqtol* forms (also called "preterite" or "imperfect with *waw*-consecutive"). Their function in narrative is to advance the main line of the story. Appendix A discusses this feature in detail.

54. Alter, *The Art of Biblical Narrative*, 80.

55. Author's translation of the Hebrew text of Genesis 22:2a.

      C. Abraham prepares to slay his son Isaac (vv. 9–10)

IV. *Resolution:* God stops Abraham from slaying Isaac and provides a ram for the sacrifice (vv. 11–14)

      A. The angel of the LORD commands Abraham not to do anything to Isaac and commends Abraham for demonstrating the fear of God (vv. 11–12)

      B. Abraham finds a ram for the sacrifice and attributes it to God's provision (vv. 13–14)

V. *Conclusion:* The angel of the LORD returns to reaffirm the LORD's blessing on Abraham and the LORD's intent to fulfill his promise (vv. 15–19)

4

❀ ❀ ❀ ❀

THE PEOPLE
WHO MAKE STORIES INTERESTING

❀ ❀ ❀ ❀

Part of the fun of going to a shopping mall is watching people. People are fascinating. A small child begs for more pennies to throw into a fountain. Two teenage girls giggle as they scope out the young males who saunter by their bench. A drama unfolds at the checkout counter in a JC Penney store where a man fusses at a sales clerk for not letting him return merchandise without a sales slip. A white-haired couple ambles along, their gait betraying their struggle with health in recent years. While shopping is centered around purchasing merchandise, it's the people that make shopping interesting.

Similarly, while Old Testament narratives focus more on action, the people involved supply the reason for our interest in stories. A rabbinic saying quips, "God made people because he loves stories." Perhaps the reverse is also true— God made stories because he loves people. Our interest in stories rivets us to the characters. We even identify stories by characters' names: the story of Ruth, the David story, and the Judah-Tamar story. Interpreting Old Testament stories requires us to pay attention to the characters and how they develop. Because plot is primary, our analysis should attempt to specify the function of characters in relationship to the plot.[1]

---

1. "The predominance of action and the lack of interest in the psychological processes of the characters are two of the main characteristics of Biblical narrative" (Jean Louis Ska, *"Our Fathers Have Told Us": Introduction to the Analysis of Hebrew Narratives* [Roma: Editrice Pontificio Instituto Biblico, 1990], 83).

Classifying the Characters

When reading an Old Testament narrative, interpreters should distinguish between major and minor characters (see table 4.1). This distinction arises from the size of a character's role in the story. Furthermore, the exegete should categorize the main characters based on the nature of their roles. Literary scholars identify the following character types: *protagonists* (central characters, those who are most indispensable to the plot), *antagonists* (the main adversaries or forces arrayed against central characters), and *foils* (characters who heighten the central character by providing a contrast or occasionally a parallel).[2]

Table 4.1
Types of Characters in Old Testament Stories

Major	or	Minor
↓		
Protagonist		
Antagonist		
Foil		

While these categories emerge from Western literary analysis, they seem to transcend Western literature and apply to stories of various cultures, including the Bible. The idea is not to reduce a character to a label but to clarify what role a narrator assigns to a particular character in a particular story.

The David story offers a prime example of how classifying characters aids exegesis. Beginning in 1 Samuel 16, David surfaces as the protagonist while Saul functions as both an antagonist and a foil.[3] Thus, while the conflict in 1 Samuel 17 occurs at one level between David and Goliath, it takes place at another level between David and Saul. Goliath provides the challenge that will reveal the contrast between David and Saul. The future king and the present king respond differently, revealing their fitness to occupy the throne of Israel.[4] In 1 Samuel 25, David remains the protagonist, Nabal functions as the antagonist who opposes David, and Abigail serves as the foil, contrasting David's thirst for retaliation with her discerning plea to let God execute ven-

---

2. Ska, *"Our Fathers Have Told Us,"* 86–87; Leland Ryken, *How to Read the Bible As Literature* (Grand Rapids: Zondervan, 1984), 43, 54.

3. Walter Brueggemann, *First and Second Samuel,* Interpretation: A Bible Commentary for Teaching and Preaching, ed. James L. Mays (Louisville: John Knox, 1990), 124–25. Herbert M. Wolf has suggested that 1 Samuel 15 to 2 Samuel 8 functions as a "dynastic defense," similar in structure and theme to a thirteenth-century Hittite dynastic defense, "Apology of Hattusilis" ("Implications of Form Criticism for Old Testament Studies," *Bibliotheca Sacra* 127 [October 1970]: 303–6). This section, then, defends the replacement of Saul's house with David's house on the throne.

4. See Brueggemann, *First and Second Samuel,* 134.

geance. David changes so that by the end of the episode he shares the same conviction as Abigail.[5]

In 2 Samuel 11–12, David continues as the protagonist while Uriah the Hittite serves as the foil. As a foil, Uriah is the hero of the story, demonstrating a level of integrity that David, the leading character, does not. Though Bathsheba is important to the story, her role is minor. Adele Berlin comments,

> Throughout the entire story the narrator has purposely subordinated the character of Bathsheba. He has ignored her feelings and given the barest notice of her actions. . . . For lack of a better designation, I will call her an "agent," an Aristotelian term which describes the performer of an action necessary to the plot.[6]

Later, however, in 1 Kings 1–2, Bathsheba assumes the role of a leading character as she works to secure the throne for her son.[7]

In Genesis 38, Judah is the central character while Tamar serves as a foil. Judah and Tamar are clearly the major characters and everyone else serves in supporting or minor roles (see table 4.2). The terms *major* and *minor* refer to a character's role in a story, not their overall importance in redemptive history. In fact, the same person can play a different role in a different story. In Genesis 37 Judah functions as an antagonist, although a more sympathetic antagonist than his other brothers. In the larger framework of the Joseph story, however, Judah functions as a foil for Joseph.

Table 4.2
Character Classification in Genesis 38

Major:	Judah—*protagonist*
	Tamar—*foil*
Minor:	Hirah, Daughter of Shua, Er, Onan, Shelah, men at Timnah, midwife, Perez, Zerah.

What do you do once you've labeled the characters? Ryken explains that readers must go through the story as a "traveling companion of the protagonist" and view this protagonist as "someone who undertakes an experiment in

5. Some foils, such as Abigail in 1 Samuel 25 and Gehazi in 2 Kings 5, play a major role in the story. Others, such as Orpah in the Book of Ruth, play a minor role.

6. Adele Berlin, *Poetics and Interpretation of Biblical Narrative* (Sheffield: Almond, 1983), 26–27.

7. Ibid., 27. Berlin notes that there is an "alternation in the narratives [of 1, 2 Samuel and 1 Kings 1–2] between David as the main character and David as subordinate character, and that these correspond roughly to the public and private domains" (33).

living."[8] The key is, "if we can see our own experience in the events and characters of the story, the story has captured something universal about life."[9]

Means of Characterization

In John Grisham's novel *The Testament,* lawyer Nate Riley searches for the surprise heir to an eleven billion dollar fortune—a missionary named Rachel Lane. Riley finally finds her deep in the jungles of Brazil. At their initial encounter, a group of tribesmen escort Rachel to Riley. Notice how Grisham describes her as he relates the encounter:

> Rachel was with them; she was coming. There was a light yellow shirt in the midst of the brown-skinned chests, and a lighter face under a straw hat. . . . She was slightly taller than the Indians, and carried herself with an easy elegance. . . . Nate watched every step. She was very slender, with wide bony shoulders. She began looking in their direction as they grew closer. . . . She removed her hat. Her hair was brown and half-gray, and very short.[10]

Similarly, Louis L'Amour paints a vivid picture of James T. Kettleman, the main character in his novel *Flint:*

> His face was lean and hard, triangular, with high cheekbones, green eyes, and a strong jaw. His sideburns were long in the fashion of the time, his hair dark brown and curly. In the light it showed a tinge of red. His skin was dark, his features, except for his eyes, normally without expression.
> James T. Kettleman, financier and speculator, had often been called a handsome man. He had never been called a friendly one.[11]

Our Western literary tradition, particularly the novel, goes to great lengths to paint character portraits. In contrast to a Louis L'Amour, John Grisham, or Charles Dickens, the authors of Old Testament narratives tell their stories in a lean, spare style.[12] Thus, characterization in Old Testament narratives resembles a quick pencil sketch. As Robert Alter notes, "We are given only the barest hints about the physical appearance, the tics and gestures, the dress and implements of the characters, the material milieu in which they enact their destinies."[13] Sternberg observes that elaborate descriptions "perform no other

8. Ryken, *How to Read the Bible As Literature,* 43.
9. Ibid., 44. See also 1 Corinthians 10:11.
10. John Grisham, *The Testament* (New York: Island Books, 1999), 254.
11. Louis L'Amour, *Flint* (New York: Bantam, 1960), 4.
12. Thomas G. Long, *Preaching and the Literary Forms of the Bible* (Philadelphia: Fortress, 1989), 78.
13. Robert Alter, *The Art of Biblical Narrative* (New York: Basic, 1981), 114. Alter refers to the "rigorous economy of biblical narrative," which is different from the "Greek tendency to narrative specification . . . that modern literary practice has by and large adopted" (129).

role than realistic fullness."[14] The biblical storytellers do not concern themselves with vivid depictions.[15]

Direct Description

The scarcity of detailed description makes it significant when it does occur. Descriptive details are highly significant because "the ratio of description in general to action and dialogue is relatively low."[16] Therefore, every detail in biblical narrative merits attention. Berlin comments,

> The purpose of character description in the Bible is not to enable the reader to visualize the character, but to enable him to situate the character in terms of his place in society, his own particular situation, and his outstanding traits—in other words, to tell what kind of a person he is.[17]

In most cases, suggests Sternberg, "epithet prefigures drama."[18] The descriptions in Judges 3:15–17 of Ehud as "left-handed" and Eglon as "very fat" prepare the reader for Ehud's successful attempt to sneak an undetected sword (because it was strapped to the side of his body opposite that of most men) into Eglon's quarters and assassinate him. The reference to Joseph's good looks in Genesis 39:6 explains the sexual advance made by Potiphar's wife. Likewise, the description of Esau as a "hairy man" (Gen. 27:11) helps the reader appreciate Jacob's effort when he disguised himself as his brother.

Actions

Generally, the biblical narrators show us rather than tell us. Thus, interpreters get insight into a character's nature by paying attention to his or her

14. Meir Sternberg, *The Poetics of Biblical Narrative: Ideological Literature and the Drama of Reading*, Indiana Studies in Biblical Literature (Bloomington: Indiana University Press, 1985), 329.

15. Shimon Bar-Efrat writes, "The absence of depictions in biblical narrative is connected with the tension which exists in a work of literature between the categories of time and space. . . . [N]arration time continues when a more or less detailed description of places or scenes is given, while narrated time comes to a standstill. By stopping narrated time a static element is introduced, and this is incompatible with the dynamic and vigorous nature of biblical narrative. The biblical narrative is wholly devoted to creating a sense of time which flows continually and rapidly, and this is inevitably achieved at the expense of the shaping of space. Because space is fundamentally static and unchanging it is an alien element in biblical narrative" (*Narrative Art in the Bible* [Sheffield: Almond, 1989], 195–96).

16. Berlin, *Poetics and Interpretation of Biblical Narrative*, 34.

17. Ibid., 36.

18. Sternberg, *The Poetics of Biblical Narrative*, 342. J. P. Fokkelman observes, "The description of people, thoughts, landscapes and buildings can take up many pages in modern narrative. In the Bible it is extremely scarce. If the narrator leaves the action for a moment and tells of a woman that she is 'fair of face,' this is never just because of this quality in its own right. He will only mention something like that if it is going to be a factor in a plot" (*Reading Biblical Narrative: An Introductory Guide* [Philadelphia: Westminster, 1999], 71).

actions. For example, a careful reading of Genesis 22:1–19 shows the reader that Abraham is a man who is so committed to obeying God that he will obey even when God's command seems outrageous. Notice how the writer describes Peninnah's actions towards Hannah in 1 Samuel 1:6–7:

> And because the LORD had closed her [Hannah's] womb, her rival [Peninnah] kept provoking her in order to irritate her. This went on year after year. Whenever Hannah went up to the house of the LORD, her rival provoked her till she wept and would not eat.

The writer does not need to inform us that Peninnah is a bitter, jealous woman. Her actions clearly demonstrate these traits.

Names

Certain cultures attach a special significance to names. I remember the first high school basketball game I watched in Montana involving a team from the Crow reservation. When the starting lineups were introduced, I heard names like Jo Jo Pretty Paint, Jonathan Takes Enemy, and Miles Fighter. At a recent high school girls tournament, the rosters of teams from the Native American schools included names like Malerie Covers Up, Staci Big Hair, Vonna Good Luck, Heather Clubfoot, and Tawny Whistling Elk. These names reflect either the circumstances attending the child's birth or a virtue that will hopefully characterize the child's life.

In Old Testament narratives, characters' names play an important role. As Ska points out, "A very common way to 'characterize' a personage is to give him or her a name."[19] Obvious examples include Abraham (a variant of his old name, Abram, which sounds more like the Hebrew for "father of many nations"), and Nabal in 1 Samuel 25 (whose name means "fool").

John Stek argues for the significance of the names in Judges 4, the account of the defeat of Sisera, the cruel Canaanite commander.[20] Ironically, the Israelite warrior, "lightning" (the meaning of Barak), remains passive, doubtful, and silent. The glory goes to two faithful and fearless women: "bee" (the meaning of Deborah) and "mountain goat" (the meaning of Jael). Stek sees the names forming a pun that captures the gist of the story. Deborah, the bee, dispensed her sweet justice under a honey tree and kept prodding (stinging?) Barak to attack Sisera. Jael, the mountain goat, provided the fleeing Sisera with nourishing milk and then stabbed him when he lay down to rest. As a result, peace is restored to the Promised Land of milk and honey.

19. Ska, *"Our Fathers Have Told Us,"* 88.
20. John H. Stek, "The Bee and the Mountain Goat: A Literary Reading of Judges 4," in *A Tribute to Gleason Archer,* ed. Walter C. Kaiser Jr. and Ronald F. Youngblood (Chicago: Moody, 1986), 53–86.

The Book of Ruth provides another example of how names contribute to characterization. Irony occurs when "My God is King" (Elimelech) flees his King's territory because of a famine.[21] If the names Mahlon and Chilion mean "sickly" and "failing," they foreshadow the early demise of these men and highlight the severe effects of the famine on Elimelech and his wife, Naomi.[22] Naomi, whose name means "pleasant one," demonstrates the irony of her name when she responds angrily to the women of Bethlehem who call out her name when she returns.[23] Ruth 1:20 may be translated, "But she said to them, 'Do not call me Pleasant One [נָעֳמִי]. Call me Bitter One (מָרָא) because Shaddai has made me extremely bitter.'"[24] Even more intriguing is the expression Boaz uses in Ruth 4:1 in reference to a potential kinsman-redeemer. Boaz addresses him with the Hebrew expression פְּלֹנִי אַלְמֹנִי. Hubbard captures the intention of this expression by translating verse 1 like this: "Boaz hailed him: 'Come over here and sit down, Mr. So and So!'"[25] The intrusion of this odd expression "serves a literary, not a historical, purpose. Perhaps the spotlight cast on the man's namelessness implied judgment: the one who refused to raise a name over the inheritance of his deceased kin deserves no name in the story."[26]

Names of characters contribute to the author's intent by highlighting character qualities, but they also form puns and create irony. In Genesis 21:1–7, Sarah's laughter of joy at her son's birth replaces her laughter of disbelief (Gen. 18:12). God, of course, gets the last laugh when Abraham follows his command (Gen. 17:19) and names the boy Isaac, which means "laughter." The delightful pun, though it contains some aesthetic value, serves to highlight God's faithfulness to fulfill promises even when he seems slow in doing it.

Designations

Designations also contribute to characterization. For instance, a designation may betray how one character is perceived by the narrator or by other characters in the story.[27] In Genesis 21:9, the narrator betrays Sarah's resent-

---

21. Robert L. Hubbard Jr., *The Book of Ruth*, New International Commentary on the Old Testament (Grand Rapids: Eerdmans, 1988), 88.

22. Daniel I. Block argues for this interpretation of the names (*Judges, Ruth*, New American Commentary, ed. E. Ray Clendenen, vol. 6 [Nashville: Broadman and Holman, 1999], 625). Hubbard, who has doubts about this interpretation of the names, provides a helpful summary of the arguments for and against it (see *The Book of Ruth*, 89–90).

23. Hubbard, *The Book of Ruth*, 89.

24. Author's translation from the Hebrew text of Ruth 1:20. Unfortunately, the meanings of Ruth and Boaz, names of two prominent characters, have not been settled. Suggestions for the meaning of Ruth range from "refreshment/comfort" to "friendship," while Boaz is most likely related to "strength." See Hubbard, 94, 134–35.

25. Ibid., 232.

26. Ibid., 234–35.

27. Bar-Efrat, *Narrative Art in the Bible*, 36. See also Berlin, *Poetics and Interpretation of Biblical Narrative*, 59–60.

ment when he withholds Ishmael's name and says, "But Sarah saw that the son whom Hagar the Egyptian had borne to Abraham was mocking." David reflects an attitude of contempt towards Goliath by referring to him as "this uncircumcised Philistine" (1 Sam. 17:26). Later the text betrays David's attitude towards Bathsheba by mentioning her as "a/the woman" (2 Sam. 11:1–5) though her name had already been given.[28]

On the other hand, suggests Sternberg, "A character's emergence from anonymity may correlate with a rise in importance. It is no accident that the text [1 Samuel 16:1–13] consistently withholds David's name . . . till the very moment of anointment and elevation."[29]

Dialogue

When studying Old Testament narratives, interpreters must also focus on the statements or speeches made by the characters. Alter speaks of "the highly subsidiary role of narration in comparison to direct speech by the characters."[30] Cynthia Miller notes that "speech permeated the Bible, from the creative word of divine speech in Genesis to the decrees of a Persian king at the end of Chronicles."[31] For example, Joshua 1 consists almost entirely of four speeches: Yahweh to Joshua (1:1–9), Joshua to the officers (1:10–11), Joshua to the Transjordan tribes (1:12–15), and the people to Joshua (1:16–18). The so-called "David-Goliath" story in 1 Samuel 17 provides another example. Brueggemann observes, "The action does not take very long. As is characteristic of Israel's narrative art, the speeches are of more interest and importance than the action."[32] Furthermore, Fokkelman makes this observation about the David-Mephibosheth story in 2 Samuel 9:

> In this section, [there is a] ratio of 25 lines of narrative to 23 lines of direct speech . . . yet it is the direct speech that carries the action. The other lines have mainly auxiliary function: some of them provide us with information about Ziba and Mephibosheth in their nominal clauses; thirteen lines are only intro-

28. Bar-Efrat, *Narrative Art in the Bible,* 37. Christo H. J. van der Merwe describes the "withholding of full reference to a participant . . . in which a persona is developed first and then finally assigned a name" as a "marked way" of "participant reference" ("Discourse Linguistics and Biblical Hebrew Grammar," in *Biblical Hebrew and Discourse Linguistics,* ed. Robert D. Bergen [Dallas: Summer Institute of Linguistics; Winona Lake, Ind.: Eisenbrauns, 1994], 35). See appendix A for an explanation of marking.

29. Sternberg, *The Poetics of Biblical Narrative,* 330.

30. Alter, *The Art of Biblical Narrative,* 65. Textlinguists point out that dialogue is embedded into the main line of a story; however, dialogue often has a significance that transcends its subordinate role in a storyline.

31. Cynthia L. Miller, *The Representation of Speech in Biblical Hebrew Narrative: A Linguistic Analysis,* Harvard Semitic Monographs, ed. Peter Machinist, no. 55 (Atlanta: Scholars Press, 1996), 1.

32. Brueggemann, *First and Second Samuel,* 133.

ductory statements ("X said to Y"); six pave the way for a meeting; and the nominal sentences at the end show how David's commands become a lasting reality.[33]

While speech dominates, interpreters should expect it to be compressed. Bar-Efrat explains that "conversations in biblical narrative are never precise and naturalistic imitations of real-life conversations. They are highly concentrated and stylized, are devoid of idle chatter, and all the details they contain are carefully calculated to fulfil a clear function."[34]

One of the functions of speech by the characters is to provide insight into their traits. Esau's blunt request for stew in Genesis 25:30 portrays him as a man controlled by his cravings. On the other hand, Uriah's refusal speech to King David's offer of a night at home during a heated battle portrays him as a man of honor and integrity (2 Sam. 11:11).

Even more significantly, conversation points to meaning. According to Alter, "Dialogue is made to carry a large part of the freight of meaning."[35] For example, when Isaac asks Abraham where the lamb is for the burnt offering, Abraham's response in Genesis 22:8 foreshadows the outcome and supplies the conviction by which he passes God's test: "God himself will provide the lamb for the burnt offering." Joseph summarizes the meaning of the entire Joseph cycle, as well as the immediate story in Genesis 49:29–50:26, when he states, "You intended to harm me, but God intended it for good to accomplish what is now being done, the saving of many lives" (Gen. 50:20). Similarly, statements by David in 1 Samuel 17:34–37 and 45–47 provide the key to the David-Goliath story, and Abigail's impassioned speech in 1 Samuel 25:24–31 moves the reader towards the theme of vengeance belonging to God. Thus, interpreters should look to speeches for clues to the author's intent.

Two more features of speech deserve attention. First, Alter observes that direct speech set in formal verse often has a summarizing or ceremonial function, such as Hannah's speech in 1 Samuel 2:1–10 and Adam's outburst in Genesis 2:23.[36] Second, Alter points out the technique of "contrastive dialogue" where the contrasting speech of two characters accomplishes "differentiation"—that is, a contrast between ideas or concepts.[37] As examples he cites "Esau's inarticulate outbursts over against Jacob's calculated legalisms in the selling of the birthright (Gen. 25); Joseph's long-winded statement of morally

33. J. P. Fokkelman, *Narrative Art and Poetry in the Books of Samuel: A Full Interpretation Based on Stylistic and Structural Analyses*, vol. 1: *King David (II Sam. 9–20 and I Kings 1–2)* (Assen, The Netherlands: Van Gorcum, 1981), 24.

34. Bar-Efrat, *Narrative Art in the Bible*, 148.

35. Alter, *The Art of Biblical Narrative*, 37.

36. Ibid., 28. For a discussion of "poetic seams" in the Pentateuch, see John H. Sailhamer, *The Pentateuch As Narrative* (Grand Rapids: Zondervan, 1992), 35–37.

37. Alter, *The Art of Biblical Narrative*, 72.

aghast refusal over against the two-word sexual bluntness of Potiphar's wife (Gen. 39); [and] Saul's choked cry after David's impassioned speech outside the cave at Ein Gedi (1 Sam. 24)."[38]

Alright, you should now have a good handle on how to study the people who make stories interesting. If you take time to classify the characters, to notice how the writer has characterized them, and to listen to their speech, you're well on your way to understanding the author's intended meaning. Nevertheless, some environmental issues await you.

38. Ibid.

5

❀ ❀ ❀ ❀ ❀

ENVIRONMENTAL ISSUES

❀ ❀ ❀ ❀ ❀

After scrutinizing the plot and the characters of a story, an interpreter needs to consider two issues related to a story's setting or environment. One issue concerns the specific place and time in which the story occurs. This is the story's historical, cultural, and geographical setting. The other issue concerns the position of the story within the flow of stories that make up a book. Scholars often refer to this as the literary setting.

These issues resemble those faced by students who research a Civil War battle. If I intend to understand the Battle of Gettysburg, I have to look at two settings. The first setting consists of the actual location and time period of the battle. The Union and Confederate armies converged unintentionally at the little town of Gettysburg, Pennsylvania, on July 1, 1863. The battle raged for three days, ending on July 3 with Confederate Major General George E. Pickett's fateful charge. Students who study the battle in more detail will observe the role of topographical features like Cemetery Ridge, Round Top, Little Round Top, Devil's Den, and Seminary Ridge.

The second setting consists of the position of the Battle of Gettysburg in the overall flow of the Civil War. The battle occurred roughly in the middle of the Civil War which ran from 1861 to 1865. The Union victory at Gettysburg, coupled with Grant's victory at Vicksburg, reversed the war. Even more significant is what happened in the aftermath of Gettysburg. Union General

George Meade missed his chance to finish off Lee's army and end the war. His caution in pursuing Lee gave Lee's troops time to recoup from their exhaustion and escape to Virginia. Understanding the Battle of Gettysburg, then, requires a look at the physical setting in which the battle took place as well as its location in the larger flow of Civil War battles.

When I work with an Old Testament narrative, I prefer to describe the two settings in terms that remind me to keep my conclusions based on the text. Thus, I distinguish between a story's *inner-textual setting* and its *inter-textual setting*.[1] Inner-textual setting refers to what literary scholars typically refer to as setting, namely, "the space in which the characters perform the actions that constitute the plot."[2] Longman observes,

> We must realize that in the historical narrative that dominates the narrative genre of the Bible, the author's choice of setting was usually restricted. Authors simply placed action where it actually occurred. Of course, these authors controlled the selectivity of detail in the description of settings, requiring the reader to pay close attention to these textual signals.[3]

On the other hand, I use inter-textual setting to describe what some refer to as literary setting, the location of a story in the larger narrative framework.

Inner-Textual Setting

An interpreter discovers the inner-textual setting by asking, Where did the story happen? Is there any significant geographical movement within the story? When did this story take place? During what season of year? What was happening in Israel's history at this time? Robert Chisholm notes that while details of physical setting serve merely to lend realism to the story or create a certain mood, "at other times physical setting can have symbolic value and contribute to the story's theme."[4] He cites an example:

> In 2 Kings 1:9, the king's arrogant officer demands that the prophet Elijah "come down" from his perch "on the top of a hill." Elijah refuses to come down

---

1. My coinage of these terms builds on the distinction between the expressions "inner-textuality" (the composition of a text; links within a text) and "inter-textuality" (the interrelationship of texts; links between texts). For a discussion of the latter two expressions, see John H. Sailhamer, *Introduction to Old Testament Theology* (Grand Rapids: Zondervan, 1995), 155, 212.
2. Tremper Longman III, "Biblical Narrative," in *A Complete Literary Guide to the Bible,* ed. Leland Ryken and Tremper Longman III (Grand Rapids: Zondervan, 1993), 74.
3. Ibid., 75.
4. Robert B. Chisholm Jr., *From Exegesis to Exposition: A Practical Guide to Using Biblical Hebrew* (Grand Rapids: Baker, 1998), 151.

and instead calls fire down on the officer and his men. Elijah's elevated position symbolizes his authority as God's spokesman over the king and his messengers.[5]

In the Book of Ruth, the movement of the setting from Israel to Moab and back to Israel is significant. By leaving Israel for Moab, Elimelech abandons the covenant community in search of a solution to his hunger. Furthermore, the temporal information that introduces the narrative, "in the days when the judges ruled" (Ruth 1:1), suggests that the physical problem Elimelech sought to escape was due to a spiritual problem.[6]

In 2 Samuel 11–12, the text identifies the story's beginning as the springtime, when kings typically go out to war. We expect, then, to find King David with the Israelite army at the battlefield. To our surprise, we learn that David remained in Jerusalem. This leads to a crisis that would not have evolved if David had been with his army.

Inter-Textual Setting

"To understand fully the significance of a narrative one must examine its placement within the larger whole of which it is a part."[7] I refer to this as the story's inter-textual setting. For example, the story of Solomon and the two prostitutes in 1 Kings 3:16–28 has a verifying function. It authenticates the previous story (1 Kings 3:1–15) which narrates how God gave Solomon a wise and discerning heart.

The story of David, Abigail, and Nabal in 1 Samuel 25 is sandwiched between two stories in which David refrains from taking revenge against King Saul. Thus, the story is part of a larger unit that hinges on the theme of revenge. In 1 Samuel 24, David refuses to take revenge against the Lord's anointed. In 1 Samuel 25, he learns not to take revenge against an ordinary (non-royal) fool like Nabal. Even more important, David learns not to take revenge when the death of the prophet Samuel (25:1) weakens his claim to the throne and when everyone seems to be against him. In this story, Abigail arises as a new prophetic voice and reminds David that he does not need to seek vengeance because God will make a lasting dynasty for him and will defeat his enemies (25:28–29). So David's attitude towards revenge comes full circle in 1 Samuel 26 where he seeks Saul out to pursue reconciliation and to emphasize his refusal to inflict harm on the king. In its broader context, 1 Samuel 25 and the immediately surrounding stories are part of a larger unit

---

5. Ibid.

6. The expression "in the days when the judges ruled" is an allusion to the book of Judges. The allusion presupposes an understanding of the cycles that Israel experienced. See Judges 2:11–19.

7. Chisholm, *From Exegesis to Exposition,* 168.

(1 Sam. 16–2 Sam. 8) that functions as a "dynastic defense," exposing Saul's failure as king and David's qualification to be king.

Another noteworthy example of inter-textual setting is Genesis 38. While the location of the story within the Joseph narrative has confused many interpreters, its location contributes to the larger story.[8] It interrupts the story just when Joseph has been sold into prison. This heightens the tension, forcing the reader to wait until the story resumes in Genesis 39 before finding out what happens to Joseph. Also, Judah serves as a foil to Joseph. Judah's sexual indiscretion contrasts with Joseph's sexual purity. Furthermore, Genesis 38 is part of the larger story of God developing in Abraham a nation through which he would bless the earth. The continuation of the line of blessing is threatened by Judah's failure to produce an heir. In the end, the righteous Tamar is responsible for continuing the line from which the Messiah would come.

Once again, I encourage you to put your conclusions in writing. This will ensure that you clearly identify both the inner-textual and inter-textual settings of a story. Getting a grasp on these settings will move you closer to discerning the author's intended meaning. All you have left to do before nailing down this intended meaning is to zero in on the perspective from which the author tells the story.

8. For a summary of the discussion about the problematic location of Genesis 38, see Steven D. Mathewson, "An Exegetical Study of Genesis 38," *Bibliotheca Sacra* 146 (October–December 1989): 373–74. Genesis 38 uses a technique called "resumptive repetition" in which the author of a Biblical Hebrew narrative interrupts a story to insert something and then resumes the original narrative by repeating the last sentence before the break (Shemaryahu Talmon, "The Presentation of Synchroneity and Simultaneity in Biblical Narrative," in *Studies in Hebrew Narrative Art throughout the Ages,* Scripta Hierosolymitana, vol. 27, ed. Joseph Heinemann and Samuel Werses [Jerusalem: Magnes Press, Hebrew University, 1978], 9–26).

6

❀❀❀❀❀

PUTTING PERSPECTIVE
IN PERSPECTIVE

❀❀❀❀❀

A storyteller's perspective determines how listeners experience and understand a story. Robert Fulgham offers a hilarious example about his neighbor's encounter with a spider web.[1] Here is the scene from Fulgham's perspective, just as he saw it happen.

> This is my neighbor. Nice lady. Coming out her front door, on her way to work and in her "looking good" mode. She's locking the door now and picking up her daily luggage: purse, lunch bag, gym bag for aerobics, and the garbage bucket to take out. She turns, sees me, gives me the big smiling Hello, takes three steps across her front porch. And goes "AAAAGGGHHH!!!" . . . At about the level of a fire engine at full cry. Spider web! She has walked full force into a spider web. . . .
>
> She flings her baggage in all directions. And at the same time does a high-kick, jitterbug sort of dance . . . Clutches at her face and hair and goes "AAAAGGGGHHH!!!" at a new level of intensity. Tries opening the front door without unlocking it. Tries again. Breaks key in the lock. Runs around the house headed for the back door.

1. This account comes from Robert Fulgham, *All I Really Need to Know I Learned in Kindergarten* (New York: Ivy, 1986), 13–14.

But then Fulgham relates a different view of the scene. Here is the encounter from the spider's perspective.

> Rather ordinary, medium gray, middle-aged lady spider. She's been up since before dawn working on her web, and all is well. Nice day, no wind, dew point just right to keep things sticky. She's out checking the moorings and thinking about the little gnats she'd like to have for breakfast. Feeling good. Ready for action. All of a sudden all hell breaks loose—earthquake, tornado, volcano. The web is torn loose and is wrapped around a frenzied moving haystack, and a huge piece of raw-but-painted meat is making a sound the spider never heard before: "AAAAGGGHHH!!!" It's too big to wrap up and eat later, and it's moving too much to hold down. Jump for it? Hang on and hope? Dig in?

How readers experience Old Testament stories depends in part on the perspective of the storyteller. Adele Berlin reminds readers that "a character is not perceived by the reader directly, but rather mediated or filtered through the telling of the (implied) author, the narrator, or another character."[2] We refer to the storyteller's perspective as the point of view. Longman explains,

> The narrator is the one who controls the story. His is the voice through whom we hear about the action and the people of the narrative. The narrator's point of view is the perspective through which we observe and evaluate everything connected with the story. In short, the narrator is a device used by authors to shape and guide how the reader responds to the characters and events of the story.[3]

So in addition to examining a story's plot, characters, and setting, interpreters must also zero in on a story's point of view or perspective.

Generally, the Old Testament narrators adopt a third-person point of view. The most notable exceptions are certain stories in Nehemiah that are cast in first-person narrative. The following description of the Gospel of Mark's "narrator" applies equally well to the narrators of Old Testament stories:

> The narrator does not figure in the events of the story; speaks in the third person; is not bound by time or space in the telling of the story; is an implied invisible presence in every scene, capable of being anywhere to "recount" the action; displays full omniscience by narrating the thoughts, feelings, or sensory experiences of many characters; often turns from the story to give direct "asides" to the reader, explaining a custom or translating a word or commenting

2. Adele Berlin, *Poetics and Interpretation of Biblical Narrative* (Sheffield: Almond, 1983), 43. Like Jean Louis Ska, I find the distinctions between "implied author" and "narrator" and between "implied reader" and "narrator" to be "practically irrelevant in most of the Biblical narratives" (Ska, *"Our Fathers Have Told Us": Introduction to the Analysis of Hebrew Narratives* [Roma: Editrice Pontificio Instituto Biblico, 1990], 42).

3. Tremper Longman III, "Biblical Narrative," in *A Complete Literary Guide to the Bible*, ed. Leland Ryken and Tremper Longman III (Grand Rapids: Zondervan, 1993), 75.

on the story; and narrates the story from one overarching ideological point of view.[4]

Focalization

A key aspect of the storyteller's point of view is called *focalization*. More specifically, this aspect observes what material in the narrative arises from the *reader's* point of view ("external focalization" or "vision from without"), what material issues from the *character's* point of view ("internal focalization" or "vision from within"), and what material comes from the *narrator's* point of view ("zero focalization" or "vision from behind").[5] The first focalization is considered an *external* point of view. The next two focalizations—character and narrator—are considered *internal* points of view (see table 6.1).

In Genesis 38, for example, the story begins with an external point of view. That is, "the reader first has the impression that the narrative is told by an external observer listing facts."[6] But in verse 7, the narrator adopts an internal perspective. More specifically, he shares information from the narrator's point of view, not the character's. The text gives us no reason to assume that the character, Er, was privy to this information. In other words, the narrator is saying more than the character knows. However, in verse 9 the narrator discloses what Onan knows. This internal perspective is assumed by the character as well as the narrator.

Table 6.1
Points of View

External
↓
• Reader—what an observer knows

Internal
↓
• Character—what a character knows (more than a reader knows)
• Narrator—what a narrator knows (more than a character knows)

Interpreters can look for three indicators of a shift in focalization (see table 6.2).[7] First, focalization is often indicated by verbs of perception (to see, to hear, to know, etc.). A second indicator is the expression "to say to one's heart" as in Genesis 8:21 and 27:41. A third indicator is the particle *wehinneh*

---

4. David Rhoads and Donald Michie, *Mark As Story: An Introduction to the Narrative of a Gospel* (Philadelphia: Fortress, 1982), 36.
5. Ska, *"Our Fathers Have Told Us,"* 66–67.
6. Ibid., 69.
7. Ibid., 67–68.

(וְהִנֵּה "behold"). This particle sometimes signals a shift from the narrator's omniscient perspective to the character's perspective.[8] That is, the narrator shows the reader a certain detail through the eyes of the character. For examples, see Genesis 24:63; 28:12–13; 29:25; Judges 3:24–25; 2 Samuel 15:24; 18:24; and 1 Kings 18:7. In Genesis 28:12–13a, the particle *wehinneh* (וְהִנֵּה) occurs three times within a short space, each time signifying what Jacob saw in his dream:

וַיַּחֲלֹם וְהִנֵּה סֻלָּם מֻצָּב אַרְצָה וְרֹאשׁוֹ
מַגִּיעַ הַשָּׁמָיְמָה וְהִנֵּה מַלְאֲכֵי אֱלֹהִים
עֹלִים וְיֹרְדִים בּוֹ׃ וְהִנֵּה יְהוָה נִצָּב
עָלָיו וַיֹּאמַר

He had a dream, and *behold*, a ladder was set on the earth with its top reaching to heaven; and *behold*, the angels of God were ascending and descending on it. And *behold*, the LORD stood above it and said . . . (NASB)

Table 6.2
Indicators of Shifts in Focalization

1. Verbs of perception (to see, to hear, to know)
2. The expression "to say to one's heart"
3. The particle *wehinneh* (וְהִנֵּה "behold")

Omniscience

Another feature of a narrator's point of view is called *omniscience*. Sternberg explains, "To say that he [the biblical writer] is omniscient is to invest him with a storytelling privilege that the same writer would hardly lay claim to in his everyday life."[9] Ska elaborates on the notion of omniscience and an omniscient narrator:

The classical narrator of ancient and traditional narratives is "omniscient." He is almost like God: he knows everything and speaks with an unabashed authority. This privilege is felt especially when he reveals the thoughts of the characters through "inside views." In modern novels the narrator often gives up this privilege and has a knowledge limited to the external world or to the interior

8. J. P. Fokkelman, *Narrative Art in Genesis: Specimens of Stylistic and Structural Analysis* (Amsterdam: Van Gorcum, 1975), 50–55; Shimon Bar-Efrat, *Narrative Art in the Bible* (Sheffield: Almond, 1989), 35–36; Berlin, *Poetics and Interpretation of Biblical Narrative,* 62–63.

9. Meir Sternberg, *The Poetics of Biblical Narrative: Ideological Literature and the Drama of Reading,* Indiana Studies in Biblical Literature (Bloomington: Indiana University Press, 1985), 68.

world of one character who is used as the "eye of the camera" or the "center of consciousness" of the narration. This narrator knows in general only what a normal person can see, hear, and experience.[10]

In Genesis 22:1–19, for example, the narrator informs the audience at the outset that the subsequent events amount to a God-given test. This piece of omniscient information functions as a sort of disclaimer. Sailhamer explains that "without it [verse 1] God's request that Abraham offer up Isaac as a 'burnt offering' would be inexplicable. By stating clearly at the start that 'God tested Abraham,' the writer quickly allays any doubt about God's real purpose."[11]

Genesis 38 provides another example of the narrator's omniscience. In Genesis 38:7, he discloses that Er was wicked in Yahweh's sight and Yahweh killed him. His omniscient perspective appears again in verse 9 when he reveals Onan's motives for refusing to impregnate Tamar. Likewise in verse 10, the omniscient narrator conveys Yahweh's feeling of displeasure about this action as well as the insight that Yahweh took Onan's life. In verse 11, the narrator exposes another piece of privileged information: Judah's reason for not giving his third son, Shelah, to Tamar. Judah believed that Shelah might die like his brothers. Further examples appear in the story: Tamar's motivations for setting up shop as a temple prostitute at a location Judah would pass (v. 14); Judah's lack of perception and failure to recognize Tamar (v. 15); and again, Judah's ignorance that the prostitute was his daughter-in-law (v. 16). Thus, the narrator can disclose a character's opinions, feelings, and intentions—whether the character is God or a human being.[12]

Irony

Another by-product of the narrator's perspective is irony. Irony refers to an incongruity or discrepancy.[13] Ska distinguishes between two types of irony in Old Testament narrative literature: verbal and dramatic.[14] Verbal irony refers to statements in which a character says one thing and intends the opposite. An example is Michal's speech to David after he returned from the parade that brought the ark of the covenant into Jerusalem. Her words are recorded in 2 Samuel 6:20:

10. Ska, *"Our Fathers Have Told Us,"* 44.

11. John H. Sailhamer, "Genesis," in *The Expositor's Bible Commentary,* ed. Frank E. Gaebelein, vol. 2 (Grand Rapids: Zondervan, 1990), 167.

12. Bar-Efrat, *Narrative Art in the Bible* (Sheffield: Almond, 1989), 20.

13. Leland Ryken, *Words of Delight: A Literary Introduction to the Bible* (Grand Rapids: Baker, 1987), 361.

14. Ska, *"Our Fathers Have Told Us,"* 57–61.

> Then David returned to bless his household. And Michal the daughter of Saul came out to meet David, and said, "How glorious was the king of Israel today, uncovering himself today in the eyes of the maids of his servants, as one of the base fellows shamelessly uncovers himself!" (NKJV)

She meant that David had *not* acted gloriously. On the other hand, dramatic irony occurs when a character says one thing but does not perceive what the reader knows to be true. Bar-Efrat explains that dramatic irony "derives from the fact that the character knows less than the reader, or unknowingly does things which are not in his or her own best interests, or from the course of events leading to results which are the reverse of the character's aspirations."[15] Sisera's speech to Jael in Judges 4:20 offers a prime example. When he seeks refuge in her tent, he instructs her, "And if any man comes and inquires of you, and says, 'Is there any man here?' you shall say, 'No'" (NKJV).

Sisera did not realize the literal truth behind the answer he instructed Jael to give. There would not be a man present because he would be dead with a tent peg driven through his temple! Uriah's response to King David provides an additional example of dramatic irony. In 2 Samuel 11:10, David asks Uriah why he had not returned home to his wife to spend the night. Uriah's reply is recorded in 2 Samuel 11:11:

> And Uriah said to David, "The ark and Israel and Judah are dwelling in tents, and my lord Joab and the servants of my lord are encamped in the open fields. Shall I then go to my house to eat and drink, and to lie with my wife? As you live, and as your soul lives, I will not do this thing." (NKJV)

Bar-Efrat comments on the "ironic sting in his words," assuming that Uriah did not know what David had done with Bathsheba, Uriah's wife, in Uriah's absence:

> To all intents and purposes Uriah simply compares his conditions with those of his comrades in the field, declaring that he will not enjoy any privilege which they cannot share. The sting, however, lies in the fact that an implicit comparison is made between his behaviour and David's. Uriah asserts that he will not go to lie with his wife, and that is precisely what David has been doing! . . . The subtle irony reaches its zenith when Uriah swears by David's life, namely, by the life of the man who did just what he will not do.[16]

Ryken mentions a third type of irony. Irony of situation occurs when a situation is the opposite of what is expected or appropriate.[17] An example would

15. Bar-Efrat, *Narrative Art in the Bible*, 125.
16. Ibid., 126.
17. Ryken, *Words of Delight*, 361. While Ska does not label this category, he seems to include it as an aspect of dramatic irony (*"Our Fathers Have Told Us,"* 60).

be Gehazi, Elisha's servant, contracting the leprosy from which Naaman had just been healed (2 Kings 5:27). An additional case including irony of situation would be the story of Saul setting out in search of lost donkeys and coming back with a kingdom (1 Sam. 9).

Table 6.3
Three Types of Irony

1. *Verbal*—The character says one thing and means something else.
2. *Dramatic*—The character says something but does not understand its full implications.
3. *Situational*—The situation is the opposite of what is expected or appropriate.

By now you will have studied the text from every major angle. Table 6.4 at the end of the chapter summarizes the major features that you will need to examine when studying an Old Testament story.[18] You might need to keep it handy at first. Eventually, looking for the features of Old Testament narrative texts will become second nature to you, and your reading of the text will be more of a fluid experience rather than a mechanical procedure. As Ska points out, "A text is like a score of music. The music remains dead unless somebody plays or sings what is written in the score. A Biblical text remains dead unless the reader interprets it."[19]

Table 6.4
A Summary List of Features to Examine in Old Testament Narrative Texts

Plot
    Interpreters who can use Hebrew start here . . .
- *Plot Lines:* Locate the main storyline (foreground) and subsidiary lines (background).
- *Marked Text:* Spot sections where clusters of rare forms and terms slow down the reader.
- *Chiasm:* Note chiastic patterns (a b c c′ b′ a′) which mark boundaries or turning points.

    Interpreters who do not use Hebrew start here . . .
- *Plot Stages:* Determine the story's exposition, crisis, resolution, and conclusion.
- *Archetypes:* Identify plot patterns or motifs (comedy, tragedy, petitionary narratives, etc.).
- *Repetition:* Notice key words, changes or duplication in command fulfillment, and unnecessary repetition of names and pronouns.
- *Time and Pace:* Compare narrative time (length of events) to narration time (length of telling).

18.   The first three items under plot are discussed in appendix A.
19.   Ska, *"Our Fathers Have Told Us,"* 63.

Characters
- *Classifications:* Identify characters as major (protagonist, antagonist, foil) or minor.
- *Direct Descriptions:* Look for the occasional statement about a character's appearance.
- *Behavior:* Observe the characters' actions for insight into their personalities and nature.
- *Names:* Notice the significance behind names of characters.
- *Designation:* Pay attention to how the narrator or other characters describe a character.
- *Dialogue:* Listen to speech for insight into characters and for clues pointing to meaning.

Setting
- *Inner-Textual:* Check the text for the story's temporal, geographical, and cultural setting.
- *Inter-Textual:* Check the content for the story's role in the larger narrative framework.

Point of View
- *Focalization:* Notice whether the perspective is external (the reader's) or internal (the character's or narrator's).
- *Omniscience:* Identify narrator statements that give inside views or priviledged information.
- *Irony:* Determine the occurrence of verbal, dramatic, or situational irony.

7

❀ ❀ ❀ ❀ ❀

Narrowing the Focus

❀ ❀ ❀ ❀ ❀

I t's time to wrap up your study of the passage. You're ready to sort through your data and draw some conclusions. This is the time to interact with some scholars and teachers who have worked through the same passage you just studied. Ideally, you have saved the bulk of your interaction with commentaries until this point in the process. Since you've done your homework, you will be much better prepared to listen to them and debate with them. Not all commentaries are created equal. Some delve so deeply into historical criticism or textual criticism that they avoid the literary dimension of the text. Appendix B lists the more useful commentaries for each narrative book of the Old Testament.

In addition to reading commentaries, plan to consult the standard works on Old Testament narrative literature for discussions of particular texts. If I am preparing a sermon on 1 Samuel 17, I will turn to the indexes of works on Old Testament narrative literature to locate any discussions of this particular text (see table 7.1). You may recognize these resources from the footnotes in earlier chapters of this book.

Here are some suggestions for your library. Every preacher who works through an Old Testament narrative book should purchase copies of *The Art of Biblical Narrative* by Robert Alter and *Narrative Art in the Bible* by Shimon Bar-Efrat. Alter, Professor of Hebrew and Comparative Literature at the Uni-

Table 7.1
Works on Old Testament Narrative Literature

1. Robert Alter, *The Art of Biblical Narrative*
2. Shimon Bar-Efrat, *Narrative Art in the Bible*
3. J. P. Fokkelman, *Reading Biblical Narrative: An Introductory Guide*
4. Adele Berlin, *Poetics and Interpretation of Biblical Narrative*
5. Meir Sternberg, *The Poetics of Biblical Narrative*
6. Jean Louis Ska, *"Our Fathers Have Told Us"*
7. David M. Gunn and Danna Nolan Fewell, *Narrative in the Hebrew Bible*

versity of California, Berkeley, published his watershed volume in 1981. It remains a classic in the field of interpreting Old Testament narrative literature, and I recommend it as a first-read for preachers who plan to preach Old Testament narrative texts. Alter writes in the style of a well-crafted *Time* magazine article. Bar-Efrat's work serves as an excellent companion volume. Bar-Efrat, the Head of Biblical Studies at the Hebrew University Secondary School in Jerusalem, provides a catalogue of literary techniques and devices found in Old Testament narratives. Neither book requires expertise in Hebrew.

If you want more than Alter and Bar-Efrat, the footnotes and bibliography in this book will give you direction. Let me share a few recommendations, though, for further resources. You may want to do more reading in the field, or you may want further works available as references. Start with J. P. Fokkelman's recent work, *Reading Biblical Narrative: An Introductory Guide*. He uses twelve Old Testament stories to help readers pay attention to narrator, character, action, hero, quest, plot, time, and space. Also get a copy of Adele Berlin's slim volume, *Poetics and Interpretation of Biblical Narrative*. Berlin focuses especially on character and characterization and point of view. She then applies these to the book of Ruth. Ambitious preachers may want to tackle Meir Sternberg's massive and at times verbose volume, *The Poetics of Biblical Narrative*. Sternberg, Professor of Poetics and Comparative Literature at Tel Aviv University, covers the entire terrain from theoretical issues to particular literary conventions. Next, try the manual titled *"Our Fathers Have Told Us": Introduction to the Analysis of Hebrew Narratives* by Jean Louis Ska, a scholar at the Pontifical Biblical Institute in Rome. Ska aims to help beginners through the forest of new terms used by specialists like Alter, Berlin, Sternberg, and others. He distills the insights of these specialists into concise summaries. Finally, preachers will find helpful insights in *Narrative in the Hebrew Bible* by David M. Gunn and Danna Nolan Fewell, professors at Columbia Theological Seminary in Atlanta and the Perkins School of Theology at Southern Methodist University, respectively. Despite their presupposition that meaning is the reader's creation rather than the author's creation, they offer help on strategies for reading, on characters and narrators, on plot designs, on the lure of language, and on readers and responsibility. Among these topics, they have interspersed chapters on specific Old Testament narratives. None of the books mentioned above require a knowledge of Hebrew.

If you possess Hebrew language skills and want to learn more about text-linguistic analysis of the Hebrew text, you will find suggestions in appendix A of this volume.

The Components of a Big Idea

One of the most challenging stages in the interpretive process is identifying the story's exegetical idea. While you may find several ideas in a story, you must ask: What is the unifying center? What message is the writer conveying through the story? Identifying this message and writing it in a clear sentence is a significant accomplishment.

Before we discuss finding the exegetical idea of a particular Old Testament narrative, we must make sure we are clear on what an idea is. Thought, whether expressed verbally or in writing, consists of ideas or concepts. An idea or concept consists of two essential elements: a subject and a complement (see table 7.2). A big idea distills the particulars into a summary by isolating what several ideas have in common. When preachers talk about the big idea of a Scripture passage, they often refer to it as an exegetical idea since it emerges from their exegetical study of the text. I'll clarify the difference between the two labels in a moment.

Table 7.2
Components of a Big Idea

✎ **Subject**—What am I talking about?
✎ **Complement**—What am I saying about what I am talking about?

To find the big idea of a thought unit (paragraph, story, etc.), determine the unit's subject. The term subject does not refer to the grammatical subject of a sentence. Rather, it refers to the complete answer to the question, What am I talking about? While a grammatical subject is often a single word, this is rarely the case with the subject of a big idea. Take a moment to read the following paragraph, and then try to identify its subject. The selection is from Neil Postman's work *Amusing Ourselves to Death*.[1]

> President Ronald Reagan is a former Hollywood movie actor. Former nominee George McGovern has hosted the popular television show, "Saturday Night Live." So has a candidate of more recent vintage, the Reverend Jesse Jackson. Former President Richard Nixon, who once claimed he lost an election because

1. Neil Postman, *Amusing Ourselves to Death* (New York: Penguin, 1985), 4.

he was sabotaged by make-up men, has offered Senator Edward Kennedy advice on how to make a serious run for the presidency: lose twenty pounds. Although the constitution makes no mention of it, it would appear that fat people are now effectively excluded from running for high political office. Probably bald people as well. Almost certainly those whose looks are not significantly enhanced by the cosmetician's art. Indeed, we may have reached the point where cosmetics has replaced ideology as the field of expertise over which a politician must have competent control.

Alright, what is the subject of this paragraph? What is this paragraph talking about? Perhaps you note that the paragraph talks about presidents and people who run for political office. You're off to a good start, but your identification of the subject is still too broad. Try again. The full subject is, *What politicians have to pay attention to if they hope to get elected.* Notice the use of the word *what* at the beginning of the subject. Using the questions that journalists ask—how, what, why, when, where, and who—will help you narrow your subject. In fact, I find it helpful to preface each subject I identify with one of these questions. If I wanted to, though, I could state the subject like this: *The area of expertise that politicians must pay attention to if they hope to get elected.* Either way, you've nailed down the subject.

Once you have nailed down the subject, you look for the complement. As the term suggests, the *complement* completes the subject. It answers the question, What am I saying about what I am talking about? In the above example from Neil Postman, the subject is, *What politicians have to pay attention to if they hope to get elected.* The complement is, *Their personal appearance, not just their platform of issues.* When you put together the subject and complement, a big idea emerges: *In order to get elected, politicians must pay as much attention to their personal appearance as they do to their platform of issues.*

Here is another example. Towards the end of Norman Maclean's *A River Runs through It*, Norman's father makes a statement that summarizes the story's idea. He comments to Norman, "It is those we live with and love and should know who elude us."[2] Take a moment to read that quote again. Before continuing any further in this paragraph, write down what you think are the subject and complement. Alright, what is the quote talking about? That is, what is the subject? I describe the subject as, *Who are the people we understand the least?* Or I could phrase it as, *The identity of the people we understand the least.* Now, what is the quote saying about the subject? In other words, what is the complement? My attempt at describing the complement is, *The people we love the most.* Put subject and complement together, and the big idea sounds like this: *The people we understand the least are the people we love the most.*

2. Norman Maclean, *A River Runs through It, and Other Stories* (Chicago: University of Chicago Press, 1976), 104.

As I wrestle with thought, I notice that I could reverse the subject and complement of the above quote. The subject could be, *What is the struggle we have with the people we love the most?* The complement then becomes, *We understand them the least.* So the big idea becomes: *The struggle we have with the people we love the most is that we understand them the least.* Deciding which way to go would require a thorough reading of Maclean's story to determine which way of stating the big idea sticks closest to his emphasis.

Developing the Big Idea

In *Biblical Preaching*, Haddon Robinson applies the big idea concept to preaching. He breaks the big idea down into two expressions: the exegetical idea and the homiletical idea. The exegetical idea is stating a biblical concept in such a way that it accurately reflects what the author intends. In a later stage of sermon development, the preacher will take this exegetical idea and state it as a homiletical idea. A homiletical idea is stating a biblical concept in such a way that it accurately reflects the Bible and meaningfully relates to the congregation.

Some of Robinson's followers have added a third expression by subdividing the exegetical idea stage into *exegetical idea* and *theological idea* (see table 7.3).

Table 7.3
Expressions of the Big Idea

Exegetical Idea
↓
Theological Idea
↓
Homiletical or Preaching Idea

While I prefer to keep things as simple as possible, I see particular value in adding this extra stage when working in Old Testament narrative literature. In the three expression approach, the first expression of the big idea is the exegetical idea. This is a sentence statement of the author's intended meaning that reflects the time and culture of the original audience. It uses the language of the text, including the names of characters in the story. The next expression is the theological idea. The theological expression of the big idea states it in timeless language that applies to God's people living in any stage of salvation history. Finally, the preacher will craft the big idea in a homiletical expression. This preaching idea or homiletical idea makes the statement in a more personal, contemporary way. We will develop the preaching or homiletical idea at a later stage of the process. For now, we are concerned with developing an exegetical idea and turning it into a theological idea.

As previously mentioned, I prefer to keep processes lean and clean. As preachers hone their skills, their minds may move directly from an exegetical idea to a theological idea, and thus they write down only the theological idea.

Clues for Nailing Down the Big Idea

To find the exegetical expression of the big idea in an Old Testament narrative, expositors must sift through the exegetical data they have amassed and attempt to identify a subject. Remember, the subject must be broad enough to account for the entire range of material—plot twists, dialogue, etc.—that makes up the story. The danger is formulating a big idea that uses the text as an illustration rather than formulating a big idea that the text actually communicates. For example, in his sermon on 2 Samuel 11–12, Paul Borden identifies the exegetical idea like this: *David learns to accept what the grace of God has given him and what the grace of God has not.* The subject of this big idea is, *What David has to learn about responding to the grace of God.* The complement is, *That he must accept what the grace of God has given him and what the grace of God has not.*

But wait! The subjects of most sermons on this text are, *How to avoid adultery,* or *What the consequences of adultery are.* As a tape screener for the *Preaching Today* tape series, I recently listened to a recorded sermon in which the preacher used Nathan's confrontation in 2 Samuel 11–12 to emphasize the importance of honesty. The subject of the sermon was something like, *Why honesty is the best policy.* My question is, does this approach really take into account the author's intention, or does it use the text to illustrate another valid point?

I'm convinced that Borden nails the big idea because he accounts for the data in the text. This underscores the need for rigorous exegesis. Without hard work in the text, the expositor will settle for pat answers. Borden did his homework. He observed that God identified a bigger sin in David's life that was behind the sins of adultery, deception, and murder. When Nathan came to David with God's message, Nathan began by rehearsing the gifts that God had given to David. We call this God's grace. Then Nathan asks, "Why did you despise the word of the LORD by doing what is evil in his eyes?" (2 Sam. 12:9). The term *despise* means "to regard with contempt." The very next verse reports Nathan's summary, and the same assessment emerges again: "Because you despised me and took the wife of Uriah the Hittite to be your own" (2 Sam. 12:10). Most sermons I've heard from 2 Samuel 11–12 stop there and do not account for the death of David and Bathsheba's first child. In his exegesis, Borden observes that through the death of this child, David learns to accept what God in his grace gives and does not give.

Obviously, determining the big idea of Old Testament narrative poses a steeper challenge than other literary genres. Stories work through indirection, conveying their ideas in a more subtle way than poetry or prophecy. Thankfully, there are a couple of additional clues that will help the preacher put the details together and determine what the author intended. Haddon Robinson counsels preachers to look for these clues when they study any text of Scripture. I find them particularly helpful in Old Testament narratives.

Vision of God

The first clue is a passage's vision of God. Most passages focus on a particular aspect of God's character, for example, God as Creator or God as Judge. In 2 Samuel 11–12, the narrator's vision of God is the giver of gifts. That's the issue in the text. Again, Nathan's message begins with a litany of the gifts God had given to David. Paul Borden describes this gift giving as God's grace. So the vision of God is the giver of gifts, or the God of grace.

Depravity Factor

A second clue to look for is what Haddon Robinson calls the *depravity factor*. What in humanity rebels against the text's vision of God? What sin keeps God's people from responding properly to a particular aspect of his character? Bryan Chapell calls this the text's FCF or *fallen condition focus*.[3] Returning to our example in 2 Samuel 11–12, the depravity factor is David's (and our) tendency to despise God by being discontent with what his grace has given us.

Determining the big idea resembles splitting wood: sometimes you get stuck in a knot. The way to get out of the knot is to identify the story's vision of God and the depravity factor that works against this vision. These clues will get you back on target.

Examples of Big Ideas in Old Testament Narratives

I have suggested that Paul Borden's exegetical idea for 2 Samuel 11–12 hits the bull's-eye: *David learns to accept what the grace of God has given him and what the grace of God has not.* But is that the only possible big idea? Yes and no. While an interpreter is bound to the author's intended meaning, there may be more than one legitimate way to describe it. Any big idea of 2 Samuel 11–12 must account for the data. So a big idea whose subject is *How to avoid adultery* or *Why honesty is the best policy* falls short of what the author is doing. On the other hand, since preaching is "truth mediated through personality," to quote Phillips Brooks's classic statement from the Yale Lectures on Preaching, each expositor will focus on the truth from a unique angle. For example, Haddon Robinson states his exegetical idea for the same passage like this:

3. Bryan Chapell defines the *fallen condition focus* (FCF) as "the mutual human condition that contemporary believers share with those to or for whom the text was written that requires the grace of the passage" (*Christ-Centered Preaching: Redeeming the Expository Sermon* [Grand Rapids: Baker, 1994], 42).

When David failed to walk with God, he put his life, family, and career in jeopardy. Like Borden, Robinson realizes that the story is about more than adultery. While Borden describes David's sin as "showing contempt for God's grace," Robinson identifies it as "failing to walk with God." The difference between these two statements is not one of content but of specificity. Both zero in on the same vision of God and the same depravity factor. Borden's exegetical idea ends up being more specific; Robinson's ends up being more general.

Now notice how these exegetical ideas from 2 Samuel 11–12 can be transformed into theological ideas. Let's start with Paul Borden's exegetical idea.

Exegetical idea: *David learned to accept what the grace of God had given him and what the grace of God had not.*

Theological idea: *Believers must learn to accept what the grace of God has given them and what the grace of God has not.*

The theological expression of the big idea assumes that what is true for David in this case is true for believers in any age. When moving from a specific character such as David to a more timeless identity such as believers, preachers must grapple with the range of possibilities (see table 7.4). One possibility is abstracting from *David* to "leaders" since David was Israel's king. This is legitimate, but nothing in the story requires that the teaching applies only to God's people who occupy leadership positions. On the other hand, changing "David" to "people" is too general. God's dealing with David is based on the covenant relationship between them, so the timeless element is "believers." Expositors, then, must search for a timeless element that is neither too specific nor too broad.

Table 7.4
Range of Possibilities for Making an Element Timeless (2 Sam. 11–12)

Person
↑
Believer
↑
Leader
↑
David

Let's see how Haddon Robinson's exegetical idea can be changed to a theological idea.

Exegetical idea: *When David failed to walk with God, he put his life, family, and career in jeopardy.*

Theological idea: *When believers fail to walk with God, they put their lives, families, and careers in jeopardy.*

Notice from this and the previous example, that past tense language shifts to present tense. Again, the theological idea moves away from event-specific description to timeless description.

Look at a few more examples. You might want to read these texts first and formulate your own exegetical ideas before proceeding. For each text, write a subject and complement. Then combine these into an exegetical idea. Remember, it will help to identify the vision of God and the depravity factor of each story. Here are the texts to read:

• Genesis 13
• Genesis 22:1–19
• 1 Samuel 17

Let's start with Genesis 13. The storyline in Genesis 13 is not complicated. Abram moves into Canaan, accompanied by his nephew Lot. Their respective holdings—flocks, herds, and tents—make it difficult for the land to support both of them. As a result, a dispute arises between Abram's herdsmen and Lot's herdsmen. A note in verse 7 about the presence of the Canaanites and Perizzites makes readers aware that neither Abram nor Lot could simply move a few miles away. Other occupants were vying for the same grazing ground. The lone statement Abram makes to Lot in verse 8 is highly significant: "Do not let there be any quarreling between me and you, or between my herdsmen and your herdsmen, because men, brothers, we are" (my translation of the Hebrew text). Abram suggests parting company and offers Lot first choice of where he will go. Abram agrees to take whatever is left. Lot chooses the cities of the Jordan plain, so Abram remains in Canaan. The story closes with God appearing to Abram and reconfirming his gift of the land to Abram and his descendants.

Identifying the vision of God and the depravity factor of this story helps interpreters isolate the exegetical idea. The vision of God is the giver who blesses his people. The depravity factor is the greed or anxiety that leads people to fight with those closest to them over the blessings or rights God has provided. As a result of this analysis, I would identify the subject of Genesis 13 as, *How Abram, a man under God's blessing, handled conflict.* The complement would be, *He took the initiative to resolve it.* When you put subject and complement together, the exegetical idea becomes, *Abram, a man under God's blessing, handled conflict by taking the initiative to resolve it.*

Determining the precise wording can be maddening. Don't let it be. Perhaps it is better to state the subject as, *How Abram preserved God's blessing when he faced conflict.* The complement remains the same, but this changes the exegetical idea to read, *Abram preserved God's blessing when he faced conflict by taking the initiative to resolve it.* When you get this close, don't spend precious time agonizing over which expression will be best. Write one down and go with it. Now, notice the development from exegetical idea to theological idea:

Exegetical idea: *Abram preserved God's blessing when he faced conflict by taking the initiative to resolve it.*

Theological idea: *God's people preserve God's blessing when they face conflict by taking the initiative to resolve it.*

In Genesis 22:1–19, the subject is, *How far did Abraham go to put obedience to God first?* The complement is, *He was willing to sacrifice his son Isaac.* Notice the exegetical idea that emerges and the resulting theological idea:

Exegetical idea: *Abraham put obedience to God first even though he faced the prospect of sacrificing his son Isaac.*

Theological idea: *Faithful worshipers of God will put obedience to God first even when there is great cost involved.*

In this example, moving from exegetical idea to theological idea involves two main abstractions. In the story, Abraham comes to Mount Moriah to worship God. The role Abraham assumes here as a worshiper of God allows us to abstract to "worshiper of God" rather than a more general element such as "believer." The key shift is from "sacrificing his son Isaac" to "great cost." Genesis 22 is the only place in Scripture where God asks a father to place his child on an altar and offer him as a sacrifice. This is a specific instance of a more abstract concept that underlies a number of situations in Scripture: God asks worshipers to sacrifice what is costly.

For a final example, turn to 1 Samuel 17, the story that culminates in the battle between David and Goliath. Keep in mind the inter-textual context of the passage. It appears towards the beginning of a series of stories that demonstrate David is more fit to be king than Saul is.

Once again, identifying the vision of God and the depravity factor helps immensely. The vision of God in this text is, "The living God who is a warrior," or more precisely, "The living God who fights for his people." What about the depravity factor? The depravity factor, I suggest, is the lack of courage to follow through with a God-given task. But is it fair to suggest that Saul should have gone up against Goliath? How do we know that would have been an act of faith rather than an act of impulsiveness, an act of obedience rather than an act of stupidity? Again, we have to rely on the inter-textual setting of the story. An original reader would have had the book of Deuteronomy in mind and would have remembered God's commands to people going into battle: "Hear, O Israel, today you are going into battle against your enemies. Do not be fainthearted or afraid; do not be terrified or give way to panic before them. For the LORD your God is the one who goes with you to fight for you against your enemies to give you victory" (Deut. 20:3–4). It's reasonable to expect that an original reader knew this command well. But there's even a textual clue in 1 Samuel 17 that may suggest it. The identity of Goliath's hometown, Gath, may have tipped off the original readers that Goliath was a leftover giant, one of the Anakites whom God had commanded the Israelites to exterminate in Deuteronomy 9:1–4. According to Joshua 11:21–22, the Israelites wiped out all but a few survivors who fled to three coastal cities, including Gath.

Armed with this data, I suggest that the subject of 1 Samuel 17 is, *Why God chose to use David instead of Saul.* The complement is, *Because David had the courage to act in faith on God's specific promise.* The full exegetical expression of the big idea is, *God chose to use David instead of Saul because David had the courage to act in faith on God's specific promise.*

Now, let's move from exegetical expression to theological expression. I will abstract from the subject, *Why God chose to use David instead of Saul,* to *The kind of person God uses.* In this move up the ladder of abstraction, I have to decide if the principle this story teaches applies only to leaders. If so, I should state the subject as, *The kind of leader God uses.* While this certainly applies to leaders, there's nothing in the passage to suggest it is exclusive to those in leadership positions. Biblical theology verifies this. For example, the list of names in the hall of faith in Hebrews 11 does not only include leaders. So I will state the subject as, *The kind of person God uses.* Or, if I want to state the subject more fully, I could write it as, *The kind of person God uses to accomplish his mission in the world.* The complement is, *The person who has the courage to act in faith on God's specific promises.* The full theological expression of the big idea is, *God uses people who have the courage to act in faith on his specific promises.* Or I could say, *The people God uses to accomplish his mission in the world are the people who have the courage to act in faith on his specific promises.*

You may have noticed several key ideas in this passage. For example, David was the first person to bring the living God into the equation (1 Sam. 17:26). In the process, he identifies Goliath as "this uncircumcised Philistine." Thus, a key idea of the story is that David operated from a perspective that included God in the equation. Furthermore, David's recollection about fighting off a lion and a bear (17:34–37) show us that he learned to trust God. A second key idea, then, is that David drew courage from reviewing past victories from

God. A third key idea emerges from David's conviction that "the battle is the LORD's" (17:47). I have taken these concepts into account in my statement of the big idea. I will develop them when I preach 1 Samuel 17, but I will enlist them to help me arrive at the idea that holds them together—the big idea that *God uses people who have the courage to act in faith on his specific promises.* I will present the three ideas noted above as means of drawing the courage needed to step out in faith and act on God's promises.

There is another way of stating this idea, however. Paul Borden, for example, sees the exegetical idea of 1 Samuel 17 like this: *David succeeded under pressure because his perspective was different, because he learned the habit of trusting God, and because he let God do the fighting.* Borden rightly notes that the real context in 1 Samuel 17 is between David and Saul. Goliath is the challenge each must face. Borden also notices the three key ideas I cited above, and he turns them into a multiple complement. The subject is, *Why David succeeded under pressure (when Saul failed under it).* The complement consists of three statements that relate the reasons for David's success. Borden chooses to build these into his big idea statement.

Nailing down the exegetical idea and theological idea is hard work. It requires wrestling with thought. Don't give up if you get stumped. You may wrestle with the data for an hour at your desk and have only a page of crossed out items on a legal pad to show for it. That's fine. Set it aside and return to it later. In fact, Eugene Lowry counsels preachers to conclude sessions of sermon preparation at points of "felt difficulty."[4] Quit for the day or for a few hours when you have *not* achieved a point of closure rather than when you feel pretty good about what you've accomplished. The reason? Your preconscious mind keeps working on the sermon and wrestling with the problem point. So shift gears and make a hospital call. Play tennis. Check your e-mail. When you return later, your thoughts may crystallize and lead you to the passage's big idea. You'll say, "It's so simple! Why didn't I see this yesterday?!" Yes, nailing down the big idea is hard work, but doing it will keep you on track to producing an effective sermon.

---

4. Eugene Lowry, *The Sermon: Dancing the Edge of Mystery* (Nashville: Abingdon, 1997), 98–100.

PART 2

From Concept to Sermon

8

❀ ❀ ❀ ❀ ❀

STARTING THE SECOND HALF
OF THE ADVENTURE

❀ ❀ ❀ ❀ ❀

Jon Krakauer cleared the ice from his oxygen mask, hunched a shoulder against the wind, and straddled the summit of Mount Everest. It was 1:17 P.M. on May 10, 1996. Krakauer, an accomplished climber and journalist, had not slept in fifty-seven hours. He had not eaten much more than a bowl of ramen soup and a handful of peanut M&Ms in three days. Still, he had reached the top of the earth's tallest peak—29,028 feet. In his oxygen-deprived stupor, he had no way of knowing that storm clouds forming below would turn into a vicious blizzard that would claim the lives of five fellow climbers. Yet he knew his adventure was hardly finished. In his book *Into Thin Air*, Krakauer describes what he felt:

> Reaching the top of Everest is supposed to trigger a surge of intense elation; against long odds, after all, I had just attained a goal I'd coveted since childhood. But the summit was really only the halfway point. Any impulse I might have felt toward self-congratulation was extinguished by the overwhelming apprehension about the long, dangerous descent that lay ahead.[1]

---

1. Jon Krakauer, *Into Thin Air* (New York: Villard, 1997), 181.

David Breashears, the first American to scale Everest twice, concurs and offers this counsel to climbers: "Getting to the summit is the easy part; it's getting back down that's hard."[2]

In this respect, the adventure of preaching Old Testament narratives resembles an Everest expedition. Arriving at the exegetical summit with the author's intended meaning is the easy part. It's getting back down to deliver the goods to the congregation that's hard. When the journey from text to concept is completed, preachers may feel a rush. There's a thrill and a sense of satisfaction that accompanies understanding what the author means. But this summit is only the halfway point. A demanding journey lies ahead as the preacher moves from concept to sermon.

The difficulty of the descent from concept to sermon calls for increased fervency in prayer. Preachers should continue to saturate their labors with prayer. The summit or halfway point in the process is a good time to pause and worship God for who he is and what he has done. A careful study of the story will have yielded new or fresh insights about God's person and work that should move a preacher to praise. Then, throughout the descent, preachers will need to pray through issues such as how the story applies to a believer's life and what communication strategies will work best when preaching the story to a particular congregation. The descent from concept to sermon is no time for a preacher's prayer life to wane.

The ensuing chapters will explore the stages of sermon development as the expositor descends from concept to sermon. The next three stages may be the most difficult in the entire process because they involve a high level of thinking. In some ways, I find them harder than studying the narrative text in Hebrew. Once you know what you're doing in Hebrew, the work is fairly objective. However, these stages require synthesis—putting back together what you've taken apart in analysis—and a more abstract type of thinking. As difficult as these stages may appear, they will make the difference between a mediocre sermon and a superb one.

Thought develops in one of three basic ways. Aside from restating a concept, you can either *explain* it, *validate* it, or *apply* it. For example, during my childhood years in central Illinois, I remember my parents and school teachers frequently communicating a particular concept during May and June: Our county is under a tornado warning.

The idea might require further explanation. I could ask, "What does this mean?" My mother or teacher would explain that a tornado warning means someone has spotted a funnel cloud in our region. It differs from a tornado watch in which a funnel cloud has not been seen but weather conditions are ripe for a tornado to appear. In this instance, a farmer spotted a funnel cloud

2. Ibid., 277.

about six miles east of our town. Furthermore, the warning took effect fifteen minutes ago and will continue for the next two hours.

In addition to requesting explanation, I may demand validation. I could say, "Give me some proof. I'm not sure I believe your report that our county is under a tornado warning." My mother or teacher would then validate the idea by divulging the source of their information: they heard it on WMBD, our local radio station. They might describe how two eyewitnesses—a doctor driving home from her office and a UPS driver making his rounds east of town—corroborated the testimony of the farmer who first identified the funnel cloud.

Once I understand the idea and accept its legitimacy, then my concern will turn to applying it. I may ask, "What difference does this make? How should I respond?" My mother or school teacher would reply, "You need to go to the basement. Sit cross-legged against the east wall, tuck your head in between your knees, and cover your neck with your hands. Wait there until the radio reports that the tornado warning has been lifted."

Thought develops the same way in Bible texts and in preaching Bible texts. As a Bible expositor, you will now take the exegetical idea of your passage and submit it to three developmental or functional questions (see table 8.1) that probe the dimensions of understanding (explanation), belief (validation), and behavior (application). You will analyze both the text and your audience with these questions. You will begin by asking, Did the author develop his point by explaining, proving, or applying? Then you will ask, Will my audience respond to this idea by saying, "Explain it, validate it, or apply it"? Notice that these questions appear in sequential order since we're dealing with how thought forms. You cannot prove or validate what people do not understand. You cannot apply what people do not accept.

Table 8.1
The Three Functional Questions

1. *Explanation*—What does it mean?
2. *Validation*—Is it true? Do I believe it?
3. *Application*—So what? How then should I live?

The payoff for wrestling with thought at this level is understanding how the writer of an Old Testament narrative developed his thought. In telling a story, a writer communicated a point. This writer may have presented the story in a way that explained, validated, or applied the idea. He may have focused on one particular dimension or on all of them. Not only will you understand how the writer developed his thought, but you will possess a better idea of how you should develop the thought of the text in light of your particular audience. Let's look at the questions in more detail.

Explanation

The first functional question zeroes in on explanation. It asks, What does it mean? When preachers bring this question to a biblical text, they are asking, Is the author of this text developing his thought primarily through explanation? Is the biblical writer telling the story in a manner that answers the question, What does it mean?

For example, the story in Genesis 13 explains how Abraham resolved the conflict between his herdsmen and Lot's herdsmen. It explains what happens when people of faith take the risk to initiate conflict resolution. The narrative in Genesis 38 explains how God worked around Judah's sin to preserve the line through which the Messiah would come. It also explains the need for God to move his chosen people to Egypt, where they could develop in a culture that was less aggressive than that of the Canaanites to assimilate outsiders. The story in 2 Samuel 11–12 explains how failure to accept God's gracious gifts in our lives can lead to major-league sins. The book of Esther explains how we experience God's presence in our lives even when we don't see him or hear his voice.

An expositor will also ask the functional question, What does it mean? in relationship to the audience. When presented with the sermon's big idea, would the audience say, "I don't understand"? Would they respond by saying, "Explain that, please" or "What does it mean?" Furthermore, are there elements in the story that may not make sense to a modern audience? Modern audiences are as familiar with siege warfare as ancient audiences were familiar with ATM machines. Modern audiences may have questions about customs, geography, theology, and language that an ancient storyteller would assume the audience knew. An expositor who preaches the story of Ruth may have to explain:

- The meaning of names like Elimelech, Naomi, Ruth, Boaz, and Obed
- The theological implications of leaving the land of Israel for Moab
- Who the Moabites were and why Israel despised them
- The plight of a childless widow in Israel
- The kinsman-redeemer concept
- The custom of allowing the poor to glean at the edge of the field
- How much an ephah of grain equals—a small or large amount?
- What the expression "loyal love" (Hebrew, *hesed*) means
- The significance of Ruth uncovering Boaz's feet
- Why Boaz sat at the town gate and what the town elders were doing there
- The sandal-removal ceremony (even the writer explains this one!)

Obviously, the expositor doesn't want to turn the sermon into an exegetical lecture. Maybe a sentence of explanation will do for some of the details. Perhaps it will require a couple minutes of the sermon to explain the custom. But preachers must wrestle with what features of the story need explanation as well as how much explanation they will require.

Validation

The second functional question focuses on validity. It asks, Is it true? In other words, Can I believe it? When directed to Old Testament narrative, this question asks, Did the biblical author tell this story to validate a particular idea or prove a point?

This second functional question lies behind the books of Kings. The writer of Kings crafts his account to argue that God's judgment is just. Israel and Judah got what they deserved. To an audience that thought, "I don't buy the idea that we deserved the destruction of Samaria and Jerusalem," the books of Kings argue, "Your history proves that you deserved this form of God's judgment."

The section running from 1 Samuel 15 to 2 Samuel 8 resembles a dynastic defense which, in the ancient Near East, defended the replacement of one dynasty with another. The writer anticipates people saying, "I'm not sure I buy the idea of David replacing Saul as king. Prove to me that this was a legitimate move." This section of Samuel, then, validates David's fitness to be king as well as Saul's unworthiness to serve as Israel's king. Similarly, the story in 1 Kings 3:16–28 has a validating function. It tells of two prostitutes who came to King Solomon with a dispute over the maternity of a baby and proves that Solomon did receive wisdom from Yahweh as the previous narrative in 3:1–15 claims.

The second functional question should be directed to the audience as well as the text. Once listeners grasp the meaning of a text and its components, they may ask, Is it true? Can we believe this? Certainly, people who take the Bible seriously value an acceptance of its truth claims. We loudly affirm, "God says it, I believe it, that settles it." Still, we struggle with emotional and intellectual doubts. We want to believe, but we need reasons or proofs. Haddon Robinson contends that this second functional question concerning validation is the dominant question of modern audiences. I once heard him comment, "C. S. Lewis is still popular today because he is the master of the second functional question."

At first, the second functional question may intimidate preachers. Why stir up more controversy in your listeners' minds? Controversy creates tension, and tension creates an interest factor. Controversy forces people to wrestle with thought at a deeper level, beyond the pat answers. The second functional question, then, turns out to be a friend, not a foe.

Skilled preachers look for tension in a text and then use it to hold interest. Often, the more controversial passages are easier to preach, at least in terms of holding your listeners. For example, in a sermon on the book of Esther, you might raise a question that your audience is thinking: How can I really be sure that God is working in my life when I can't see or hear him? Suppose your big idea for Esther is, *Even when you can't see or hear God, he is still in control of your destiny.* When confronted with that idea, a listener might respond, "Is it true? Can I buy this?" Your answer to the listener's question comes right out of the text. From the story of Esther, you can show how God overcomes the poor spiritual climate around you, the impossible people, the unpredictable events of life, the circumstances you can't change. He does all of this in ways you won't recognize if you don't look closely.

For another example, think about preaching a sermon from Genesis 13. We've already noted that the biblical writer seems to pursue explanation in his telling of the story. But as you think about your audience, you think they will challenge the notion that believers should initiate conflict resolution. Perhaps they got burned when they tried to settle an argument with a spouse. Maybe some of them lost jobs because they tried to initiate resolution. Instead, they initiated the process of being terminated. When they hear you say, "Believers should take the initiative to resolve conflict," they may respond, "Is it true? I'm not sure I buy it." By anticipating this question, you can use the latter part of the story to validate the idea that God blesses his people when they take the initiative to resolve conflict. You can point out to people that while the short-term payoffs may be deceiving, the long-term payoffs will reward the risk you take to resolve a conflict.

Application

The third functional question tackles application. It asks, So what? What difference does it make? Once again, expositors will begin by asking this question of the text. Did the writer shape the story to show the implications of the story's big idea? Preachers must realize, though, that the narrative form does not lend itself to the kind of application possible in the didactic literature of the New Testament Epistles. For example, in 1 Peter 4:7, the apostle submits this idea: "The end of all things is near." Then, with the word *therefore*, he launches into a series of applications. What difference does it make if the end is near? Peter sketches applications in the areas of praying, loving, sharing, and serving. While stories rarely apply their ideas this directly, they sometimes apply ideas subtly. For example, the author of Chronicles shapes his material to encourage loyalty. While Kings and Chronicles rely on the same pool of historical events, the writer of Kings chooses material validating the idea that Israel and Judah deserved punishment. Chronicles, on the other hand, speaks to the exiles who return from captivity, assuring them that obeying God will make a difference. Because God blesses loyalty, they should pursue loyalty. To be sure, this development happens subtly as the various stories in Chronicles provide pictures of what loyalty looks like.

In preaching Old Testament narratives, the third functional question makes its most significant impact when the preacher relates it to the audience. When related to the audience, this question asks, What will this truth look like when it is fleshed out in the lives of my hearers? What is God calling people to do through this story?

Application is the area where preachers most often run into trouble when preparing sermons from Old Testament narrative literature. To be sure, "All Scripture is God-breathed and is useful for teaching, rebuking, correcting and training in righteousness, so that the man of God may be thoroughly equipped for every good work" (2 Tim. 3:16–17). But how do preachers extract legitimate applications from a story? Haddon Robinson quips, "More heresy is preached in application than in Bible exegesis."[3]

Moralizing

Some preachers who swing for the application green end up in a bunker called moralizing. Eugene Peterson describes and laments this approach:

> Somewhere along the way, most of us pick up bad habits of extracting from the Bible what we pretentiously call "spiritual principles," or "moral guidelines," or "theological truths," and then corseting ourselves in them in order to force a godly shape on our lives. That's a mighty uncomfortable way to go about improving our condition. And it's not the gospel way.[4]

Listen to Graeme Goldsworthy criticize evangelicals for moralizing Old Testament narrative texts instead of basing application on the author's intent:

> We must not view these recorded events [historical narrative] as if they were a mere succession of events from which we draw little moral lessons or examples for life. Much that passes for application of the Old Testament to the Christian life is only moralizing. It consists almost exclusively in *observing* the behaviour of the godly and godless (admittedly against a background of the activity of God) and then *exhorting* people to learn from these observations. That is why the "character" study is a favoured approach to Bible narrative—the life of Moses, the life of David, the life of Elijah and so on. There is nothing wrong with character studies as such—we are to learn by others' examples—but such character studies all too often take the place of more fundamental aspects of biblical teaching.[5]

3. Haddon Robinson, "The Heresy of Application," *Leadership Journal* 18 (fall 1997): 21.
4. Eugene Peterson, *Leap over a Wall: Earthy Spirituality for Everyday Christians* (New York: HarperCollins, 1997), 4.
5. Graeme Goldsworthy, *Gospel and Kingdom: A Christian's Guide to the Old Testament* (Minneapolis: Winston, 1981), 24.

For example, a typical sermon on 2 Samuel 11–12 might extract the following applications from the story:

- Times of idleness can make us more vulnerable to temptation. If King David had gone out to war with his army in the spring (the usual custom of kings), he would not have put himself in a circumstance where he faced sexual temptation. Likewise, it's the down times in your life that place you in a vulnerable spot. When you decide to quit teaching your Sunday school class, or stop volunteering as an aide in your daughter's kindergarten class, or take a break from singing in your church choir, you can create idleness that leads to boredom and heightened vulnerability to temptation.

- Create a parable when you need to confront someone with their sin. Nathan did this. If he had started by pointing his finger at David and accusing him of committing adultery and murder, David might have committed another murder! However, the parable caught David off guard. Like good stories do, Nathan's parable snuck past David's defenses and nailed him with the truth before he realized what had happened. When you need to confront your sixteen-year-old son or daughter about drinking, create a parable that will lead your teen to see how dangerous and foolish it is before directly confronting him or her for involvement in this activity.

These applications fail because they amount to "don't do what David did here" and "follow Nathan's example." But why reject them? Old Testament scholar Carl Kromminga notes that the moralizing that voices like Peterson and Goldsworthy reject is a "wrong *kind* of 'lesson-making' on the basis of Old Testament narrative. They do *not* reject a 'do' or 'don't' application on the basis of the text; they reject a certain *type* of 'do' or 'don't' application."[6] After all, the apostle Paul recognized the validity of looking at Old Testament narratives for examples of how or how not to live (1 Cor. 10:6, 11).

The problem with these applications is that as powerful as they seem, they are peripheral to the author's intent. David's decision to stay home from battle provided the occasion for temptation, but it doesn't explain why David, the man after God's heart, would stoop to adultery and murder. The writer wants us to see that behind the bigger package of sins was the sin of despising God's grace. Applications must flow from that intent. Does Nathan's parable illustrate the power of a parable? Certainly. But that's not where the author goes with the incident. I'm not arguing that a preacher should remain silent about these elements of the story. I don't suggest that a preacher should never draw an application from them. But any mention of them should be in passing if the preacher's goal is to preach a sermon that communicates the author's intended meaning.

6. Carl G. Kromminga, "Remember Lot's Wife: Preaching Old Testament Narrative Texts," *Calvin Theological Journal* 13 (1983): 35.

❀ ❀ ❀

A More Excellent Way

How does a preacher extract an application based on the author's intended meaning rather than peripheral (though important) incidents in the storyline? I find it helpful to begin by asking, What does this story teach me about God and his relationship with human beings? Haddon Robinson reminds preachers that "the purpose of Bible stories is not to say 'you must, you should.' The purpose is to give insight into how men and women relate to the eternal God and how God relates to them."[7]

This takes us back to two concepts we worked with earlier: a story's vision of God and depravity factor. We should build application around the contours of these concepts. This is what distinguishes God-centered application from mere moralizing. Like the maxims in the book of Proverbs, our applications may sometimes sound like good business advice. They may resemble hints from Heloise, advice from Dear Abby, or concepts from Stephen Covey. But like the maxims in Proverbs, solid applications must be rooted in the fear of God.

Identifying the vision of God and the depravity factor helps the interpreter move from the ancient situation to the theological principle it conveys. The preacher can then bring the theological principle into the modern world and examine what it looks like when a listener lives his or her life in response to it (see figure 8.1). The exegetical idea you have already developed will usually express the ancient situation. The theological principle will be closely related or identical to the theological expression of the sermon's big idea.

Figure 8.1
The Process of Application

Theological
Principle

Ancient
Situation

Modern
Situation

The real challenge consists of moving from the more abstract theological principle to some concrete situations in the modern world. It's easy to get tunnel vision here. We tend to think in terms of applying the theological principle to people like ourselves. The challenge is to think outside our immediate circumstances. As a middle-aged husband and father, I have to think about how a theological principle will intersect with the world of a retired couple in their seventies who deal with grandchildren as well as children. I have to imagine how a theological principle informs the Christian life of a

7. Robinson, "The Heresy of Application," 27.

single mother who drops off her two boys at day care, works all day as a secretary in the university's chemistry department, then picks them up and spends her evenings trying to function as father and mother. As a male whose world involves fly-fishing, basketball, power tools, and *Outdoor Life*, I have to think about how a theological principle will affect the life of a female whose world may revolve around flower-arranging, aerobics, kitchen appliances, and *Good Housekeeping*. As a pastor with a modest income, I have to think about how a theological principle relates to a doctor who must decide whether she should plunk down cash for a sports car or a sport utility vehicle. I have to put myself in the world of the young husband and father who supplements the pittance he receives teaching third grade at a private school with a night job at a sawmill.

Notice how a theological principle takes shape when applied to the grid of people who make up a congregation listening to a Sunday morning sermon. Suppose the sermon is from Genesis 13. We've already expressed the theological idea as, *God's people preserve God's blessing when they face conflict by taking the initiative to resolve it.* Where would this principle crop up in different people's lives? How might they apply it in their particular situation?

A single mom with two children might be embroiled in a dispute over when the children's father may visit them. He's clamoring for more time on weekends. That's the only time she can spend with her children since she works Monday through Friday. Who's going to give? To honor God, she might take the initiative by calling her children's father and offering him Saturdays from 1:00–8:00 P.M.

The young father who works a teaching job during the day and a sawmill job at night may be at odds with a couple who disagree with how he is handling their son, Andrew. The parents think Andrew might suffer from attention deficit disorder. The young teacher thinks Andrew's problem is his insistence on getting his own way. Andrew's parents want the teacher to meet with them and their family physician; they want the teacher to lighten up on their son. The teacher wants Andrew's parents to butt out and let him handle his classroom as he sees fit. He is willing to discuss the issue, but he wants to wait until the parent-teacher conferences scheduled six weeks down the road. To honor God, the young teacher might write a note to the parents explaining his busy schedule but also indicating his willingness to find an hour some afternoon when he can visit with them and Andrew's physician.

A seventy-year-old couple is at odds with their unmarried son, Rick, for leaving the family accounting firm and taking a job with D. A. Davidson and Company selling investment securities. Rick is annoyed at his parents' unwillingness to let him run his life as he sees fit. The parents think that Rick has left them in the lurch. The parents have made some snide remarks, and Rick unleashed a torrent of angry words. Both sides have cooled off, but a tension remains. Although they live only twenty minutes apart, they rarely speak, let alone see each other. To honor God, the parents decide to take the initiative to resolve the conflict. Although Rick's angry words still sting, they decide to invite him over to eat grilled burgers and watch a World Series game.

Thinking about those in your congregation who are different from you in sex, race, generation, socioeconomic status, marital status, and career will help you identify realistic ways of bringing the truth to bear on people's lives.

9

❀ ❀ ❀ ❀ ❀

PACKAGING THE BIG IDEA

❀ ❀ ❀ ❀ ❀

People act on ideas. But ideas stick only when a communicator packages them properly. So a company like the United Parcel Service (UPS) funnels thousands of dollars towards advertising agencies who deliver slogans. Slogans make the ideas stick. If you read a magazine ad that claims, "UPS is the most dependable, reliable company in the delivery industry," you may not give the idea another thought. Even if UPS's claim is true, it's quite forgettable. But you remember a UPS advertisement that claims, "We run the tightest ship in the shipping business." As one advertisement specialist claims, "A good slogan tries to sell an idea. It slaps you round the face, thrusts its chin forward, and dares you to reply. But of course, if it's a really good slogan, it is so eloquent that you are stunned into silence."

Preachers must do for their big idea what a good slogan writer does for an idea that a company is trying to sell. They must figure out how to get their ideas to stick. This means wrestling with how to state the big idea in a creative, contemporary way. Haddon Robinson remarks, "People are more likely to think God's thoughts after Him, and to live and love and choose on the basis of these thoughts when they are couched in memorable sentences."[1]

1. Haddon W. Robinson, *Biblical Preaching: The Development and Delivery of Expository Messages,* 2d ed. (Grand Rapids: Baker, 2001), 104.

Table 9.1
Big Idea Development in 1 Samuel 17

Exegetical idea: *God chose to use David instead of Saul because David had the courage to act in faith on God's specific promise.*
Theological idea: *The people God uses to accomplish his mission in the world are the people who have the courage to act in faith on his specific promises.*
Preaching idea: *When God has big business, faith always gets the contract.*

A primary concern is to state the big idea in a condensed, memorable sentence. Proverbs and aphorisms linger in listeners' memories because they are short and catchy. Take 1 Samuel 17 as an example (see table 9.1). The theological idea I suggested is accurate, but cumbersome: *The people God uses to accomplish his mission in the world are the people who have the courage to act in faith on his specific promises.* Chances are, it won't stick like a bur in a listener's mental socks. However, stating it in a catchy, ten-word sentence makes it stick: *When God has big business, faith always gets the contract.* How do you dream up catchy statements like this? Pay attention to television commercials and magazine advertisements. Notice how they capture an idea in a catchy slogan. Roche Laboratories Inc., a pharmaceutical company, uses a catchy slogan to deliver its message to readers of *Time* magazine and *Sports Illustrated.* Advertisements in these magazines push a weight-loss medication called Xenical. The message is that Xenical blocks digestion of about one-third of the fat contained in a meal that is nutritionally balanced, reduced in calories, with no more than 30 percent of the calories from fat. Read that last sentence again. It communicates the message clearly. But it doesn't stick like Velcro in a listener's mind. To communicate the message in a memorable way, someone coined the slogan, "We do our best work after a good meal." This slogan dominates the two-page spread, appearing at the top of the advertisement in bold-faced, inch-high letters. Whenever you can put a twist on a popular slogan, listeners zone in on it. For example, you could change the slogan, "You're in good hands with Allstate" to "You're in good hands with the Almighty." I like to read the Quotable Quotes section in *Reader's Digest.* It stimulates my creativity, gives me ideas, and occasionally provides a quote I can modify or use. The preaching idea I shared above for 1 Samuel 17 originated from a quote in this section. It's also helpful to have a copy of quotation books such as *Bartlett's Familiar Quotations.* Again, scanning quotes on a particular topic will stimulate your thinking and will sometimes provide you with a quote to borrow or adapt.

For another example, consider Exodus 33:12–34:7. In this narrative, Moses asks to see God's glory. God consents to let Moses view his "backside" from a cleft in the rock. He says, "I will cause all my goodness to pass in front of you, and I will proclaim my name, Yahweh, in your presence" (33:19). Notice the progression from exegetical to theological to preaching expressions of the big idea in this story. The move from theological idea to preaching idea whittles down the word count from twenty-six to twelve words. It also uses a crisp image.

> Exegetical idea: *Although God is so powerful that Moses cannot handle a look at his presence, God is driven by compassion, grace, patience, love, and forgiveness.*
> Theological idea: *Although God is so powerful that a human being cannot handle a look at his presence, God is driven by compassion, grace, patience, love, and forgiveness!*
> Preaching idea: *The God who has the power to fry you is incredibly good!*

Going back to Genesis 13, an expositor could adopt the following preaching idea for the sermon: *God's people guard God's blessing by operating on a "no conflict" basis.* The progression from exegetical to theological to preaching idea looks like this:

> Exegetical idea: *Abram preserved God's blessing when he faced conflict by taking the initiative to resolve it.*
> Theological idea: *God's people preserve God's blessing when they face conflict by taking the initiative to resolve it.*
> Preaching idea: *God's people guard God's blessing by operating on a "no conflict" basis.*

Another tactic for moving from theological idea to preaching idea is to paint a verbal picture. Haddon Robinson does this with 2 Samuel 11–12 (see table 9.2). He tightens up the word count and provides a vivid image when he phrases the big idea as, *When you fail to walk with God, you walk on the edge of an abyss.*

Table 9.2
Big Idea Development in 2 Samuel 11–12

Exegetical idea: *When David failed to walk with God, he put his life, family, and career in jeopardy.*
Theological idea: *When believers fail to walk with God, they put their lives, families, and careers in jeopardy.*
Preaching idea: *When you fail to walk with God, you walk on the edge of an abyss.*

Sometimes an expositor will not need to modify the theological idea. It may be clear and catchy enough as it is. The strategy is not to be clever; simply communicate the big idea so that it gets remembered. For example, as we noted earlier, Paul Borden's theological idea for 2 Samuel 11–12 is, *Believers must learn to accept what the grace of God has given them and what the grace of God has not.* It's hard to improve on that. In this case, a preacher may want to expend creative thinking on some other phase of the sermon. The theological idea here will preach as it stands.

At times, a preacher may want to craft a preaching idea that reflects application to a particular life situation or to a particular people group. The preaching idea must be in line with the theological idea, but it will apply the idea to a specific situation or audience. For example, a message on Genesis 22:1–19 directed to fathers on Father's Day may convey this idea: *The greatest thing you can do for your children is to worship God, not your children.* The progression looks like this:

Exegetical idea: *Abraham put obedience to God first even though he faced the prospect of sacrificing his son Isaac.*
Theological idea: *Faithful worshipers of God will put obedience to God first even when there is great cost involved.*
Preaching idea: *The greatest thing you can do for your kids is to worship God, not your kids!*

In this instance, the preaching idea takes the theological idea and applies it specifically to child rearing. The sacrifice or great cost involves saying no to our children. We may idolize them to the point that we fudge on our giving to buy them designer jeans. Or we let our children's soccer or basketball schedule keep us from worship and fellowship with other believers. The preaching idea is true to the theological idea, but it reflects a particular area of application.

Developing your big idea in this way requires high-level thinking. But the result is an idea that will stick in your listeners' minds. Once you give your big idea sticking power, you are ready to move on and think about your sermon's purpose.

10

❀ ❀ ❀ ❀ ❀

DETERMINING THE SERMON'S PURPOSE

❀ ❀ ❀ ❀ ❀

Wise preachers take the time to wrestle with a sermon's purpose. Forming a purpose statement forces preachers to think through what they expect to happen within their hearers as a result of hearing the sermon.[1] If the sermon's big idea resembles an arrow, the sermon's purpose resembles the target (see figure 10.1). The big idea states the truth. The purpose describes what the truth should accomplish.

Figure 10.1
The Relationship between Big Idea and Purpose

Big Idea   **Purpose**

1. For a fuller discussion, see Haddon W. Robinson, *Biblical Preaching: The Development and Delivery of Expository Messages,* 2d ed. (Grand Rapids: Baker, 2001), 107–12.

In order to discipline their thinking, preachers should write out the purpose statement in a sentence that describes the intended outcome. Ask what should happen in the listeners as a result of hearing the sermon. Then write this in a sentence. Effective purpose statements exhibit at least two characteristics.

First, effective purpose statements reflect the purpose of the author. A preacher should start with the author's purpose by asking, What did the writer expect to accomplish by putting this story here and telling it in this manner? With the answer in hand, the second step is to ask, What do I expect to happen in the lives of my audience after listening to this story? The preacher's purpose should be in line with the biblical author's purpose.

In 1 Samuel 17, the writer's purpose is to show the audience that David was more qualified to serve as Israel's king than Saul was because David had the courage to act in faith when facing a crisis. To put it another way, the writer's purpose for including this story in the larger narrative is to show the audience what kind of person God uses in major positions of leadership. The author's purpose was not to present three strategies for slaying the giant of lust when it attacks a believer's life. Such a statement does not line up with the author's purpose because it deals with overcoming temptation rather than overcoming a crisis in one's life. What about a sermon that will help listeners recite three strategies for preparing to handle crisis situations? This does line up with the writer's purpose, even though the writer's purpose is a bit more specific.

The purpose of your sermon can be different than the author's purpose as long as it is in line with the author's purpose. Sometimes the composition of your audience dictates this. The author of Genesis 22:1–19 did not intend to address a group of fathers on Father's Day about the need to discern whether or not they are worshiping their children instead of God. However, if you are speaking to a group of fathers on Father's Day, it's legitimate to craft your purpose so that it becomes audience specific. Your purpose for a sermon on Genesis 22:1–19 could be, *Fathers will write out a list of sacrifices they make for their children that steal time or money rightly belonging to God.*

When moving from the author's intended purpose to your sermon's purpose, you can move from apples to oranges because you are still talking about fruit. Moving from apples to baseballs is too large a stretch, even though both objects are roughly the same shape and size. The key is, does your purpose line up with the author's? The purpose statement for Genesis 22:1–19 lines up with the author's purpose since it builds on the idea of putting God first when obedience may seem to threaten a blessing or a solution he has previously given you. On the other hand, it's unlikely that the author envisioned using 2 Samuel 11–12 as an example of why honest communication is important. That amounts to going in a completely different direction than the author did. You must always ask, Would the author be comfortable with the way I am using his story to address this particular situation? Would the author have done that?

Second, effective purpose statements describe measurable results. Stating the sermon's purpose as an instructional objective gives the preacher a means of gauging the sermon's effectiveness. This requires stating the purpose in measurable terms. It's too vague to say, "Listeners should love God more." How can you measure a purpose statement like this? You can't. A measurable purpose statement specifically describes the performance of the listener. It's too general to say, "My listeners should encourage two people this week." You arrive at a measurable statement by saying, "My listeners should send two cards to two people, thanking them for their contributions to the church's ministry." Or, if you want to make explicit the idea of encouragement, you could merge the two examples into a statement such as, "My listeners should encourage two people this week by sending two cards to two people, thanking them for their contributions to the church's ministry."

Think about the story in Genesis 13. We already identified a preaching idea for a sermon from this story: *God's people guard God's blessing by operating on a "no conflict" basis.* Look at the following two examples of purpose statements for a sermon on Genesis 13. The first attempt is too general. The second makes the changes necessary for the statement to be measurable.

> *Not measurable:* Hearers should initiate conflict resolution when conflict arises.
>
> *Measurable:* Hearers should set up one lunch appointment or make one telephone call to suggest a solution for resolving a conflict.

As you think about your audience, you may conclude that many of them have blind spots when it comes to recognizing conflicts with other people. They are so used to conflict that they can't seem to spot it. For them, the first step in initiating resolution will be identifying the conflict. So the outcome you envision involves recognizing or identifying conflicts they have with other people. This happens internally rather than externally. The intended outcome takes shape in their minds before it works out in their visible behavior. The previous examples of purpose statements have worked with visible or overt performance. If present, you can observe someone writing a thank-you note or making a phone call. A listener can easily say, "Yes, I did that," or "No, I did not follow through on that." But how can you craft a measurable purpose statement when an attitude is involved? How do you express in measurable terms a purpose that involves understanding, appreciating, recognizing, or hating? Now we are dealing with invisible or covert performance. The trick is to add an indicator behavior that reveals how the covert performance can be detected.[2] Look at the two sample purpose statements from a sermon

2. Robert F. Mager, *Preparing Instructional Objectives,* 3d ed. (Atlanta: The Center for Effective Performance, 1997), 77.

on Genesis 13. The preacher wants listeners to move from an unawareness of conflict to a recognition of conflict. The first statement includes an invisible, covert performance. The second makes the performance visible by adding an indicator behavior.

Not measurable: Hearers should identify people with whom they need to initiate conflict resolution.

Measurable: Hearers should write out a list of five to ten people with whom they have some sort of conflict.

If your purpose is for listeners to know or understand God's loyal love, then your indicator behavior will involve reciting a definition, writing a list of examples, or preparing a lesson on God's loyal love for a third-grade Sunday school class. If your purpose is for listeners to appreciate God's loyal love, then your indicator behavior might involve writing a psalm of thanksgiving or a love letter to God. Whether or not the hearers actually recite a definition, write a list, prepare a lesson, or write a psalm of thanksgiving, you will preach more directly if you preach as though they will.

Try this example. The preaching idea for Paul Borden's sermon on 2 Samuel 11–12 is, *Believers must learn to accept what the grace of God has given them and what the grace of God has not.* Suppose the intended outcome of your sermon is for listeners to appreciate what God's grace has given them and what it has withheld. How could you add an indicator behavior to a covert, invisible performance like appreciating? Try writing a measurable purpose statement of your own before looking at the example I propose.

Did you write out a statement of your own? Here is a purpose statement that describes what appreciating God's grace will look like when it happens in a listener's life: *Listeners will write out a list of God's specific gifts to them and then offer daily, five-minute prayers of thanksgiving to God for these gifts.* Here is another possible example: *Hearers will use their mealtime prayers to recite God's specific blessings in their lives and to request from him contentment.*

Whether or not your listeners will actually write out a list of items or use their mealtime prayers to recite God's blessings, you should preach as if they will. The Spirit of God may even use your sermon to accomplish a different purpose than you intended. But identifying the purpose for your sermon will help you aim your big idea more accurately.

11

SHAPING THE SERMON

❀ ❀ ❀ ❀ ❀

For years, aspiring preachers have received this sage advice: "Tell them what you plan to tell them; tell them; then tell them what you've just told them." This turns out to be lousy advice when preaching a story. To preach an Old Testament narrative effectively, preachers must wrestle with the most effective means of shaping their sermon. This brings us to the next stage in the sermon development process.

At this point the preacher must ask, What kind of form will I use to accomplish the purpose I determined based on the big idea? What shape will my sermon take?

Many pastors opt for shaping their sermons around a list of principles they have combed during their study. During a recent trip to a seminary library, I perused a year's worth of issues from a popular magazine on preaching. Most of the published manuscripts on Old Testament narrative texts followed this tactic. One pastor shaped a sermon from Exodus 3:1–12 around three keys to impossible living gleaned from Moses' life. Another pastor preached Genesis 45:1–13 by listing the techniques Joseph used to put his painful past behind him. Still another preacher handled the story of Abraham's test in Genesis 22 by sharing four principles about the testing of our faith. Yet another preached the Genesis 39 account of Joseph overcoming temptation by highlighting four reasons why we should say no to sexual temptation. As previously noted,

112   ❀ ❀ ❀

this approach usually does not reflect the strategy or style of the authors who composed Old Testament narratives. Often, it does not do justice to the author's intention but uses a story to illustrate principles a preacher reads into a text.

What shape should a sermon from an Old Testament narrative take? The story form is the obvious choice. As David C. Deuel argues, "If the preacher's goal is to be expositional, what is more expositional than preaching the text in its storyline form?"[1] This is not as easy as it sounds, however. Sidney Greidanus explains, "The narrative form has to strike a delicate balance between simply narrating the story and providing explicit statements for right understanding."[2] Haddon Robinson elaborates:

> Narrative preaching however does not merely repeat the details of a story like recounting a pointless, worn-out joke. Through the story you communicate ideas. In a narrative sermon, as in any other sermon, a major idea continues to be supported by other ideas, but the content supporting the points is drawn directly from the incidents in the story. In other words, the details of the story are woven together to make a point, and all the points develop the central idea of the sermon.[3]

Preaching the text in its story line form means following the plot elements of a story: exposition, crisis, resolution, and conclusion. You will plot your sermon by taking your cue from the way the story unfolds. While you will do more than retell the story, you will not do less than that. Ideally, you will follow the same set of tracks as the biblical storyteller. What implications does this have for the development of your sermon's big idea?

Inductive Preaching

For one thing, following the contours of the storyline means preaching inductively rather than deductively. Remember the terms *inductive* and *deductive* from your preaching and philosophy courses? They describe the way people reason and present ideas (see figure 11.1). In deduction, you start with the conclusion or the whole and then work to the specific pieces. The answer is

1. David C. Deuel, "Expository Preaching from Old Testament Narrative," in *Rediscovering Expository Preaching*, ed. John MacArthur Jr. (Dallas: Word, 1992), 275. By "storyline," Deuel refers to the plot or general plan of a story. Likewise, Sidney Greidanus observes, "The most appropriate form for a sermon on a narrative text is, not surprisingly, the narrative form" (*The Modern Preacher and the Ancient Text* [Grand Rapids: Eerdmans, 1988], 226).

2. Greidanus, *The Modern Preacher and the Ancient Text*, 225. Haddon Robinson comments, "Narratives are most effective when the audience hears the story and arrives at the speaker's ideas without the idea being stated directly" (*Biblical Preaching: The Development and Delivery of Expository Messages*, 2d ed. [Grand Rapids: Baker, 2001], 130).

3. Robinson, *Biblical Preaching*, 130.

front-loaded, and then you break it down. Arranging a sermon deductively can make it clear. It can also make it boring. Unless your idea creates tension, your listeners will check out. Don Sunukjian preaches an effective deductive sermon on 2 Corinthians 12:7–10 in which he develops the big idea, *The thing you pray most that God would change is the thing you most want to keep.* When listeners hear that idea, their response is not, "Good, I've got the answer. Let's go home." Their response is most likely, "No way. That's outrageous." They are ready to debate, to argue, and, yes, to listen to your defense of the idea.

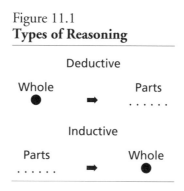

Figure 11.1
Types of Reasoning

The opposite approach is induction. Induction starts with the specific pieces and then works its way through them to the conclusion or the whole. The answer is unknown at the beginning. The idea does not emerge until the end. When done poorly, induction can be unclear. Your listeners may struggle to stay on track since they're not sure where you're going. When done well, though, induction gives the preacher an edge. Arranging a sermon inductively creates suspense and produces a sense of discovery.

One evening, my teenage daughter, Erin, and I watched an episode of Dick Van Dyke's hit television series *Diagnosis Murder.* In the first five minutes, a priest intentionally drove his car onto a sidewalk to hit a man who was standing on a street corner. The man lived, but the priest murdered the victim by sneaking into the victim's hospital room and tampering with his IV. My daughter groaned, "Oh, I don't like it when they show us at the beginning who committed the murder." She explained to me that *Diagnosis Murder* usually does not reveal the identity of the murderer until the final segment. She prefers it that way because it creates more suspense. In other words, she prefers an inductive arrangement. In this episode, the producers used a deductive arrangement to tell the story. They relied on other means of creating suspense. The story raised questions designed to hold the viewer's interest. Why did a priest commit a murder? How could Dr. Mark Sloan, the leading character played by Dick Van Dyke, prove that the good guy—a man of the cloth—was actually the bad guy? Still, my daughter expressed her preference for an inductive shape.

Since stories operate inductively, most sermons that preach Bible stories should operate inductively as well. A preacher should maintain the story's sense of "strategic delay." In other words, the big idea is not front-loaded but saved for the end. Early in my preaching of Old Testament narratives, I always told the congregation up front what I planned to tell them. I was so concerned they might miss my big idea that I distrusted the story form and gave away my big idea at the beginning of the sermon. I would say something like, "This morning, we're going to see in 1 Samuel 5–7 that *God is not just a power source you can exploit, but a powerful person you must worship.*" In essence, I was saying, "Before I tell you the story this morning, let me skip to the last chapter and read you the ending."

Imagine that your favorite baseball team, the St. Louis Cardinals (okay, my favorite team), will battle the New York Yankees in the seventh game of the World Series. The problem is, game seven will be held on Sunday night and you're preaching at an evening service. So you set your VCR to record the game. You anticipate dashing home after the service as soon as it's polite to leave. You won't turn on the radio because you might hear how the game ended. You want to experience the same sense of discovery that the fans and announcers and players had as the innings piled up. The last thing you want is for somebody to come running in after the church service and say, "Hey, I just heard the final score from game seven!" If you don't plug your ears in time, you'll hear the outcome. And knowing the outcome before you watch the game will suck the life and energy right out of the experience. The same happens with a sermon from an Old Testament narrative. If you tell people the destination before you start, the journey will be less exciting.

Paul Harvey is a master of strategic delay. For years, he has charmed his radio audience with his "rest of the story" anecdotes. Author Paul Aurandt has compiled these stories in three paperback volumes.[4] I urge preachers to get copies of these. Not only do they provide an astounding source of illustrations, but they teach preachers how to maintain tension and save key details for the end. The same detail that might only produce a whimper earlier in the sermon can produce a bang at the end.

For example, read the following account written by Paul Aurandt, describing how he came to work for Paul Harvey:

> I've always been a fan of Paul Harvey. The quality of his voice and the timing of his words never failed to mesmerize me, even as a young boy who understood little of the News. I listened to him every day, at the encouragement of my par-

---

4. Paul Aurandt, *Paul Harvey's The Rest of the Story* (New York: Bantam, 1977); Paul Aurandt, *More of Paul Harvey's The Rest of the Story* (New York: Bantam, 1980); Paul Aurandt, *Destiny* (New York: Bantam, 1983).

ents. And I suppose you might say that the Paul Harvey timing even influenced my music later. The dramatic pauses, the careful, warm pacing.

Anyway, I had known for quite some while that Paul Harvey, my childhood hero, was looking for a writer. On an impulse day . . . when I was practicing for an upcoming concert . . . I sat down and wrote a Rest of the Story just as I imagined Paul Harvey would have written it. The topic was a musical one . . . something I'd researched once.

When I was finished, I showed the story to my mother . . . another Paul Harvey devotee. And she was impressed! "It sounds just like him!" she told me.

To make a long story short, I applied for and got the job. I've had to set aside a lot of concerts, but I'm really having fun. So far, at least.

Oh, there's something you might be interested in learning about Mr. Harvey. When you work for someone, you learn things about him no one else knows.

Paul Harvey is not his complete name.

Now, don't tell anybody you heard it from me, but Harvey is his middle name. He dropped his last name because it was difficult to spell and to pronounce.

I kept it.

I'm his son.

And now you know the rest . . . of The Rest of the Story.[5]

Now imagine the lack of impact the same information would have if Paul Aurandt had simply written a preface saying, "It's a privilege to serve as editor and writer for my father, Paul Harvey. Just so you know, Paul Harvey is not his complete name. It is his first name and middle name. His last name, like mine, is Aurandt. He simply dropped it because it doesn't work as well on the radio." The intrigue is gone. The journey is over.

In his sermon on 2 Samuel 11–12, Paul Borden does a masterful job of placing details about Uriah the Hittite at the end of the sermon. By doing so, he brings the sermon to a stunning conclusion. Uriah emerges as the hero. He ends up losing his life because he had the integrity to do what David did not.

Following the contours of the storyline means placing the big idea at the end, but it also means riding the tension created by the crisis or complication of the story. As a storyteller, tension is your best friend. Keeping your listeners in suspense keeps them listening.[6] So plan to play up the tension rather than downplaying it. For example, in Genesis 22:2 the tension builds when God commands Abraham to offer Isaac as a sacrifice. A wise expositor will point out how Abraham's apprehension must have increased with each level of spec-

5. Aurandt, *Paul Harvey's The Rest of the Story*, 179–80.
6. Eugene L. Lowry has proposed five sequential stages for a sermon that develops like a story unfolds: (1) upsetting the equilibrium, (2) analyzing the discrepancy, (3) disclosing the clue to resolution, (4) experiencing the gospel, and (5) anticipating the consequences (*The Homiletical Plot: The Sermon As Narrative Art Form* [Atlanta: John Knox, 1980], 25). In his most recent work, Lowry slightly modifies his earlier sermon plot, opting for four stages rather

ificity: your son . . . your only son . . . the one you love . . . Isaac. Perhaps the preacher will take the time to draw an analogy of how God today puts us in situations that leave us apprehensive, afraid, or even angry. Instead of rushing to the resolution, the preacher will allow the hearers to experience the tension in the text.

Paul Borden perfectly describes how an inductive sermon from an Old Testament story should flow to create tension and then to release it. The starting point is developing the crisis or spiritual disease of the story:

> Your job as a preacher is to develop for your congregation how people relate, interact, and struggle with the same spiritual disease. You pick those aspects of the story that enable you to illustrate this disease. Rather than thinking of which verses do this, demonstrate how the plot, character development, scenes, actions, design, tone, and so on develop the disease. You use these elements to state, elaborate, and build the first half to two-thirds of your sermon.[7]

According to Borden, the final one-third to one-half of the sermon will develop the remedy:

> You demonstrate how God's people successfully or unsuccessfully embraced the divine remedy for their spiritual sickness. This idea is applied to your congregation. In this way, your preaching idea becomes the reversal (the remedy) to the disequilibrium you have created (the spiritual sickness).
>
> Last, you use the closing minutes to demonstrate the implications of accepting or rejecting this remedy. You show how acceptance brings spiritual health, while rejection brings further illness. You appeal to people to choose health (life) over disease (death).[8]

Borden then explains the payoff for using this kind of an inductive flow to preach an Old Testament narrative:

> Preaching this way enables you and your people to feel the story as drama. The sermon, which has its own plot, uses the pieces of the story that reflect the disequilibrium, reversal, and resolution they felt when they first read or heard the story. However, you have used the story as story, and the idea of the story has caused the congregation to wrestle with the disequilibrium of humanness, to

---

than five: (1) conflict, (2) complication, (3) sudden shift, and (4) unfolding. He notes that the gospel component of his previous plot diagram can fit after the sudden shift, or sometimes it is the sudden shift. Sometimes the good news even takes place before the sudden shift (*The Sermon: Dancing the Edge of Mystery* [Nashville: Abingdon, 1997], 81–89).

7. Paul Borden, "Is There Really One Big Idea in That Story?" in *The Big Idea of Biblical Preaching,* ed. Keith Willhite and Scott M. Gibson (Grand Rapids: Baker, 1998), 78.

8. Ibid., 79.

understand and feel the reversal of divine truth, and choose the resolutions that provide life. Both the sermon and the text (a narrative) have been treated as story.[9]

The Flashback Approach

A variation of the inductive approach would be to use a flashback. In other words, start at the conclusion and show how the character arrived there. For example, Haddon Robinson begins a sermon on David's life as a father with his lament over Absalom's death (2 Sam. 18:33). Then he goes back to the beginning and traces the course of events that led to this cry of grief. This technique works particularly well with tragic stories. The story of Samson in Judges 13–16 could begin with the implosion of the Philistine temple that took blind Samson's life.

The flashback technique can also work with comedy. The expositor could begin the story of Esther with Esther on the throne and ask, How did a Jewish girl whose nation was in jeopardy of a holocaust end up on the Persian throne? Or the expositor might start the story of Ruth with the ending: How did a Moabite widow end up being part of the line from which King David would come?

The Inductive-Deductive Approach

Occasionally, if the big idea requires an extra dose of explanation or validation, a preacher may choose an inductive-deductive arrangement. Suppose a preacher decides to preach the following big idea from the book of Esther: *Even when you can't see or hear God, he is still in control of your destiny.* Ordinarily, the preacher will work through the story inductively, and this big idea will emerge at the end. However, a preacher may determine that the hearers will not readily buy into this idea. Maybe several teens from their church died in a bus accident. Or perhaps listeners live in a community where God has never done anything dramatic. No revival has taken place there. No Christian leaders or missionaries have arisen from the congregation. The preacher may sense the need to tell the story, let the idea emerge about halfway through the sermon, and then go back to point out more specifically from the story that circumstances don't stop God from controlling one's destiny. God is still in control despite the insensitivity of people around you. He's still in control even though you face impossible people in prominent places. What's more, he still guides your destiny when unpredictable events take place. And finally, God remains in control in spite of circumstances that no human being can change.

This arrangement is inductive-deductive because the first part of the ser-

9. Ibid.

mon tells us the story inductively, while the second part spends time developing the idea. In this case, the development takes the form of validation.

The Semi-Inductive Approach

Sometimes sermons from Old Testament narratives can take a semi-inductive form. This happens when the big idea has a multiple complement. The sermon is semi-inductive because the big idea emerges in sections. The expositor raises the subject in the introduction. Then the complement emerges as a series of ideas. For example, Paul Borden preaches a sermon on 1 Samuel 17 in which his big idea is, *David succeeded under pressure because his perspective was different, because he learned the habit of trusting God, and because he let God do the fighting.* The subject of this sermon— *Why David succeeded under pressure*—is introduced at the beginning of the sermon. The three parts of the complement emerge throughout the sermon at the appropriate places in the storyline.

First-Person Narratives

Another decision the expositor must make relates to perspective. Usually, the expositor will adopt the third-person point of view and tell the story from the perspective of the biblical narrator. This approach gets its name from the third-person pronouns that dominate the narration: *she* wept, *he* went up, *she* ran, *he* said.

Another option is to tell the story as a major or minor character in the story, similar to Dr. Watson relating a Sherlock Holmes story. This is called a first-person narrative because telling the story as a participant requires using the first-person pronoun: *I* came to the throne, *I* waited eagerly, *I* kept quiet. Some refer to this kind of sermon as a "dramatic monologue." While this form should not be overdone, mixing in a first-person narrative once or twice a year can add some zing to a preacher's homiletical stew.[10]

In most cases, the sermon will develop along the lines of the story as in a traditional third-person narrative. The form allows the preacher to relive the story in greater depth, seeing what the character sees and hearing what the character hears. But does this form communicate a Bible-shaped word in a Bible-shaped way? John MacArthur appears to challenge this form when he responds to a question about drama in the pulpit:

> I was at a pastor's conference where one of the speakers came out in diapers with a doll under one arm, a pacifier around his neck, and a baby bottle in his hand. He proceeded to talk about baby Christians. In my judgment I would have to say that such a performance appears to be a crutch, and it seems that

10. Jeffrey Arthurs, "Performing the Story," *Preaching* 12 (March-April 1997): 30.

only a weak preacher would need such a crutch. You have to believe the power of God's Word will be more effective than any human drama or communication gimmick. Nothing is as dramatic as the explosion of truth on the mind of a believer through powerful preaching.[11]

Aside from using a rather bizarre example to dismiss the whole, MacArthur's answer fails by assuming that human drama is antithetical to the power of God's Word and is therefore a "communication gimmick." Why, then, would God use a communication gimmick to relate his word to the prophet Jeremiah? In Jeremiah 13:1–11, God told Jeremiah to buy a linen belt, put it around his waist, then bury it in some rocks, and eventually dig it up and observe its worthlessness. The ruined belt served as a picture of Judah—bound to God like a belt around one's waist but useless. Furthermore, why did God command Jeremiah to use a communication gimmick to communicate to the priests and people of Judah? In Jeremiah 27–28, God commanded Jeremiah to make a yoke out of straps and crossbars and to put it on his neck. He wore this yoke when he gave a message to King Zedekiah and when he spoke to the people and the priests. Eventually, the prophet Hananiah broke this yoke as he and Jeremiah explained that God would break the yoke of the king of Babylon. Warren Wiersbe comments, "The episodes involving the linen belt (chap. 13), the potter (chaps. 18–19), the yokes (chaps. 27–28), and the burial of the stones in Egypt (chap. 43) were in a sense 'action sermons' for the communicating of abstract truth."[12] Likewise, Ezekiel used drama to communicate God's Word. Wiersbe observes,

> As a sign, he [Ezekiel] was bound with ropes (3:24–27); he "played war" (4:1–17); he played barber (5:1–17); he clapped his hands and stamped his feet (6:11; see 21:14); he acted like he was going on a trip (12:1–16); he trembled as he ate (12:17–20) and groaned like a man in grief (21:6, 12); he played road-builder (21:18–23); he was not allowed to mourn his dead wife (24:15–27); and he made two sticks into one (37:15–17).[13]

To be sure, drama can be done poorly, or it can be overdone. Sermons from Old Testament narrative texts do not always need drama to communicate truth. Yet the way in which the prophets communicated God's truth seems to give biblical and theological credence to a creative form such as a first-person narrative. The Bible does not stifle the limits of a preacher's creativity as long as the form complements the content. The next chapter will explore how to fill in a first-person narrative sermon.

11. John MacArthur Jr., "Frequently Asked Questions about Expository Preaching," in *Rediscovering Expository Preaching*, ed. John MacArthur Jr. (Dallas: Word, 1992), 345.

12. Warren W. Wiersbe, *Preaching and Teaching with Imagination: The Quest for Biblical Ministry* (Wheaton: Victor, 1994), 145.

13. Ibid., 147.

Finding a Place for Application

Another issue a preacher faces when shaping a sermon to fit his purpose concerns finding a place for application. Basically, a preacher has two choices. Save application for the end when the big idea fully emerges, or weave application throughout the sermon. The decision depends on when principles or ideas come into focus.

The point at which the crisis emerges or picks up steam is a logical place for an application image. The preacher wants the hearer to understand that her situation is not unlike Jael's (Judg. 4) or Ruth's predicament. So the preacher sketches what this predicament or disease looks like in the life of a twenty-first century listener. At this point in the sermon, the application does not consist of a principle to practice. Rather, it's a picture of what the problem looks like in the life of a modern listener. It's an attempt to get hearers to see themselves in the story. Later, when the resolution surfaces, it's time to picture how the reader will put the remedy into effect for the disease developed in the story.

Obviously, this stage in the process forces you to wrestle with thought. But thinking yourself clear at this stage will equip you to do well at the next stage. Once you have in mind the way you will develop your purpose, you are ready to plot out in detail your plan for preaching the story. You are ready to prepare an outline.

12

❀ ❀ ❀ ❀ ❀

OUTLINING THE SERMON

❀ ❀ ❀ ❀ ❀

Twenty students and two professors stared at the handwriting on the wall. One by one, students in a seminary preaching class were projecting their first attempts at a sermon outline from an assigned passage. I nervously sat waiting for my turn. My friend Rod was up first. Rod looked at the transparency he placed on the overhead and read aloud his main points for a potential sermon on 1 Samuel 17, the David and Goliath story:

I. Goliath Challenges God's People
II. Saul Cowers with God's People
III. David Conquers for God's People

After a silent pause, Haddon Robinson, the lead professor, growled, "That sounds like it came out of a book called *Simple Sermons for Sunday Evening*." The class erupted with laughter. Nervous laughter. Sympathetic laughter. "Nobody talks like this anymore, except in the pulpit," he continued. Duane Litfin, guest professor, chimed in, "What Haddon is saying is that he's afraid you might go out and actually preach that sermon!" More laughter.

The outline stage in sermon preparation is, for some, the most intimidating step in the process. Bryan Chapell relates, "In the classroom and in seminars around the country, I find that preachers have more questions about structure than they do about any other aspect of preaching."[1] This stage resembles the hole on the back nine with a narrow fairway, a water hazard to your right, and bunkers pinching the fairway as you approach the green. It's intimidating. Most preachers can relate to feature writer Jon Franklin's frustration about putting stories in the standard outline form. Franklin, a two-time Pulitzer Prize winner, laments,

> As near as I can figure it, such outline systems were specifically designed to convince budding writers that outlining is impossible, and that the only way they can create worthwhile copy is to hack their way through the words like a hunter slashing a path through a seven-canopy jungle. . . . The Roman numeral type of outline will . . . be recognized for what it is, the English Teacher's Revenge, or ETR for short.[2]

Tips for Effective Outlines

Let me share some tips that will help you relax and relate to an outline as a friend rather than a foe (see table 12.1). First, don't try to create outlines that people will remember. It took me years of preaching to figure this out.

Table 12.1
Tips for Effective Outlines

1. Don't try to create outlines that people will remember.
2. View main points as endings, not beginnings.
3. State your outline points in full sentences.
4. Think in terms of moves rather than points.

I sincerely believed that listeners would be improved for taking my outline points home with them—either in their heads or, better yet, on paper. Without a captioned survey of either the passage or the principles in it, how would people get the text into their lives? For years, I heard preachers like Warren Wiersbe say, "An outline is not a sermon." But I didn't get it. Eventually, I learned that an outline resembles a map. It gives preachers directions. It offers a plan. The preacher has to have it in mind but the congregation does not. Donald McDougall recalls,

> One of the greatest compliments ever paid me was given inadvertently when a lady commented after a message, "I came to realize that you didn't have an outline; it just flowed." Actually I did have an outline I was following, but it was inconspicuous; that is how it should be.[3]

1. Bryan Chapell, *Christ-Centered Preaching: Redeeming the Expository Sermon* (Grand Rapids: Baker, 1994), 157.
2. Jon Franklin, *Writing for Story: Craft Secrets of Dramatic Nonfiction by a Two-Time Pulitzer Prize Winner* (New York: Plume/Penguin, 1986), 110.
3. Donald G. McDougall, "Central Ideas, Outlines, and Titles," in *Rediscovering Expository Preaching*, ed. John MacArthur Jr. (Dallas: Word, 1992), 234.

When people relate to me on a personal level, is my skeleton important? Absolutely. Without it, I could not sit, stand, walk, or embrace. But do the people to whom I relate need to see my skeleton? Absolutely not. In fact, it's better when they don't see my bones protruding through the skin. An outline works the same way. It must be there for the sermon to have structure, but the outline does not need to be "Exhibit A." I want people to leave with ideas formed in their minds. Ideas gel in people's minds through images and pictures, not outlines. I want people to go home with God's truth in mind, and particularly with a picture of what that truth looks like when lived out in their lives. While I need my outline to help me communicate the ideas and pictures, the audience doesn't need to see my outline any more than they need to see the two-by-four studs supporting the sheetrock wall in my living room. The contractor who framed my house occasionally reminded me and some of the volunteer help, "We're not building a piano." In other words, we want a sturdy frame, but it doesn't have to be a polished work of art. It will not be visible when we're all done. When I preach, I may or may not say the statement exactly as I have it worded in my first point. The key is, by the time I'm done with the first main point, the idea it expresses will have formed in the hearer's mind, or I will have related the section of the story it describes.

Related to this is a second tip: View main points as endings, not beginnings. I used to struggle constantly with outlining story sermons. The reason, I eventually discovered, is that while stories work inductively, outlines work deductively. Jon Franklin explains the difference between an outline of a story or drama and the typical "English Teacher's Revenge" (ETR) outline:

> The statements in the ETR outlines represent topic sentences and therefore specify what comes at the *beginning* of the section they are supposed to represent. The first sentence in the outline expresses the thought that opens the piece. That's because in "logical" writing the writer states his premise first, then develops it.
>
> In storytelling, on the other hand, the dramatic action that makes your point comes at the *end* of each section, where climaxes belong. That means your statements represent endings, not beginnings.[4]

Typically, a preacher will move out of an introduction and state the first main point. After stating the main point, the preacher will move to subpoint A, then to subpoint B, and so on. However, in the outline of a story sermon, the preacher will often move out of the introduction into subpoint A, then to subpoint B, and then through further subpoints. Only at the end of the subpoints does the idea in the first main point emerge. When you prepare your outline, you should indicate which main points will be developed inductively.

4. Franklin, *Writing for Story*, 117–18.

Simply put "develop inductively"—italicized in parentheses—after the statement of the main point (see table 12.2 for an example).

Table 12.2
Sermon Outline of Genesis 22:1–19

I. God tests his people by forcing them to choose between worshiping him or the children he has given them (*develop inductively*).
   A. God tests Abraham with the stunning command to sacrifice Isaac (vv. 1–2).
   B. This test will force Abraham to choose between worshiping God or Isaac.
   C. Today parents face the choice of worshiping God or their children.
II. (*Big idea*) The greatest thing you can do for your kids is to worship God, not your kids (*develop inductively*).
   A. Abraham makes the worship of God his priority (vv. 3–10).
   B. God intervenes and acknowledges Abraham's obedience (vv. 11–14).
   C. God returns to reaffirm his blessing and promise (vv. 15–19).**
   D. Worshipping God and not your kids requires the conviction that God will provide (vv. 8, 14).

A third tip is to state your outline points in full sentences. Haddon Robinson explains the rationale for this practice:

> Keep in mind that each point in the outline represents an idea, and thus should be a grammatically complete sentence. When only words and phrases stand as points, they deceive us because they are incomplete and vague. Partial statements allow thought to slip through our minds like a greased football.[5]

Writing an outline is a way of thinking. You will short-circuit the thinking process if you do not write out your points in complete sentences.

Finally, think in terms of "moves" instead of points. Mainline preacher David Buttrick, who championed this shift from points to moves, describes it like this:

> Sermons are a movement of language from one idea to another, each idea being shaped in a bundle of words. Thus, when we preach we speak in formed modules of language arranged in some patterned sequence. These modules of language we will call "moves."[6]

Buttrick's approach has attracted the label "phenomenological" because of his interest in the way language forms in human consciousness.[7] He claims: "Group consciousness simply cannot handle rapid shifts in subject matter. To

---

5. Haddon W. Robinson, *Biblical Preaching: The Development and Delivery of Expository Messages*, 2d ed. (Grand Rapids: Baker, 2001), 134.
6. David Buttrick, *Homiletic: Moves and Structures* (Philadelphia: Fortress, 1987), 23.
7. Ibid., xii.

move along from subject to subject every few sentences would 'freak out' an audience. . . . To form five different subject matters in group consciousness would require at least fifteen minutes of speaking time."[8] Thus, Buttrick advocates developing sermon moves, lasting about four minutes each, to form, image, and explore a conceptual idea.[9] Buttrick emphasizes the presentation of ideas through word pictures, because, "homiletic thinking is always *a thinking of theology toward images.*"[10]

Evangelicals will find that Buttrick's approach serves narrative sermons quite well. The preacher wants to do more than make a point. He or she wants to let various elements of the story—a certain scene, a conversation, a theological idea—form in the minds of the hearers. The goal is to plot out the movements in the preaching of the story: "First, I need to tell them this. Second, I need to tell them this. Next, I plan to tell them this."

Preparing Your Sermon Outline

To build your sermon outline, go back to your exegetical outline and review the flow of the story. You will decide how to arrange the details to fit the shape you have chosen for communicating the sermon's big idea. While you will generally follow the same set of tracks as the storyteller, you may decide to rearrange some of the details. For example, when Paul Borden preaches his sermon on 2 Samuel 11–12, he chooses to save his description of Uriah's heroics for the end of the sermon even though Uriah's actions take place in the middle of the story.

My sermon on Genesis 22:1–19 provides another example. Here is the exegetical outline developed earlier:

    I. *Exposition:* The narrator explains God's intent to test Abraham (v. 1).

    II. *Crisis:* God commands Abraham to sacrifice his son Isaac (v. 2).

    III. *Rising Tension:* Abraham responds to God's command with obedience (vv. 3–10).

        A. Abraham travels to the mountain of sacrifice to worship God (vv. 3–6).

        B. Abraham replies to Isaac's question about the lamb by asserting that God will provide (vv. 7–8).

        C. Abraham prepares to slay his son Isaac (vv. 9–10).

    IV. *Resolution:* God stops Abraham from slaying Isaac and provides a ram for the sacrifice (vv. 11–14).

        A. The angel of the LORD commands Abraham not to do anything to Isaac and commends Abraham for demonstrating the fear of God (vv. 11–12).

8. Ibid., 25.
9. Ibid., 26.
10. Ibid., 29.

B. Abraham finds a ram for the sacrifice and attributes it to God's provision (vv. 13–14).

V. *Conclusion:* The angel of the LORD returns to reaffirm the LORD's blessing on Abraham and the LORD's intent to fulfill his promise (vv. 15–19).

For my sermon on Genesis 22:1–19, I decide to save Abraham's conviction that "the LORD will provide" for the latter part of the sermon. As I move through the story, then, I will not dwell on Abraham's reply in verse 8. I will not necessarily skip over it, but I may only mention it in passing. I want to save it for the peak moment in the story, when Abraham witnesses God's provision.

After deciding whether or not to rearrange any elements of the story, begin sketching out the main ideas that you will record on paper as your main points. Look for places in the story where major ideas show up. These usually occur along the crisis (disease) and resolution (remedy) of the story. Turn them into main level points. Typically, the subpoints will relate the actual episodes of the story and will fall under the major ideas communicated by the story. If the sermon is inductive, the last main point will often express the sermon's big idea. Paul Borden takes this approach in the outline for his sermon on 2 Samuel 11–12. The major points of his outline look like this:

I. God severely punishes David for committing a sin greater than murder and adultery (11:1–12:12).

II. God forgives David because he faces his sin head-on (12:13).

III. (*Big idea*) David learns to accept what the grace of God gives him and what the grace of God does not (12:14–25).

This outline plots out the direction the sermon will take. Obviously, several episodes make up the first outline point. The preacher can list these episodes as subpoints A, B, C, and so on. The key is for the ideas to emerge out of these episodes. When he preaches his sermon, Paul Borden never says, "Point number one is, 'God severely punishes David for committing a sin greater than murder.'" However, the episodes he relates will express this idea. As we noted earlier, main outline points in an inductive sermon serve as endings, not beginnings. Borden will not say, "I want you to notice in the next chapter and a half how God severely punishes David for committing a sin greater than murder and adultery." Rather, he allows the events themselves to lead listeners to that conclusion. Notice, too, that Borden chose to reflect the ancient story in his own wording rather than stating the points as theological ideas. This is fine, because the story is the vehicle, and stories work by indirection. The outline highlights the story. If Borden tells the story effectively, listeners can make the connection between their lives and David's experience. Borden will help listeners do this.

Now let's return to Genesis 22:1–19 (see table 12.2). Let me explain how I move from exegetical outline to sermon outline. As I prepare a sermon from this text, I decide the idea I want to convey first is that God tests his people by forcing them to choose between worshiping him or the children he has given them. This statement is a theological principle that grows out of the story. To arrive at this idea, I start by working through the first two verses of the story. I describe this in subpoint A under my first main point. By the way, placing the verse numbers in parentheses after the outline statement reminds me that I am telling the biblical story at this point in the process.

After relating the action in verses 1–2, I decide to explain that this test will force Abraham to choose between worshiping God or Isaac, God's gift. I explain how Isaac was God's means of blessing Abraham and fulfilling the covenant promise to him. I indicate this on the outline in subpoint B. Then, I needed to bring this into the twenty-first century and remind parents that they face a similar situation. While God's tests may not come in such a severe form, he tests us in the same area he tested Abraham. He wants to see if we will make our worship of him a priority over worshiping our children. I need to explain that in our culture, kids rule. We tend to place them before anything else. This move in the sermon is expressed in subpoint C. By the time I am through with subpoint C, my first main point will have emerged. Again, my first point is an ending, not a beginning.

The next major idea I want to communicate happens to be the big idea: *The greatest thing you can do for your kids is to worship God, not your kids.* I state this as my second main point, but again, this will be an ending, not a beginning. Chronologically, when I finish subpoint C of roman numeral I, I will proceed to subpoint A of roman numeral II. As noted by the verse numbers in parentheses, I am telling the story at this point. Subpoints A and B show that Abraham chooses to worship God and passes the test. At this point in the sermon, I will raise the questions, Is this really the way to go? What's the payoff for worshiping God instead of idolizing your children? Is worshiping God really the greatest thing you can do for your kids? Here I am dealing with the second functional question—Is it true? Letter C indicates that I will now deal with the episode in verses 15–19. In this episode, God reaffirms his blessing and promise to Abraham. That means the answer to the previous questions is, Yes, worshiping God over your kids is the best thing you can do. Your children will come out ahead, even though it may not seem so at the time. By this time in the sermon, the big idea will have emerged. For my own benefit, I marked the place where the big idea emerges with two asterisks (**).

I want to do one more thing before I finish. I want to raise the question, How do I do this? It seems so hard. I'm not sure I can put God before my children. So what will it take for me to do this? As you might suspect, this is the form of the third functional question dealing with application: What difference does it make? The answer will be found in going back through the story and noticing that obedience in this area requires the conviction that God will see to it. When you bank your life on this conviction, you will have the strength to do whatever it is that God asks you to do, even when that may seem to jeopardize your children's future.

In my outlining, I usually reserve the main points to state theological ideas and use the subpoints to advance the storyline. Another option, as in Paul Borden's example, is to use the main points to describe events in the story, with the last point being the major idea. The key is not to stifle creativity. You want to plot a sermon that tells the story well but also drives home the theological ideas—and particularly the big idea—of the text.

The following sermon outline from Exodus 15:22–17:7 provides an example of what an inductive-deductive sermon looks like on paper. The big idea emerges halfway through the sermon. The remainder of the sermon attempts to validate it by answering the second functional question, Is it really true?

I. God's people easily slip from praise into a complaining mode when they face trials and inconveniences (develop inductively).
   A. Israel complained over a lack of water (15:22–27; 17:1–7).
   B. Israel complained over a lack of food (16:1–36).
   C. You, too, may find yourself complaining shortly after God comes through for you.
II. (Big idea) Complaining is the worst way you can respond when you face trials and inconveniences.
   A. When you complain, you call God's integrity into question (15:24; 16:3, 7–8; 17:7).
   B. When you complain, you create a climate for disobedience (16:20–28).
   C. When you complain, you fail a test God wants you to pass (15:25b–26; 16:4; 17:2).

This sermon tackles three complaining stories all at once. Notice that the two major moves or points state timeless theological principles extracted from the stories. The first move in the sermon advances the idea that God's people easily slip from praise into a complaining mode when they face trials and inconveniences. Subpoints A and B recap the stories of Israel's fall from praise into a complaining mode. Subpoint C then moves into the twenty-first century and makes it clear that people today act the same way. Once again, the first main point serves as an ending, not a beginning. The idea stated in roman numeral I fully emerges only after the sermon moves from the ancient Israelites to twenty-first century believers.

At this place in the sermon, I will go ahead and disclose the big idea as it appears in roman numeral II. This is a different tactic. Rather than serving as an ending, my second main point serves as a beginning. I will start with it because I want to raise the second functional question, Is it really true? Can I really believe it? As the outline shows, the remainder of the sermon is validation. It involves going back through the story and noting details or statements that verify and support the idea. Notice, too, that I have stated the subpoints as timeless principles. However, it would not be a sin to leave them in the past. For example, subpoint A could read, "When the Israelites complained, they called God's integrity into question." Expositors will have to make this decision at every point in the sermon. At what moment do you abstract from then to now? Whenever possible, I try to turn statements into theological principles if that's where I plan to arrive anyway.

While an outline is not a sermon, the outline you create allows you to see on paper the shape your sermon will take. It allows you to track the sermon's basic movements in thought and to evaluate how well your sermon will flow like a story. If you like the flow of thought, you can use your outline as the framework on which to build your actual sermon.

13

✸ ✸ ✸ ✸ ✸

MASTERING THE STORYTELLER'S CRAFT

✸ ✸ ✸ ✸ ✸

The same story can either bore or thrill an audience. What makes the difference is the storyteller. Preachers who hope to communicate stories with flair must master the storyteller's craft. The time has come to fill in the sermon outline. As Haddon Robinson puts it, it's time to make dry bones live.

As a preacher, your task is to preach a sermon, not an outline. An outline is not a sermon; it resembles a skeleton without flesh. How do you go about putting flesh on the skeleton? More important, how do you go about putting flesh on the skeleton to make the final product attractive rather than bland?

Preparing a Sermon Manuscript

The most reliable tool for filling in your sermon outline is a manuscript. Write out your sermon word for word. You don't need to memorize it. Preferably, you will not even take the manuscript with you to the pulpit. Haddon Robinson explains:

> Agonize with thought and words at your desk, and what you write will be internalized. . . . When you step into the pulpit, your written text [sermon manuscript] will have done its work to shape your use of language. Much of the wording will come back to you as you preach, but not all. In the heat of your delivery, your sentence structure will change, new phrases will occur to you,

and your speech will sparkle like spontaneous conversation. Your manuscript, therefore, contributes to the thought and wording of your sermon, but it does not determine it.[1]

The purpose of the sermon manuscript is to assist you in your thinking. Writing is a way of thinking. You are trying to capture on paper what will come out of your mouth when you preach the Old Testament narrative you have prepared. The trick is to write in an oral style. That is, what you produce should resemble a transcript of your sermon as the audience hears it. Try to write as if you are speaking. This means the sentence fragments that angered your English teacher are okay. Contractions aren't a problem.

With outline in hand, you're ready to write your oral transcript. But what goes into the mix? How do you flesh out your sermon outline?

Telling the Story Well

Preachers usually flesh out their sermon outlines by adding a variety of supporting materials that attempt to explain, prove, or apply their ideas. Some typical devices a preacher may use include restatement, explanation, definition, statistics, quotations, storytelling, and illustrations.

In a sermon on an Old Testament narrative, the preacher's primary tactic will be telling the story well. To be more precise, the preacher's primary tactic will be retelling the story well. The authors of Old Testament stories tell them in a rather spare, lean style. You won't find any throwaway lines. Every detail serves a purpose. Meir Sternberg points out that elaborate descriptions "perform no other role than realistic fullness."[2] In Old Testament narrative, other concerns overshadow the need for realistic fullness. However, a modern preacher may need to pursue realistic fullness to connect with a modern audience. Preachers need to engage listeners with sensory details.

The trick is to strike a balance between economy and detail. The preacher's retelling of the story must bring the story to life. This means placing sensory details at strategic places in the narrative. It also means avoiding excess. The temptation is to add too many details and descriptions—to pursue elegance rather than simplicity. Ernest Hemingway models the balance between economy and detail in his classic novel *A Farewell to Arms*. At the end of chapter 9, Hemingway describes the ambulance ride of Frederic Henry, a wounded American soldier who is en route to a field hospital during World War I. Another wounded soldier lies on a stretcher above him.

1. Haddon W. Robinson, *Biblical Preaching: The Development and Delivery of Expository Messages,* 2d ed. (Grand Rapids: Baker, 2001), 186.

2. Meir Sternberg, *The Poetics of Biblical Narrative: Ideological Literature and the Drama of Reading,* Indiana Studies in Biblical Literature (Bloomington: Indiana University Press, 1985), 329.

I felt something dripping. At first it dripped slowly and regularly, then it pattered into a stream. . . . The stream kept on. In the dark I could not see where it came from the canvas overhead. I tried to move sideways so that it did not fall on me. Where it had run down under my shirt it was warm and sticky. I was cold and my leg hurt so that it made me sick. After a while the stream from the stretcher above lessened and started to drip again and I heard and felt the canvas above move as the man on the stretcher settled more comfortably.

"How is he?" the Englishman called back. "We're almost up."

"He's dead I think," I said.

The drops fell very slowly as they fall from an icicle after the sun has gone. It was cold in the car in the night as the road climbed.[3]

A statement Hemingway once made about prose also applies to retelling Bible stories: "Prose is architecture, not interior decoration." While modern readers are used to fuller descriptions than Bible stories contain, they do not demand as many details as one might expect. Writer Oakley Hall observes that modern fiction can omit more details than the fiction of a century ago: "More economy is necessary because the reader's threshold of irrelevancy is lower. Part of the irrelevant is what is obvious, or what the reader can supply out of his own imagination, experience, or past reading."[4]

Reading well-crafted stories can enhance a preacher's storytelling skills. In addition to reading classics by Hemingway, Faulkner, Hawthorne, and others, preachers would do well to read the best contemporary storytellers. I recommend books such as Garrison Keillor's *Lake Wobegon Days*, Robert Fulgham's *All I Really Need to Know I Learned in Kindergarten*, and *The Good Samaritan Strikes Again* by outdoor humor writer Patrick McManus.[5]

Preachers should attempt to tell a Bible story as a responsible writer of a historical novel might tell it. Paul Maier provides a model in his biographical novels *Pontius Pilate* and *The Flames of Rome*. The first book, as the title suggests, looks at Christ's death from the perspective of Pontius Pilate, the Roman prefect who publicly washed his hands of the blood of Jesus. The second book chronicles the rise of the early church under the leadership of Peter and Paul. It does so from the vantage point of a Roman lieutenant commander who rises to power in the Roman government. In the preface to *Pontius Pilate*, Maier assures his readers that unlike a work of historical fiction, his documentary novel takes no liberties with the facts.[6] He uses them as discovered, with-

---

3. Ernest Hemingway, *A Farewell to Arms* (New York: Charles Scribner's Sons, 1929), 61.

4. Oakley Hall, *The Art and Craft of Novel Writing* (Cincinnati: Story, 1989), 117.

5. Garrison Keillor, *Lake Wobegon Days* (New York: Viking, 1985); Robert Fulgham, *All I Really Need to Know I Learned in Kindergarten* (New York: Ivy, 1986); Patrick F. McManus, *The Good Samaritan Strikes Again* (New York: Holt, 1992). McManus has published several books of humorous outdoor stories. Reading any one of his titles will benefit storytellers.

6. Paul L. Maier, *Pontius Pilate* (New York: Doubleday, 1968; reprint, Wheaton: Living Books, 1983), 7.

out alteration. He simply fills in the gaps. While preachers should use their imaginations when retelling stories, they should also allow the rigorous exegesis they have done to keep their imaginations in check.

Eugene Peterson models the kind of storytelling that preachers should pursue when retelling a Bible story. He relates David's meeting with Saul in the wilderness cave near En-Gedi like this:

> David and a few of his men are hidden in a cave cut in the cliffs above the Dead Sea. The day is hot and the cave is cool. They're deep in the cave, resting. Suddenly there's a shadow across the mouth of the cave; they're astonished to see that it's King Saul. They didn't know that he was that close in his pursuit. Saul enters the cave but doesn't see them: fresh from the hard glare of desert sun, his eyes aren't adjusted to the darkness and don't pick out the shadowy figures in the recesses of the cave. Besides, he isn't looking for them at that moment; he has entered the cave to respond to the call of nature. He turns his back to them.[7]

Read Creative Descriptions of Old Testament Stories, Characters, and Culture

A good place for preachers to start is to read creative descriptions of Old Testament characters, stories, and culture. Preachers can learn from these and even adapt them as they craft images that bring the stories of the Old Testament to life. Paul Maier's documentary novels *Pontius Pilate* and *The Flames of Rome* provide a good starting point. Even though these novels relate New Testament events, they model the kind of storytelling that sticks to the facts while painting a vivid picture.

James Michener's tome, *The Source*, sweeps back and forth between the fictional account of an archaeological excavation in western Galilee and the ancient stories behind the artifacts it uncovers. The first 373 pages supply vivid images from Jewish history through 605 B.C., particularly the daily routines of family life, farming, and Canaanite religious practice.[8] Michener's depiction of a Canaanite child sacrifice ritual is particularly stunning.[9] Notice how Michener describes the scene when an Israelite farmer, Urbaal, and his wife, Timna, receive the news that their six-month-old son was chosen to be sacrificed:

> When Urbaal reached home he received the ugly news that Timna had feared. The priests of Melak had returned to deliver their decision: "The stars indicate that we shall be attacked from the north. By a host larger than before. It is therefore essential to take steps and we shall have a burning of first sons tomorrow." With a red dye obtained from the seashore they stained the wrists of Urbaal's son

---

7. Eugene Peterson, *Leap over a Wall: Earthy Spirituality for Everyday Christians* (New York: HarperCollins, 1997), 76.

8. James Michener, *The Source* (New York: Fawcett Crest, 1967).

9. Ibid., 132–42.

and then directed the farmer to halt the screaming of his wife. Proving by their implacable detachment that there could be no appeal from their decision, they stalked from the house and proceeded to seven others, where they similarly stained the wrists of children from the leading families of Makor.[10]

John Hercus tells Old Testament stories with flair, reflecting his interest in people and his passion for God. Expositors who preach from Judges or the David stories can pick up ideas for picturing scenes from his books *God Is God: Samson and Other Case Histories from the Book of Judges* and *David*.[11] Hercus's style is almost sermonic. His descriptions of characters and scenes bring them to life, although his use of colloquial language and homespun expressions may seem a bit dated and overdone to some preachers. The following sample is from the story of Ehud:

The Moabite servants bowed and silently slipped out of the room. Only Eglon, huge mountainous Eglon still reclining back in his padded chair, and Ehud, left-handed Ehud kneeling on his left knee with that so-businesslike little dagger still strapped to his right thigh, remaining.

And the distance is still not quite right. It will take both a lunge and a step to reach Eglon with the sword. About two seconds too much time is needed, it's just not right, even now!

And Ehud hasn't moved. Not a fraction of an inch. His voice is still a hoarse whisper, as with downcast eyes he speaks. "Yes sir, it's from God. I had to come and tell you."

"Speak up, man! I can't properly hear you. Tell me, what is it the gods want me to know?"

Was it greed? Was it conceit? Was it something more than greed, something greater than conceit? Was it perhaps fear, the fear man always has when finally confronted by his God? Was it this that swept this caution aside? Perhaps that is the real answer, perhaps that properly explains why his two hands gripped the arms of his chair so strongly, why there was that sudden heave as he raised his whole lumbering bulk on to feet that could just barely carry him—and there he was, half-standing, just above Ehud, just that half-pace closer that Ehud needed.

A sudden flash, a slight hiss of breath as the Benjamite springs, a single muffled gasp from the stricken king, and it's over. Eglon is dead. Collapsed in a ghastly mountain of fat-enveloped flesh. . . . The dagger has disappeared completely into the great belly of the Moabite king, the flesh has closed over the blade and haft alike. Eglon now has it! Only the small trickle of blood and the large stream of bowel contents give out the secret at all. That and the stench that now no nostril could mistake. Eglon is dead.[12]

10. Ibid., 134.
11. John Hercus, *God Is God: Samson and Other Case Histories from the Book of Judges* (London: Hodder and Stoughton, 1971); idem., *David*, 2d ed. (Chicago: InterVarsity, 1968).
12. Hercus, *God Is God*, 39–40.

A more recent attempt to retell the stories of Scripture appears in *The Book of God* by Walter Wangerin Jr. Wangerin succeeds at capturing the passion, color, and grit of the Bible's stories as he narrates them. His volume follows the storyline of the Bible, and he dramatizes most of the major Old Testament narratives in the process. For example, here is Wangerin's depiction of the fall of Jericho in Joshua 6:

> On this day, Israel circled Jericho not once, but seven times, from dawn to late afternoon. Suddenly, in the midst of their seventh passage, the sound of the ram's horns changed. It rose to the shrieks of eagles. And all the voices, all the throats of Israel opened. Ten thousand warriors turned inward, roaring, and charged the city. The city walls themselves began to shudder. The king felt a terrible agitation in the stones beneath his feet. His archers leaped up. Spearmen reached for spears. Women brought smudgepots to ignite the oil in sheets of fire. But just as Israel entered the range of Jericho's arrows, the city walls rose three feet into the air, bellowed like a living thing, cracked at every join and mortar, then collapsed—a great crush of stones on all the people below.
>
> The king of Jericho tumbled down into his dying city. The burning oil spilled inward. Fire and timber and rock fell with him. And the final vision vouchsafed unto the king was a piece of wall which neither crumbled nor burned, a slim finger of stone with one window two stories up from which hung a scarlet cord.
>
> In his last instant of life all the world seemed to the king a bitter joke—for why should that one live at last and not another? The window belonged to an outcast! A whore named Rahab.[13]

In *Peculiar Treasures: A Biblical Who's Who*, Frederick Buechner offers brief, witty character sketches that will pique the imaginations of preachers who want to breathe color into Bible characters. For example, Buechner portrays the story of Naaman in 2 Kings 5 like this:

> Naaman was a five-star general in the Syrian army and also a leper. His wife had working for her a little Jewish slave-girl who mentioned one day that there was a prophet named Elisha back home who could cure leprosy as easily as a toad cures warts. So Naaman took off for Israel with a letter of introduction from the king and a suitcase full of cash and asked Elisha to do his stuff.
>
> Elisha told him to go dunk in the Jordan seven times, and after some initial comments to the effect that there were rivers back in Syria that made the Jordan look like a cow track, Naaman went and did what he was told. When he came out, he could have passed for an ad for Palmolive soap. Naaman was so grateful that he converted on the spot and reached into his suitcase for an inch of fifties, but Elisha said he was a prophet of Yahweh, not a dermatologist, and refused to take a cent.[14]

---

13. Walter Wangerin Jr., *The Book of God* (Grand Rapids: Zondervan, 1996), 134.

14. Frederick Buechner, *Peculiar Treasures: A Biblical Who's Who* (New York: Harper and Row, 1979), 112–13.

In *Leap over a Wall: Earthy Spirituality for Everyday Christians*, Eugene Peterson offers reflections on the life of David. Peterson's primary interest is spiritual formation, but his reflections will stir the imaginations of preachers who want to tell the stories well. Peterson is a first-rate wordsmith, as demonstrated by his description of Shammah in the story of David's anointing from 1 Samuel 16:

> Shammah was a mincing little sophisticate in Calvin Klein jeans and alligator cowboy boots. He hated living in backwater Bethlehem. He could hardly get across the street without getting cow flop on his boots. Mingling with all these common people, their vulgar games and coarse entertainment, was torture for him. He didn't know what Samuel was up to, but it looked as if it could be a ticket to a finer life—a life of culture and taste. But Samuel dismissed him with one shake of the head.[15]

The previous examples raise a question: should preachers use colloquial language, particularly the kind that imports modern images into the story? Preachers may take this liberty as long as their exegesis informs and limits it and as long as they do not overuse it. Like overdone humor, excessive use of colloquial language and modern images will come across as corny, to use a colloquial term. Preachers bring the story to life when they describe Boaz praising Ruth for choosing him instead of chasing all the young bucks wearing Wranglers.[16] Placing the statement in modern terms helps readers to grasp more fully what Boaz was saying. It does not mislead or confuse hearers; they recognize what the preacher is trying to do.

Do Ample Historical-Cultural Research

Painting scenes like the ones above requires ample historical-cultural research in Bible dictionaries, Bible encyclopedias, Bible atlases, and archaeology books. Such research supplies concrete details and keeps one's imagination in line with the biblical text. For example, half an hour of research on the Jordan River valley can lead to the following portrayal of the scene in Joshua 3:

> When the first rays of the sun peeked over the mountain plateau and lit up the Jordan valley, the air was already sticky with humidity. It was springtime in this geological gash in the cellar of the earth, a sunken valley between two fault lines, at this place about one thousand feet below sea level. Thousands and thousands of Israelites were getting ready to enter the Promised Land. But crossing the valley at this time of year is virtually impossible. A river runs through it. Not Old Man River, which just keeps meandering and rolling along. Not even Grumpy Old Man River. But angry, violent, ticked off, snort-

15. Peterson, *Leap over a Wall*, 15.
16. This image is adapted from Buechner, *Peculiar Treasures*, 148–49.

ing, out-to-get-you Old Man River. The Jordan isn't a terribly wide river. At most places it resembles the Gallatin or Madison Rivers in south-central Montana. But in the springtime, the snow runoff sends it snarling and raging down the Jordan Valley Rift. It's a swollen, chocolate brown mess, tearing off chunks of cliff as it twists and turns and spits and thrashes. But Israel is going to have to cross it to get the land God promised.

Follow the Accepted Elements of Style

Storytellers in our culture have developed a style that draws hearers or readers into the story. While some matters boil down to preference, preachers should follow the basic rules. Telling a story is an art form, so rules need to be bent at times. Nevertheless, preachers should master the rules before bending them.

1. Use concrete, specific words. Feature writer Jon Franklin says, "The key to word choice, as well as to the inherent power of active images, is specificity."[17] What preaching professor Wayne McDill observes about preaching in general is especially true of preaching in Old Testament narrative literature:

> If the sermon doesn't have the particulars, with specifics like broccoli and cheesecake, it seems abstract and dull. It is too heavy with generals. These rather generic attempts at development are often announced with preacher talk like "We live in a world that . . ." Or "Oftentimes . . ." Or "Many times. . . ." What follows is usually a bland, flat generalization instead of a specific, concrete particular which makes the concept come alive.[18]

Generalities and cliches fail to grab the listener's interest. So start by enlisting strong verbs. Instead of saying, "David goes to the front of the cave," try "David creeps to the front of the cave." Choosing verbs like "stifle" instead of "held back" or "slugged" or "jabbed" in place of "hit" may make the difference between an engaging story and a bland one. Sometimes a thesaurus will get you out of a verbal rut, but be careful to choose an appropriate word. Specific nouns help, too. Instead of trying to boost a noun like "rock" with a generic modifier like "big," use a word like "boulder." Instead of "flowers" choose the appropriate designation like "daisies" or "lilies" or "roses." Rather than "unpleasant smell," try "stench." Instead of "food," use "corn bread" or "figs" or "grapes." "Alarm" or "terror" works better than "great fear."

2. Avoid excessive modifiers. Some communicators use adjectives and adverbs to try to pick up the slack left by weak verbs and nouns. However, modifiers tend to litter the story. Ernest Hemingway learned to distrust adjectives, and Voltaire considered them the enemies of the noun. Similarly, Carl Sand-

17. Jon Franklin, *Writing for Story: Craft Secrets of Dramatic Nonfiction by a Two-Time Pulitzer Prize Winner* (New York: Plume/Penguin, 1986), 181.
18. Wayne McDill, *The 12 Essential Skills for Great Preaching* (Nashville: Broadman and Holman, 1999), 225–26.

burg confessed, "At 61 I am more suspicious of adjectives than at any other time in all my born days." Adjectives like "fine," "bad," "good," "big," and "nice" fail because they are too general. Notice how excessive modifiers clutter the following description of the prostitute Rahab.

> One of the many dwellings attached to Jericho's inside wall housed the Calamity Jane of Jericho. She really excelled at her shady profession. She could easily turn on the charm, cunningly flash a grand smile, and smooth-talk vulnerable men with her words. But she was very shrewd and extremely calculating, and she could skillfully read the lustful desires of most men who knocked quietly on her door. Some of them desperately wanted her services as a prostitute. Others merely sought lodging. She offered very cheap lodging. It was a strategic part of her business strategy. She knew that most men who merely wanted lodging couldn't resist her delightful charm and would end up paying the price for an hour or two of physical pleasure.

Removing excess adverbs and adjectives accomplishes for the above paragraph what losing twenty or thirty pounds does for an overweight body. Notice how striking out certain modifiers tightens up the description.

> One of the ~~many~~ dwellings attached to Jericho's inside wall housed the Calamity Jane of Jericho. She ~~really~~ excelled at her ~~shady~~ profession. She could ~~easily~~ turn on the charm, ~~cunningly~~ flash a grand smile, and smooth-talk ~~vulnerable~~ men with her words. But she was ~~very~~ shrewd and ~~extremely~~ calculating, and she could ~~skillfully~~ read the ~~lustful~~ desires of most men who knocked ~~quietly~~ on her door. Some of them ~~desperately~~ wanted her services as a prostitute. Others merely sought lodging. She offered ~~very~~ cheap lodging. It was ~~a strategic~~ part of her business strategy. She knew that most men who merely wanted lodging couldn't resist her ~~delightful~~ charm and would end up paying the price for an hour or two of ~~physical~~ pleasure.

The adjectives "lustful," "strategic," and "delightful" get the axe because they are redundant. Other adjectives, such as "many," "shady," "vulnerable," and "physical," add details that the hearers' imaginations will supply. Adverbs like "really" and "very" are lame. However, some modifiers remain. An adjective like "most" remains to clarify that not all men who knocked on Rahab's door wanted sexual favors. The adverb "merely" makes the same point. The adjective "inside" is necessary to specify location. While a speaker could dispense with the modifier "grand," it seems to evoke a more precise picture of Rahab's smile. Notice how the adjectives "shrewd" and "calculating" follow the pronoun "she." Writer Oakley Hall claims that since a sentence is linear, moving from left to right, modifiers work best when they occur on the right—after the noun or verb. Notice how well the description flows after shedding its verbal flab.

One of the dwellings attached to Jericho's inside wall housed the Calamity Jane of Jericho. She excelled at her profession. She could turn on the charm, flash a grand smile, and smooth-talk men with her words. But she was shrewd and calculating, and she could read the desires of most men who knocked on her door. Some of them wanted her services as a prostitute. Others merely sought lodging. She offered cheap lodging. It was part of her business strategy. She knew that most men who merely wanted lodging couldn't resist her charm and would end up paying the price for an hour or two of pleasure.

Concise always wins the day. Keep your sentences short. Weed out the clutter. But be careful. As the previous sentences betray, your descriptions will appear choppy if you don't vary shorter sentences with an occasional longer one.

3. Eliminate the deadeners. Like rainfall on a campfire, certain elements smother the flicker of life in a story. For instance, the passive voice sucks out the vigor. A passive verb receives the action and consists of "is," "was," "were," or "has been" plus the past participle of the verb. Note the two passive verb forms in the following sentence: Goliath's forehead *was struck* by a stone that *had been hurled* from David's sling. Using active verb forms provides more zip. An active verb describes the action that the subject is performing. The following sentence uses active verbs to visualize David's conquest of Goliath: David *hurled* a stone from his sling and *struck* Goliath's forehead.

Furthermore, the term "there" deadens prose and can bog down the story. Notice the following examples. The use of "there" weakens the first one. The second one corrects the problem.

- There was something ironic about Sisera's instructions to Jael.
- Sisera's instructions to Jael dripped with irony.

Of course, a preacher could break the rule and use a "there was" construction when the intent is to linger on a particular point. Also, the term "that" frequently resembles a piece of deadwood. Notice how the term "that" can be chopped from the first sentence with no loss of meaning.

- Naomi hoped that her two daughters-in-law would remain in Moab.
- Naomi hoped her two daughters-in-law would remain in Moab.

4. Refrain from being too clever. Too many creative words and descriptions have the same effect as pouring too much maple syrup on pancakes. The temptation is to use overly sensational descriptions. In their quest to avoid stale words, some speakers opt for terms that try to do too much. While "Goliath said" is too lame, "Goliath bellowed" may be too sensational. The term unwittingly communicates: "How do you like this word?! I found this one in my thesaurus." Perhaps "Goliath shouted" makes the point most effectively. The word "shouted" is vivid, yet it doesn't take on a life of its own. Preachers will have to wrestle with language usage. You may make a different decision than another preacher would make, but wrestling with word choice will make the overall description more effective.

In a similar vein, Oakley Hall warns, "Varying speech tags is *not* a way to insure against monotony in long exchanges of dialog, and many a writer has made a fool of himself by being discontented with *said*." Consider Hall's example:

> "If you're wondering what's good, the chili's our specialty," she grinned.
> "That sounds good," I agreed. "But I've been longing for a good cup of homemade soup."
> "Oh, I wouldn't have the soup if I were you," she counseled. "The chili's better."
> "Okay, chili," I conceded.[19]

5. Show the reader rather than tell. Cause readers to conclude or feel something for themselves rather than telling them. For example, instead of saying, "Goliath was a huge man," or even "Goliath was an incredible hulk of a man," say, "When Goliath stood in a doorway, he filled the entire frame." Or you could say, "Goliath's bronze jacket tipped the scales at about 125 pounds, and the tip on his spear weighed as much as a shotput." For another example, a preacher describing David's feelings in the guard tower waiting for a report on the battle against Absalom could say, "David was extremely nervous as he waited to hear what had become of his son. He was impatient as he waited with a city guard in the little guard room between the two city gates leading into Mahanaim." But the preacher will do better to show David's emotions by telling the story like this:

> David paced, sweated, fumed, and fumbled with his shoelaces. A city guard waited with him in the little guard room between the two city gates leading into Mahanaim, and David was driving the poor guy nuts! The guy must have dropped five pounds scaling up and down the rungs that led to the top of the guard tower. Like a little boy or girl in your back seat on vacation who asks, "Are we there yet?" every ten minutes, David kept asking, "Do you see anybody yet?" The guard kept scanning the countryside and hollering down, "Nope. Nobody's coming."

Notice how the previous description slips from drama to explanation because of the past tense verbs and a couple additions of "would":

19. Hall, *The Art and Craft of Novel Writing*, 105.

David paced, sweated, fumed, and fumbled with his shoelaces. He was accompanied by a city guard in the little guard room between the two city gates leading into Mahanaim. This guard was driven nuts by David! The guy must have dropped five pounds scaling up and down the rungs that led to the top of the guard tower. Like a little boy or girl in your back seat on vacation who asks, "Are we there yet?" every ten minutes, David would keep asking, "Do you see anybody yet?" The guard would scan the countryside and holler down, "Nope. Nobody's coming."

By now, you may be sighing and thinking, "I'll never have enough time to compose a manuscript that tells the story well. I don't have hours to agonize over word choice and to trim the excess." Here is a solution. I suggest working with a key paragraph or two of your manuscript for each sermon. If you try to polish an entire manuscript of four or five thousand words, you will bite off more than you can chew. But you can devote thirty to sixty minutes polishing three or four hundred words. If you work with a key section or two in each sermon, this will help you in the long run. You will hone your communication style. Writing will force you to develop concrete, specific images that will work themselves into your pulpit conversation. Your storytelling will become vivid, yet lean.

Images

Aside from retelling the story, preachers who tackle Old Testament narrative texts will want to spend some time developing images. Pictures must form in the listeners' minds. People respond to the pictures that hang in the gallery of their minds. In addition to visualizing the action of the story itself, what else do you need to visualize for your listeners?

Explanatory Images

Some details in a story require explanation. Suppose you are preaching on Josiah's response to God's covenant in 2 Kings 23. In verse 10, you read that Josiah "desecrated Topheth, which was in the Valley of Ben Hinnom, so no one could use it to sacrifice his son or daughter in the fire to Molech." You assume correctly that the Canaanite custom of child sacrifice is foreign to your listeners. You need to explain it. Often, preachers will begin by saying, "In ancient Canaanite religion . . ." There is a more effective way, however. Paint the scene with your listeners in it. You could adapt James Michener's description quoted earlier in this chapter to form an image like this:

Imagine arriving home from a day's work in your olive groves and finding the priests of your village. They relate the ugly news that you and your spouse have feared: "The stars indicate that we shall be attacked from the north. By a host larger than before. It is therefore essential to take steps and we shall have a burning of first sons tomorrow." With a red dye obtained from the seashore they stain your infant's wrists and then direct you to halt your sobbing.

In a sermon on Joshua 6, you will probably need to explain a bit about siege warfare. You could introduce the information by saying, "Based on archaeological data, Bible scholars can accurately describe how the ancients conducted siege warfare." However, an image would convey the information in a more interesting way.

> The city of Jericho is tightly shut. That's what you expect, but it's not what you want to hear. It's tough to attack a fortified city once the gates have been closed and the people are holed up inside. Perched high upon the walls are guard towers or stations with guards ready to shoot arrows, pour hot oil, and dump boulders on you if you get close to the wall. Guards watch the entrance from their towers. Since the gate system is potentially the weakest part of the wall, the entrance consists of a series of two or three gates. Punch through one, and you still have one or two left. So you hope to get some battering rams close enough to start whacking at the wall. But punching a hole through can take weeks, even months. Scaling the wall is horribly difficult, too. Like General Custer, you'll be wearing an arrow shirt before you climb very far up the wall.

Application Images

Effective preachers also paint pictures of what the truth looks like fleshed out in a listener's life. I'll never forget attending the closing arguments of a murder trial in our community. A young man stood trial for deliberate homicide in the shooting death of a longtime friend. Both the prosecutor and the defense attorney told stories. Each attorney crafted a story of the defendant's involvement in the murder. Each attorney left out a lot of technical data— ballistic reports, crime lab analyses of bloodstains, and so on. Each attorney asked the jury to act on his particular story of the crime.

Preachers follow the same approach. They punctuate their storytelling with application images that either raise questions or offer solutions. The following application image from a sermon on Judges 4 helps the reader relate to Barak. The image shows what Barak's approach to his unique situation looks like when we face our own unique situations.

> It's easy to be passive like Barak when we receive God's commands. For Barak, the command was to lead the Israelite army against Jabin's army. For you, it might be God's call for you to discipline your children, to train up your children in the way of wisdom. But you slink from the task. You're afraid to set boundaries. You're reluctant to hold your child to standards. You don't have the courage to say, "We're not going to watch this television program in our home." You hesitate to say, "There's a song on this CD we're not going to allow in our home." There's no way you're going to announce, "You can't go out with this boy or with this girl."

Illustrations, Quotations, and Factual Information

Sermons on Old Testament stories will not rely as heavily on illustrations, quotations, statistics, and similar types of factual information. They will at least use such materials differently. The following are some examples of supporting materials that work when retelling Old Testament stories.

Illustrations

Regardless of the literary genre you are preaching, the illustrations you choose work most effectively when they come out of your own reading and your real-life experiences. Illustrations lifted out of illustration books usually sound stale.

In Old Testament narrative literature, the story carries its own weight. It does not need an illustration to add interest or stir emotion. However, an illustration can help a preacher explain, validate, or apply a concept. The trick is to keep the illustration as concise as possible so you don't get too far from the storyline. For example, after reading or describing the military strategy God lays out in Joshua 6:25, I would say,

> Now I am no expert on military strategy, but it doesn't take an expert to see that this is really odd. I have read a lot about the Civil War battles, and I've never encountered a strategy like this. It's almost like a coach saying to his basketball team, "Here's the game plan. I want you to go out and hold the ball for four quarters. Don't take any shots. Even if you have an open layup, don't take it. In the last seconds of the game, throw the ball up in the air, and it will end up going through the hoop and we'll win!" Seems ridiculous, doesn't it?

Quotations

Generally, save quotations for the introduction or conclusion of a sermon. They don't interface well with the flow of the story. In a sermon on 2 Samuel 11–12, Haddon Robinson effectively uses a quote from John Knox as he approaches the climax of the sermon: "I will keep the ground that God has given me, and perhaps in his grace he will ignite me again. But ignite me or not, I will by his grace and his power, hold the ground." Robinson uses this quote to advance the idea that men and women of God need to walk with God in their middle years when life flattens out.

Factual Information

While preachers must not allow their Old Testament narrative sermons to atrophy into exegetical lectures, audiences appreciate insight into the inner workings of the text. When I preach Genesis 22:1–19, I take a minute or two to point out how the tension builds in God's identification of Isaac (v. 2). In Joshua 3, I will point out how the narrative slows to a crawl in verses 14–17. Usually, I choose one or two key grammatical features to mention. I do this succinctly, and I show the significance for experiencing the story. As mentioned earlier, don't use shop talk. Describe it in a way that an intelligent person without a background in biblical studies can grasp.

Historical-cultural information is necessary, too. Listeners need to understand who the Philistines were, how ancient warfare happened, and so on. But remember, these are not the issues that keep people awake at night. You may need to explain them on your way to answering a question that keeps someone awake at night, but don't belabor the point. You may be fascinated by the Philistines, but the seventeen-year-olds in the second row are not.

What about commenting on individual words? Usually, this is unnecessary. When appropriate, though, do not bog down the advance of the story. Nor should you squeeze words until they bleed. However, in the story of Ruth, as well as in the story of David and Mephibosheth in 2 Samuel 9, the term "loyal love" *(ḥesed)* plays a key role. There's reason, then, to discuss it. Likewise, the story of Nadab and Abihu in Leviticus 10 requires an understanding of the term "holy." Package your discussion so it doesn't sound like a bland exegetical lecture. Use pictures and modern analogies to describe what the term means.

The goal in this step of sermon preparation is to fill in your sermon outline with the kind of supporting material that enables you to tell the story well. You finish the stage when you complete a manuscript for the body of your sermon. Now you are ready to prepare an introduction and conclusion. Logically, this step happens last. Of course, ideas for the introduction and conclusion often strike preachers earlier in the process, and you may occasionally prepare one or the other before your manuscript is finished. However, forming both an introduction and conclusion before you finish the body of the sermon makes no more sense than preparing an advertisement for a product that has not been fully developed. The next chapter will guide you through the process of creating an effective introduction and conclusion to your sermon.

14

✹ ✹ ✹ ✹ ✹

ENTERING AND EXITING

✹ ✹ ✹ ✹ ✹

Below Tower Falls in Yellowstone National Park, Tower Creek empties into the Yellowstone River. About a half mile upstream from this confluence, the Yellowstone rushes out of a heavily timbered ravine. Near the mouth of the ravine, two fir trees that toppled into the river slow the flow of water near the bank, creating a deep, green pool only six or seven feet in diameter. The branches sticking up from the partially submerged trees discourage any fisherman from landing a fly in the pool. But on this particular October afternoon, I peek over one of the fallen fir trees and suddenly decide to try.

A wide, cream-colored body with red spots rolls through the surface film. Then it rolls again. And again. It's one of the largest cutthroat trout I've ever seen in the Yellowstone. It's rolling through the surface film to slurp tiny gray bugs about the size of a kernel of corn. The bugs are fluttering on the surface film. I search my flybox and find just the right fly—a size 18 parachute Adams. After tying on a smaller piece of tippet material, I attach the fly with an improved clinch knot. The pool is surrounded by branches waiting to grab my fly, so I can't make a full cast. Gingerly, I dangle the fly over one of the fallen fir trees and gently drop it on the surface film. Bam! I see the cream-colored body roll over again as the trout gulps the offering of hackle and yarn. After a five-minute tussle, the trout is played out, and I lift it from the pool.

Twenty-two inches. It's the largest cutthroat I've ever caught in the Yellowstone River.

Around the next bend, another cream-colored body with red spots rolls through the surface, right at a seam separating the swift current from a slower pocket of water near the bank. My heart begins to beat rapidly, and I get myself in position for a cast. Once again, I'm sure I have the right fly. More bugs hover on the surface, dancing this way and that way until the cream-colored body rolls through the surface film and slurps them through its gills. I let out some line and toss the fly backwards until the line unfurls, then I shoot it forward. When it unfurls, I bring it back again and strip out more line. On the forward cast, I aim carefully and angle the fly to land a few yards upstream from the trout. When the fly goes over the trout's window, I'll watch for the cream-colored body to roll again, and then I'll set the hook. But this time I let out a little too much line. Some of it rolls out into the swift current. When the fly is about two feet in front of the trout's window of vision, the line in the swift current begins to drag the fly. The movement looks unnatural. The trout begins to rise but then retreats to the bank as the fly unnaturally ploughs through the surface.

In fly-fishing, a graceful entrance is everything. You can have the right fly with the perfect size and color, but if the fly is not properly introduced, the fish is gone. That trout makes the decision in a matter of seconds.

This same dynamic takes place when a preacher stands before an audience. The preacher may have a "can't miss" sermon from an Old Testament narrative, but if the entrance is not appealing, the listener checks out. The first few seconds are critical. Like a trout analyzing a fly, a listener takes only a short window of time to decide whether or not to accept the preacher's offering. That's why preaching professors often tell their students that the length of a sermon's introduction is disproportionate to its importance.

The most vulnerable, dangerous times for airline flights are the takeoffs and landings. Sermons from Old Testament narrative texts share the same points of vulnerability.

The Entrance

The effective sermon introduction will accomplish three things (see table 14.1). First, it gets people's attention. As Haddon Robinson quips, "When you stand up to preach, people are bored and expect you to make it worse." A good introduction must also surface a need. People listen to sermons because they want to learn how to deal with their money, their suffering, their anger, or their sexual urges. When you show them that the text you plan to preach deals with the concerns they face, they are ready to listen. Finally, an effective introduction orients people to the text or to the body of the sermon. It eases people into the Bible story you plan to tell.

Table 14.1
Marks of an Effective Introduction

1. It commands a listener's attention.
2. It surfaces a need for the listener to listen.
3. It orients the listener to the text.

Generally, expositors find the grist for sermon introductions in stories, illustrations, quotations, questions, poems, song lyrics, or personal experiences. In the introduction to a story sermon, however, there are some differences. Since you are already about to tell a story such as Deborah and Barak, Samson and Delilah, or Ruth and Naomi, you may make your sermon too "story-intensive" by introducing it with another story about Princess Diana or Bill Gates. You may do better with a pointed question like, *Why is it that when you ask God for your daily bread, he often seems to eat your lunch?* With a few more sentences, you can sketch out a picture of what this looks like in your listener's lives. *Around the breakfast table, you ask God to provide $248.00 to send your son or daughter to high school camp at Northwoods Christian Camp. A half hour later, the water pump on your minivan goes out, and you have to fork out $167.00 to get it fixed. You've asked God to provide. All he does is send you another bill.* Then you're ready to orient them to a text that will deal with this dilemma. *There's a story in Genesis 22 that helps us understand why God appears to eat our lunch when we've asked him for our daily bread.*

A quotation might work well, too. For example, you could introduce a sermon on 1 Samuel 17 with this quote by William Arthur Ward: "Adversity causes some men to break, others to break records." You could use a quote from Beryl Markham's book *West with the Night* to introduce a sermon on the book of Ruth: "If a man has any greatness in him, it comes to light—not in one flamboyant hour, but in the ledger of his daily work."

Often, a "cold open" is an effective way of starting. Essentially, this means jumping right into the story with a carefully crafted description of a scene. You will need to visualize the scene for your listeners. A sermon on Joshua 2 might begin like this:

It was late in the day when the knock came at the door. The afternoon sun lengthened the shadows of the men standing in the doorway. The prostitute adjusted her silver bracelets and the gold hair net that covered her braided hair. She had accented her upper eyelids with black eye paint, and her lower lids sported a narrow green streak. The smell of frankincense wafted up from a small incense burner. There were two men at the door. Short, bearded, they weren't from town. Their feet were covered with dust. Little did the prostitute know that her life would never be the same.

A cold open works especially well in a flashback sermon. The preacher opens the sermon by painting a vivid picture of a dramatic moment, perhaps the climax, of the story. The preacher then retreats to the beginning and relates the scenes leading up to this climax or dramatic moment. Usually, the preacher stops short of sharing all the details or of fully resolving the dramatic moment. For example, Haddon Robinson will sometimes introduce his sermon on 2 Samuel 13–18 by quoting 2 Samuel 18:33: "The king was shaken. He went up to the room over the gateway and wept. As he went, he said: 'O my son Absalom! My son, my son Absalom! If only I had died instead of you—O Absalom, my son, my son!'" While this approach seems to give the answer away too quickly, it has the effect of raising a rather tension-filled question: How did David end up in this situation? Sure, we learn up front that Absalom dies. But how? Why? By whom? How come David could not prevent his son's death? These questions create a tension that carries the story. Once you've painted the picture of a dramatic moment in the story, you can go back and raise questions and help your listeners understand why this story is important and what message it provides.

In a first-person narrative, the preacher can start in one of two ways. One option is starting with a formal introduction. This introduction should be brief. Either you can do the introduction, or you can get someone else to do it. If someone else gives the introduction, then you can assume the role of the character from your very first word. If you give the introduction yourself, then you need to make a clear signal that you are assuming the role of a particular character. Both your words and your body language must signal this change. You might say, "If Samson showed up today to tell his story, it would sound something like this." Or, "Today, I want to tell you the story of Naomi and Ruth from the perspective of one of the elders of the city. Here is his account." Your body language should then reinforce this verbal signal. You may simply bow your head and remain in that posture for a couple of seconds. When you look up at the audience again, you look at them as David or Samson, not as Reverend Johnson.

When Daniel Buttry gives a brief introduction to his first-person sermons, he follows the introduction by taking a step back, pausing, and then stepping to the pulpit in the character of the biblical or historical figure.[1] Don Sunukjian negotiates the transition from introduction to monologue by briefly turning his back on the congregation. When he turns around to face his audience, he assumes the character. To signal a change from introduction to monologue, you may move to another place on stage, or you may move from standing to sitting on a stool. In most cases, you will not want to adopt an accent or a different tone of voice.

1. Daniel L. Buttry, *First-Person Preaching: Bringing New Life to Biblical Stories* (Valley Forge, Pa.: Judson, 1998), 22.

Another option is to begin immediately as a character and introduce yourself in a dimension of the character's life that you want to highlight.[2] For example, you might introduce a first-person narrative sermon on Samson from Samson's perspective by saying, "I never intended for my life to end the way it did. I was a tragic failure. My name is Samson." Or, "I always figured that the movie based on my life story would be called *The Natural*. But a more appropriate title would be *The Jerk*. My name is Samson."

The Exit

Like the final bars of a symphony, a conclusion attempts to arrive at a grand finish. Haddon Robinson says that the conclusion should bring the sermon to its burning focus. I sometimes use a flying metaphor; the conclusion resembles landing a plane. Of course, you don't want to mix these two metaphors. Your conclusion should not resemble a plane crash! You want to exit in a way that leaves the big idea of your sermon lingering like the fragrance of expensive perfume when a woman exits a ballroom.

To form conclusions, preachers usually draw from the same spring of material that feeds introductions: stories, illustrations, quotations, questions, poems, song lyrics, or personal experiences. Once again, using a story may not work effectively as it can steal the spotlight from the Bible story you have just related. Something more brief, such as a quotation or a line from a song, may complement the story more effectively. In some stories, application works best at the very end, after the full idea emerges. In this case, the preacher may need to sketch some application images or raise some concluding questions. Whenever possible, let your last line or two return to the story. You might save a key detail for the end, like Paul Borden does in his sermon on 2 Samuel 11–12. At the end he returns to Uriah, identifying him as the real hero of the story—the one who embodies the integrity David did not achieve. This is why I encourage preachers to listen to or read Paul Harvey's stories. He is a master of withholding a key detail—such as a person's full name or a chronological or geographical item—until the very end. The key is to not wander away from the story you've just related.

When concluding a first-person narrative, should you conclude as the character relating the story, or should you break away from the character back to yourself? If you started the sermon as the character, breaking back to yourself may confuse the audience. Of course, if you started the sermon as yourself and then broke into character, it is easier to break out of character at the end of the sermon. You must decide whether or not your character can relate some

2. David M. Brown argues that "the most effective introduction of a narration is to begin in character" (*Dramatic Narrative in Preaching* [Valley Forge, Pa.: Judson, 1981], 40).

applicational material without undermining the realism you have achieved. If so, consider using your character to share it.

If you decide to break away from the character and back to yourself as the preacher, make this shift clear. Generally, break out of character the same way you broke into character. If you bowed your head for a few seconds, do that motion and then return the floor to yourself as the preacher. If you turned around with your back to the audience, repeat that gesture. When you turn back to face the audience, you will no longer be delivering an eyewitness account but speaking as yourself.

Of course, finishing as the main character and sitting down is highly effective. Someone else can offer a closing prayer or a few words of reflection if needed. However, if you have done your job well, a few words of reflection may be anticlimactic. Haddon Robinson closes his sermon on 2 Samuel 13–18 by returning to the pain-drenched words of 18:33 and adding a final remark. Beginning and ending with the same scene or words forms a satisfying union.

When developing a sermon manuscript, pay special attention to the introduction and conclusion. Initial words set the pace. They determine how the hearer will listen to the rest of the sermon. Last words get remembered first. So take time to polish both of these elements. Labor a little bit longer over word choice and phrasing. Entering and exiting well will enhance your story.

15

✹ ✹ ✹ ✹ ✹

DELIVERING THE GOODS

✹ ✹ ✹ ✹ ✹

Now it's time to deliver the goods. You've polished your sermon manuscript. You've pored over it and prayed over it. You've invested hours and days to get to this moment. You're ready to tell the story with conviction and style.

What to Forget

To get off to a good start, remember to forget your notes. That's right. Leave the manuscript in which you invested so many hours on your desk. The payoffs for preaching without notes are enormous compared to the advantages you think you have with notes. Notes are a security blanket; we're afraid we'll stumble or ramble without them. Communicating "eyeball to eyeball" is essential in a television age. Notes get in the way. The Bible story you tell will seem more alive and more personal when you leave home without them.

Your mind is more reliable than you realize. Try telling someone the story of your favorite childhood Christmas morning. You'll recall all of the sights and smells as well as the feelings of anticipation, euphoria, or disappointment. You'll remember details such as sizes, colors, and flavors. You don't need an outline. You lived the situation, so all you have to do is reach back into the recesses of your mind to relive it. When you have the story inside of you, you don't need notes. If you've ever listened to Bible teacher R. C. Sproul, you know that his presentations are chock-full of data. Yet Sproul preaches and teaches without notes, and he counsels preachers to follow suit:

> We do this all the time when we're talking with each other. We don't have notes in front of us. We call upon our normal vocabulary patterns and our minds to think ahead of our mouths. . . . Notes are a terrible barrier to communication.[1]

Perhaps you fear what happened to George W. Truett, pastor of the First Baptist Church in Dallas. After expounding for only seven minutes on "Ye are the light of the world," he said, "My little light went out."[2] But he recovered from the trauma to go on preaching without notes.

How do you learn to preach without notes? Just do it. There are no surefire formulas or steps; however, there are some things you can do (see table 15.1).

Table 15.1
Preparing to Preach without Notes

1. **Organize** your sermon well.
2. **Internalize** it, but don't try to memorize it.
3. **Pray** through it.
4. **Rehearse** it.

First, make sure to *organize* your sermon well. Haddon Robinson tells his homiletics classes, "A good sermon remembers itself." Writing out a word-for-word manuscript forces you to organize your sermon. Writing is a way of thinking.

Second, *internalize* your material. That is, go over it again and again. This is the meaning of the word *meditate*, which occurs in both Joshua 1:8 and Psalm 1:2 and is applied to the way people treat Scripture. Originally, *meditate* described the sound of an animal growling or moaning. Eventually, it was used to describe any repeated sound, including the sound of reading. Meditating on Scripture means reading over it again and again and again and again. You don't have to memorize your sermon manuscript. In fact, it's better if you don't try to do this. A memorized story is "as impotent as one that is read."[3] Besides, listeners don't know when you forget an image or misspeak. They do not have your manuscript in front of them.[4] To internalize your manuscript, review it over and over again. Getting your manuscript done a

1. Michael Duduit, "Theology and Preaching in the 90s: An Interview with R. C. Sproul," *Preaching* 9 (March-April 1994): 23.
2. Clyde E. Fant, "Memory," in *Concise Encyclopedia of Preaching*, ed. William H. Willimon and Richard Lischer (Louisville: Westminster John Knox, 1995), 330.
3. David M. Brown, *Dramatic Narrative in Preaching* (Valley Forge, Pa.: Judson, 1981), 41.
4. Ibid.

few days before you preach gives you an edge—you can read through it every night before you turn in for bed.

Third, *pray* through your manuscript. Turn the major moves of your sermon into prayer requests. Ask God to help you communicate each section clearly and, if necessary, to help you say something differently.

Finally, *rehearse* your delivery. Take your manuscript with you into the empty worship center where you will preach. Start by reading a section through. Then, set aside the manuscript and deliver the section without it. If you slip, you can refer to the manuscript and find out what you forgot and perhaps why you forgot it. The closer you get to delivery day, run through the whole sermon without notes. If you stumble over the same area, you may need to work on a transition or revise a section that does not flow.

What to Wear and Wield

What about costumes and props? Should the preacher use these, particularly in a first-person narrative sermon? As noted earlier, prophets like Jeremiah and Ezekiel made use of both costuming and props, so there's no theological reason to avoid them. The question becomes a practical one: Will the use of a costume or a prop work for or against my communication of this sermon?

My personal preference is to avoid costuming. Jeffrey Arthurs cites at least two practical reasons to forego the use of costumes:

> Costumes tend to communicate to the audience that the message is more entertainment than edification. When it comes to costuming, less is often more. That is, the more that audience members use their imaginations, the more they will participate in the sermon.[5]

On two separate occasions, I attended worship services in which Haddon Robinson and Don Sunukjian delivered first-person narrative sermons. Robinson preached part of the David story from David's perspective, while Sunukjian told the story of Esther from the viewpoint of one of the minor characters in the book. Neither of the men wore costumes. Both preached in traditional garb—a suit and tie. Both delivered their sermons effectively.

On the other hand, friends have told me how effective it was when Paul Borden preached a first-person narrative from an Old Testament story and dressed the part of Jacob or Abraham. Each expositor will have to make the call. A costume is not necessary. If one is used, however, it should be more than a bathrobe and slippers. A preacher's resources, time, and skill will help determine whether or not to try any costuming.

5. Jeffrey D. Arthurs, "Performing the Story," *Preaching* 12 (March-April 1997): 35.

As far as props, less is probably more. There's no substitute for painting a verbal picture. On occasion, though, a sword, animal jawbone, scroll, or piece of broken pottery might serve the telling. Props tend to attract attention and take on lives of their own, though, so be careful.

On Stage

You should think about the platform or stage on which you will deliver your sermon. The first question is how to work around the pulpit. There's good reason to move out from behind the pulpit when delivering *any* sermon, but especially sermons from Bible stories.

Several years ago, I had the privilege of inviting the late Ray Stedman to preach at a church I pastored. I remember Ray moving out from behind the pulpit and standing in front of it. He joked about hiding behind what Spurgeon called a "coward's castle." Through the years, I've watched preachers improve their communication by getting out from behind the pulpit. As Don Sunukjian tells his students, "There is no communication advantage to standing behind a box. Jay Leno doesn't do it. David Letterman doesn't do it. When you have something important to say to your daughter, you don't go look for a box behind which you can stand."

So get out from behind the pulpit. Think about replacing the physical pulpit with a music stand or a smaller lectern that you can move off to one side when you preach. If the pulpit is a permanent fixture in your church, physically or emotionally, then figure out how you can stand beside it or in front of it.

For a sermon from an Old Testament narrative, particularly a first-person narrative, you will want a little more space than normal for moving around. The area does not have to be large. But in a sermon on the book of Ruth, you will probably want a spot on the stage for Moab and a spot on the stage for Bethlehem. If you do not have a large area, Moab and Bethlehem can be separated by a couple of steps. When recreating a conversation, turn about forty-five degrees from center to the right for one character's speech. Then turn about forty-five degrees from center to the left for the other character's speech. You don't have to change physical location when the speakers change. Reserve changes in physical location for changes in scene.

You may choose to speak or not to speak while you are moving from one location to another. If you are moving from one scene to another, it may work best to be silent. The combination of a verbal pause and a physical shift from one place to another will signal the change. If you do have reason to speak as you move, that's alright. However, beware of pacing while you speak. Deliver your material from a fixed point. Change that point as often as the story demands it, but don't wander back and forth as you talk.[6] At times, you may

---

6. For more elaborate details on staging, see Reg Grant and John Reed, *Telling Stories to Touch the Heart* (Wheaton: Victor, 1990), 68–70.

even want to use a stool, particularly if you plan to deliver part of the sermon standing and part of the sermon sitting.

Delivery

In any preaching event, how you use your voice is important. You have the opportunity for vocal variety and punctuation in your pitch, punch (volume), progress (rate of delivery), and pause.[7] Whether you preach from a first-person or third-person perspective, you will have the opportunity to deliver lines from characters in the story. Use a combination of these variables to convey the emotion of the speech. As a general rule, you're not being as dramatic as you think you are. For example, if you are moving from loud to soft, it may seem to you like the volume drops from level 9 to level 2. When your audience hears it, however, or when you listen to yourself on tape, the volume level only drops from level 9 to level 6. The pause that seems like four seconds to you only takes one second. So don't be afraid to overexaggerate your contrasts.

When you deliver your story, use large gestures. Large gestures help preachers get rid of nervousness. They also add realism to your story. Storytelling lends itself to gesturing more than any other form of communication. Using your hands, you can toss wheat into the air with a pitchfork. You can draw a bowstring and shoot an arrow. You can point to Jerusalem or Bethlehem or a well or the field of Boaz. You can shield the sun from your eyes.

There are a couple of other things you can do to help your audience visualize the scene you're constructing. Remember to keep Jerusalem or Shechem at the same spot throughout the whole sermon. If you point to your left at the imaginary city of Jerusalem, you must always point to your left when indicating Jerusalem. If you point to your left the first two times and to your right the third time, you will create visual confusion. Furthermore, remember that your congregation sees everything backwards. When you draw a line from left to right, your audience sees a line being drawn from right to left. So if you are trying to construct a timeline and talk about the past, you will want to start the line on the congregation's left, which happens to be your right.

Eye contact is also important. Haddon Robinson notes, "Almost without exception, a congregation will not listen attentively to speakers who do not look at them."[8] He counsels looking at and talking with one listener at a time for a second or two. Look that listener in the eye, then turn to someone else. The goal is not simply looking at listeners but talking with them.

However, storytelling is the one time a preacher may momentarily gaze over the audience and look into space. As Fred Craddock observes, "A good storyteller seldom looks at anyone."[9] A preacher may want to look beyond the

---

7. Haddon W. Robinson, *Biblical Preaching: The Development and Delivery of Expository Messages,* 2d ed. (Grand Rapids: Baker, 2001), 213–18.

8. Ibid., 212.

9. Fred B. Craddock, *Overhearing the Gospel* (Nashville: Abingdon, 1978), 117.

audience when relating a dialogue between two characters. In a first-person narrative, the preacher might look beyond the listeners when delivering the reminiscences or reflections of a character in the story. Essentially, you are looking beyond the audience to the scene you are imagining. The trick is to reestablish eye contact with your listeners as soon as you are finished. You cannot afford to spend your whole sermon staring off into space.

Like a Christmas present you ship via Federal Express, the Old Testament story you plan to deliver must arrive at its destination or the sermon has miscarried. Remember, people's lives are at stake. Proclaiming a well-studied story in a well-prepared way will do what good stories intend to do: sneak past the listener's defenses to penetrate the heart.

PART 3

❊❊❊❊❊❊

Sermon
Manuscripts

❊❊❊❊❊❊

16

The Greatest Thing You Can Do for Your Kids

A Sermon by Steven Mathewson on Genesis 22:1–19

Foreword

A friend who belonged to the Peoria (Ill.) Camera Club invited me to a club-sponsored seminar featuring a professional photographer. During one of the sessions, the photographer explained how to create special effects when photographing a mountain stream. To get a cascade effect that looks like cotton candy oozing over the rocks, he told us to use a slow shutter speed such as a fifteenth or an eighth of a second. Because a slower shutter speed makes the exposure longer, a photographer must adjust the camera lens to let in a smaller stream of light. The professional suggested waiting for the sun to go behind the clouds and then closing down the aperture (f-stop setting) on the lens to its smallest opening. To get the opposite effect and freeze the water droplets in midair, he suggested using a fast shutter speed, perhaps a thousandth of a second. To compensate for the shorter exposure time created by a fast shutter speed, he told us to wait for bright sunlight and then to open the aperture (f-stop setting) to let in a larger volume of light. While this technique made sense, it really registered when the professional photographer pulled out some of his pictures and showed us the finished product.

The next five chapters will show you the finished product. Each chapter features a manuscript from a sermon on an Old Testament narrative. Although these chapters do not allow you to see or hear the preacher, they will give you a glimpse of what you're aiming for when you preach an Old Testament story. I begin with a sermon of my own, but I also include manuscripts from some masters of the craft: Don Sunukjian, Paul Borden, Haddon Robinson, and Alice Mathews. By the way, leading off with my manuscript is not an act of showmanship. The arrangement of the manuscripts simply follows canonical order.

The format is the same for each chapter. A *foreword* precedes each sermon and introduces the preacher and message. After the *sermon manuscript* itself, I have added an *afterword* that provides a brief analysis of the sermon. Finally, I offer a short *interview* with each preacher about his or her sermon and about the challenges of preaching from Old Testament narrative texts.

My sermon from Genesis 22:1–19 applies the text specifically to parenting. I prepared it for Father's Day. While the story speaks to a larger issue than parenting, it certainly encompasses it. After all, God selected this area of Abraham's life to test his devotion. In the manuscript, I use bold print to identify the statements of the sermon's big idea.

Sermon Manuscript

When a child enters your life, your life begins to revolve around your child. Remember when your son or daughter was born? You immediately started packing six times the baby's weight in paraphernalia. Every time you went to visit friends or family, you lugged along items such as a stroller, a swing, a baby seat, a backpack, and a high chair. I could hardly cram all the necessities in the car when our first daughter was born. Then, when we had twins, I threatened to buy a utility trailer.

As your little Timmy or Susie grows older, you're still packing necessities: bicycles, skiing equipment, and band instruments. You do it because life revolves around your child. You allow your home to become a sports complex and an activity center for slumber parties and Super Bowl parties. Suddenly, your calendar revolves around Little League, piano lessons, skiing lessons, soccer, 4-H meetings, Girl Scouts, hunter safety, and swimming lessons.

Then, to capture these precious moments, you plunk down cash for a camcorder. Your life revolves around your child, so you've got to capture her cuteness and his exploits on video.

One day, your teen is ready to take driver's education. At this point, you get the shock of your life when your insurance premium skyrockets. But you'll pay it for Tim. You'll pay it for Sue. It's a joy and a privilege to center your life around your children's lives. You don't want to deprive them of anything.

But this quest to give our children everything has its downside. As a believer living in a culture where kids rule, a time will come in your life when you face a conflict. If you are a Christian father or mother, and if your life revolves around your child, you may find yourself facing a dilemma. It's the same dilemma faced by a father who lived in the ancient Near East. I want to tell you his story this morning.

This father had a son, and life revolved around that son. The father's name was Abraham, and his son's name was Isaac. The story is in Genesis 22. Please find the story in your Bibles.

You can't blame Abraham for revolving his life around Isaac. You can't blame him for doting on this boy. After all, Isaac was Abraham's miracle baby. When Abraham was seventy-five years old, God promised Abraham that he would be the father of a great nation. But when Abraham celebrated his eightieth birthday, he still had no child. In Genesis 15:3, Abraham, then known as Abram, said, "You have given me no children; so a servant in my household will be my heir." God said, "A son coming from your own body will be your heir." But at eighty-five, Abraham had no son. He finally got so desperate that he followed the custom of his day and fathered a son through his wife's maidservant, Hagar. Instead of producing the God-promised heir, Abraham created a whole new set of problems. At ninety, Abraham had no son by his wife, Sarah. At ninety-five, Abraham had no son by his wife, Sarah. At age ninety-nine, Abraham still had not fathered a son by his wife, Sarah.

In Genesis 17, when Abraham was ninety-nine years old, God appeared to Abraham and said, "You and your wife are going to be the proud parents of a son." What was Abraham's response to that? He found it humorous. He fell down and laughed. Why, he and Sarah were thinking about checking into a nursing home, not about what color to paint a nursery! There was no way he was going to be a father when he turned one-hundred years old. In Genesis 18, God reappeared to Abraham and said, "Next year at this time, Sarah, your wife will have a son." Sarah overheard this, and she laughed, too. Like Abraham, she laughed in disbelief.

But God got the last laugh. As the narrator tells us in Genesis 21, God was gracious to Sarah, she became pregnant, and she bore Abraham a son in his old age. And per God's prior instructions (Genesis 17:19), Abraham named him "Isaac." Guess what the Hebrew name *Yitzhak*, or Isaac, means? It means "laughter." Now Sarah was laughing in joy and wonder, not in disbelief. Genesis 21:6 records her words: *God has brought me laughter, and everyone who hears about this will laugh with me.* I imagine that every time Abraham and Sarah called "laughter" in for supper, they remembered how God had turned their laughter of disbelief to laughter of joy. What a happy ending!

But then we come to Genesis 22. What we read next catches us off guard. Look at how the narrator begins the story: *Some time later God tested Abraham. He said to him, "Abraham!" "Here I am," he replied. Then God said, "Take your son, your only son, Isaac, whom you love, and go to the region of Moriah. Sacrifice him there as a burnt offering on one of the mountains I will tell you about"* (22:1–2).

Oh my! God's instructions to Abraham catch us off guard and shock us. They resemble a telephone call at 3 A.M. The ringing phone jolts us from our sleep, and the caller shatters our world with bad news. There's nothing in the story of Abraham that prepares us for God's stunning command. In fact, this is so disturbing that the narrator prefaces the account by telling us what God is doing. He's testing Abraham. We know from the Old Testament that God condemns child sacrifice. Some of the pagan cultures were doing that, but God detests it. He doesn't intend for Abraham to take Isaac's life. He wants to test him. But Abraham doesn't know what we know as readers of this story.

I can only imagine the anguish Abraham felt as he listened to God's instructions. He must have been floored! He must have been crushed! You can feel the tension mount as each phrase in verse 2 gets more specific and narrows the focus. The Hebrew text of verse 2 says, "Take your son . . . your only son . . . the one you love . . . Isaac." Incredible! Here is the boy for whom Abraham and Sarah waited for twenty-five years. They rejoiced at his birth. And now God says, "I want you to sacrifice him as a burnt offering." How devastating.

Now, what's the nature of this test anyway?! What is God after? Well, offering a sacrifice is all about worship. God's test will force Abraham's hand and find out whom Abraham will worship. This test will force Abraham to choose between worshiping God or Isaac. At this point, there's no way Abraham can do both. He will have to say, "I won't offer Isaac. I've waited twenty-five years. God, you must understand, everything in my life is wrapped up in this boy. I can't worship you by offering him as a sacrifice." Or Abraham will have to say, "Alright, God, I'll worship you and offer Isaac as a sacrifice."

I believe this is the same dilemma Christian parents face today. Will we worship Jesus Christ, or will we worship our kids? That dilemma is bound to rear its ugly head in a culture where kids rule. Now, I'm thankful that our culture places a premium on children. That's one of the good things about our culture. Our children are our future. So we revolve our lives around them. Isn't that true of your family? Your lives revolve around your children, don't they?

But sometimes our culture crosses the line. It conditions us to worship our kids instead of worshiping God. And so, God has to test us periodically to find out where our allegiance really is. Make no mistake about it, God will test you in this area just as he tested Abraham. You can miss the test, though, because it happens so subtly—unlike the mega-test that Abraham faced.

God may be testing you with the opportunity for your son to get involved in an all-star baseball league. The problem is, this opportunity will force your son and you to miss the next eight Sunday morning worship services. You may not like to admit it, but you are being forced to choose between worshiping God and worshiping your child.

Or God may test you in the area of finances. You need to cough up four hundred bucks to send your child with her science class for a dream trip to Florida to see the space shuttle and to visit NASA. You don't have the money. But four hundred dollars happens to be the monthly amount you give to God as part of your worship. If you took one month's offering, you could pay for the trip. After all, you might glorify God by helping your child better understand God's universe, right? You may not like to admit it, but you are being forced to choose between worshiping God and worshiping your child.

Perhaps your son or your daughter wants to go steady with a good-looking junior in his or her algebra class. But you know the good-looking junior is not a believer in Jesus Christ. He or she holds values that butt heads with your Christian values. However, you don't want to alienate or offend your child and say, "I will not give you permission to go steady with this boy or girl." Why, this might turn them off to Christianity, and then you would have a problem. But like it or not, you are being forced to choose between worshiping God and worshiping your child.

Friends, God tests his people by forcing them to choose between worshiping him or worshiping the children he has given to them. Abraham faced it. And you face it too. So what choice did Abraham make?

The story continues in verse 3: *Early the next morning Abraham got up and saddled his donkey. He took with him two of his servants and his son Isaac. When he had cut enough wood for the burnt offering, he set out for the place God had told him about. On the third day Abraham looked up and saw the place in the distance. He said to his servants, "Stay here with the donkey while I and the boy go over there. We will worship and then we will come back to you"* (22:3–5).

Now, I've been on some miserable camping trips, but nothing that would rival this. Imagine taking a camping trip and knowing that arriving at the destination will mean the loss of your child's life! The trip from Beersheba was about fifty miles, roughly a three-day journey. God in his sovereignty must have planned it this way to give Abraham some time to think, some time to change his mind. But Abraham had made a choice. Did you catch the statement Abraham made to his servant, recorded in verse 5? *He said to his servants, "Stay here with the donkey while I and the boy go over there. We will worship and then we will come back to you."* What an amazing statement. Apparently, Abraham believed that God would raise Isaac back from the dead, because Isaac was the promised heir. But I'm just as intrigued by his first statement, when he says, "We will worship." The Hebrew term translated in your Bibles as "worship" means "to lie face down on the ground in front of a superior." Today, we do standing ovations to honor people. In Abraham's day, you hit the ground. Abraham realized that he was being asked to worship God, even at the cost of his son's life. He was prepared to do it because he was committed to worship.

Verse 6 says, *Abraham took the wood for the burnt offering and placed it on his son Isaac, and he himself carried the fire and the knife.* Talk about foreshadowing what is about to happen!

Finally, Isaac asks the dreaded question. You just knew this young man would say this. It must have broken Abraham's heart. Look at the end of verse 6: *As the two of them went on together, Isaac spoke up and said to his father Abraham, "Father?" "Yes, my son?" Abraham replied. "The fire and wood are here," Isaac said, "but where is the lamb for the burnt offering?" Abraham answered, "God himself will provide the lamb for the burnt offering, my son."* And the *two of them went on together* (22:6b–8).

Do you feel the tension building? As the story continues to unfold, the narrator piles up action verbs, hurrying up the story towards the anticipated, awful moment: *When they reached the place God had told him about, Abraham built an altar there and arranged the wood on it. He bound his son Isaac and laid him on the altar, on top of the wood. Then he reached out his hand and took the knife to slay his son* (22:9–10). This flurry of verbs brings us to the awful moment where Abraham severs Isaac's carotid artery with the slice of the knife blade.

But something happens before Abraham presses the steel of the knife blade against the flesh of Isaac's neck. Verse 11 says, *But the angel of the LORD called out to him from heaven, "Abraham! Abraham!" "Here I am,"* he replied. For the second time in this story, God interrupts and calls on Abraham. For the second time, Abraham says, "Here I am." Talk about a welcome interruption! *"Do not lay a hand on the boy,"* he said. *"Do not do anything to him. Now I know that you fear God, because you have not withheld from me your son, your only son." Abraham looked up and there in a thicket he saw a ram caught by its horns. He went over and took the ram and sacrificed it as a burnt offering instead of his son. So Abraham called that place The LORD Will Provide. And to this day it is said, "On the mountain of the LORD it will be provided"* (22:12–14).

God intervenes. He provides an alternative. But most important of all, he says, "Abraham, you passed my test. You get an A+. Now I know that your worship for me is unlimited and unqualified. You have not held anything back, not even the most important person in your life. Abraham, you feared me rather than fearing the consequences of sacrificing your child."

That's a problem in our culture, isn't it? We fear the wrong things. Last week, Priscilla and I stopped at Taco Bell to grab something to eat. The Taco Bell in Bozeman is about the size of your hall closet, so our table was about the length of a taco from another table where a dad and his two boys were seated. His two sons reminded me a lot of our boys, Ben and Luke. The younger son, who looked to be eight or nine asked his father a question that we couldn't help overhearing. He said, "Dad, are you going to report the accident?" Now that got my attention. I sipped my Coke and pretended not to be listening. But, of course, I was! There was no response, so the little guy asked his dad the question again: "Dad, are you going to report the accident?" This time, the dad mumbled, "Well, I might call the insurance company and check with them, but there wasn't any damage done." This man feared the consequences of acting in integrity more than he feared the consequences of not acting in integrity. By contrast, Abraham feared God. Whatever fears he had about sacrificing Isaac—and you know that he had them—he was more afraid of not putting God first than he was afraid of not putting Isaac first. So Abraham made the choice to worship God, not his child, Isaac.

Perhaps, as you listen to this story, you are wondering if it's really the way to go. If there are times in my life when saying yes to God means saying no to my child, is there a payoff?

Look at the conclusion to this story, beginning in verse 15: *The angel of the LORD called to Abraham from heaven a second time and said, "I swear by myself, declares the LORD, that because you have done this and have not withheld your son, your only son, I will surely bless you and make your descendants as numerous as the stars in the sky and as the sand on the seashore. Your descendants will take possession of the cities of their enemies, and through your offspring all nations on earth will be blessed, because you have obeyed me." Then Abraham returned to his servants, and they set off together for Beersheba. And Abraham stayed in Beersheba* (22:15–19).

What's the payoff for worshiping God instead of your kids? Is it going to hurt their future? No. God said, "Abraham, because of your obedience, your commitment to worship me, your son will be better off. You've just assured my blessing on your descendents. You've positioned yourself so that your son will be better off." Fathers, make no mistake about it. **The greatest thing you can do for your kids is to worship God, not your kids**. Your culture says, "You've got to give your kids this experience, that opportunity, those lessons . . . whatever the cost, or they won't succeed in life."

Of course, your children are important. But they were not designed to fit the throne that God alone is fit to occupy. In our culture, kids rule. But God demands our allegiance. Remember Deuteronomy 6:4–9, one of the greatest statements in the Bible on child rearing? It begins with, "Hear O Israel, Yahweh is our God . . . Yahweh alone. Love Yahweh your God with all your heart and with all your soul and with all your strength." Then you'll have something to give your children. You'll put your children in a position where God can bless their lives and use them in his kingdom program.

Mark it well, God is going to test your allegiance. He's going to see how committed you are to worshiping him. And he may put you in situations where you have to choose between allegiance to his son, Jesus, or allegiance to your kids. When that happens, **the greatest thing you can do for your kids is to worship God, not your kids**. Yes, your son or daughter will be better off if you say, "I'm sorry. Although I want you to play in the all-star volleyball league so that you get some looks for a college scholarship, it would be wrong to duck out on corporate worship for the next two months just to let you play."

Yes, your son or daughter will be better off if you say, "I'd love to send you with your class to Florida to visit NASA. But we don't have the funds. Even if we can't earn them some other way, we're not going to rob God of the money we've committed to give to his kingdom work."

Yes, your son or daughter will be better off if you say, "I'm sorry, but I will not give you permission to go out with the gorgeous girl or the hunk of a guy you met in your algebra class. Your relationship with God is too important to sacrifice for a romance that isn't right."

Yes, **the greatest thing you can do for your kids is to worship God, not your kids**. I can't tell you how God will honor you. Perhaps your daughter will get another opportunity to develop her volleyball skills. Perhaps God will intervene at the eleventh hour and provide money for your son to take the Florida trip to visit NASA. Or maybe God won't. He may have another opportunity in mind. He may be protecting your son by not letting him go. The possibilities are endless. Perhaps your son or daughter will get angry at you for a season when you put the damper on their chance to have a high school flame. But you'll protect them. You'll teach them.

But there's one more question you may have this morning. How can you muster up the strength to do this? What God is asking you to do is hard. He's asking you to go against the commitment your culture has made—to put our kids first no matter what. How can you do this? How did Abraham do this? Wouldn't you like to know how Abraham maintained his resolve to worship God first before his child, even when it meant putting his child's life on the line? What was Abraham's secret?

Abraham's secret was a conviction he held. Go back to verse 8 for a moment. Remember Abraham's answer to the gut-wrenching question that Isaac asked? Dad, where is the lamb for the burnt offering? *Abraham answered, "God himself will provide."* Literally, "God himself will see to it." After the fact, in verse 14, Abraham called the name of the place *"Yahweh Yireh,"* that is, "Yahweh will see to it." The LORD will provide. *And to this day it is* said, "On the mountain of the LORD it will be provided." Friends, that's the conviction that will give you the courage to worship God instead of your kids when it seems unreasonable to you and to your kids. "God will see to it" is the conviction that will help you keep your worship priorities straight when your kids don't understand and end up getting mad at you. It's the same conviction that got you started walking with God in the first place. In the larger story of the Bible, Genesis 22 foreshadows the provision of another sacrifice. The same God who provided a sacrificial lamb so that Isaac might live provided the ultimate sacrificial lamb, Jesus Christ, so that God's people might live. The same God who invited you to trust in the Lord Jesus Christ to receive eternal life may test your trust. He may test you to see if you really trust him to provide when worshiping him puts you in a tight spot with one of your children.

On this Father's Day, we could spend time talking about parenting tips and techniques that could help both dads and moms. There's a place for that. But what you need most is a commitment to worship God first. The bottom line is, walk with God first, then you'll be a better parent.

In one of the early scenes in the movie *Forrest Gump*, Forrest's mom, played by actress Sally Field, visits Mr. Hancock, the principal of the Greenbough County Central School. Mrs. Gump wants to enroll her son, but the principal informs her that the state of Alabama requires a minimum IQ of eighty to attend public school. Forrest has an IQ of only seventy-five. But Mrs. Gump insists on enrolling Forrest in the Greenbough County Central School. She says, "My boy, Forrest, is going to get the same opportunities as everyone else. He's not going to a special school to learn how to retread tires. We're talking about five little points. There must be something that can be done." There is. Forrest's mom ends up in bed with the principal, Mr. Hancock. Later, the principal tells Forrest, "Your mama sure does care about your schooling, son." That scene reflects the philosophy of our age: "If the kid gets his chance, it doesn't matter what it takes."

Genesis 22 says, Dead wrong! You better believe it matters. The most important thing you can do for your son is not to worship him. The greatest thing you can do for your daughter is not to worship her. The greatest thing you can do for your children is to worship their Creator, the living God who provides for those who fear him.

Afterword

This sermon starts off in the twenty-first century A.D. before traveling back to the twenty-first century B.C. The introduction paints a picture of modern family life with which most listeners can identify. In fact, it uses a touch of humor with the expression "packing six times the baby's weight in paraphernalia." Most listeners will chuckle and think, "Been there, done that!" As the introduction unfolds, it refers to a conflict that arises when Christian parents revolve their lives around their children. This provides the bridge into the story of a father who faced the same conflict.

Since the sermon is inductive, the preacher has adjusted his introduction accordingly. Notice that the introduction does not raise the subject of the sermon—*What is the greatest thing parents can do for their children.* It simply establishes the presence of a conflict in the story. Even then, the introduction does not identify this conflict. The listener will only discover this conflict as the story starts to unfold. The advantage of this kind of inductive approach is that it keeps the listener in suspense. The downside is that the same withholding of details that can create suspense can also create confusion. The preacher must work to guide listeners while keeping them blindfolded for a time.

If the preacher wanted to, he could start the sermon immediately in the twenty-first century B.C. This is called a "cold open." With this approach, the preacher starts with the story and vividly describes one of its scenes. A cold open works best when the scene is dramatic. Often, the preacher will choose the opening scene. For example, a sermon on Genesis 22:1–19 might start like this: "The command came out of nowhere. Oh, Abraham knew it was God's voice. But nothing prepared him for those awful words. The specificity increased with each phrase. So did the agony. 'Take your son . . . your only son . . . the one you love . . . Isaac.' How crushing. Here is the miracle boy for whom Abraham and Sarah waited for twenty-five years. They rejoiced at his birth. And now God says, 'I want you to sacrifice him as a burnt offering.'"

Sometimes, the preacher will choose a scene towards the end of the story to use as a cold open. This scene is usually the peak moment or the point of highest tension. This strategy resembles a flashback. For example, a sermon on Genesis 22:1–19 might start like this: "It was the most awful moment of his life. Abraham took the knife and prepared to press the steel blade against his son's neck. With one quick slice, he could sever Isaac's carotid artery. Blood would gush out, and Isaac would be gone in a matter of seconds." After this dramatic opening, the preacher then retreats to the beginning of the story and develops how and why this peak moment evolved.

In the sermon manuscript you just read, the big idea is, *The greatest thing you can do for your kids is to worship God, not your kids.* The preacher restates this idea several times. However, while he states it plainly, he introduces it subtly into the flow of the sermon. He never comes out and says, "Here is the point of the story."

The sermon develops along the contours of the following outline:

I. God tests his people by forcing them to choose between worshiping him or the children he has given them *(develop inductively)*.
   A. God tests Abraham with the stunning command to sacrifice Isaac (vv. 1–2).
   B. This test will force Abraham to choose between worshiping God or Isaac.
   C. Today, parents face the choice of worshiping God or their children.

II. *(Big idea)* The greatest thing you can do for your kids is to worship God, not your kids *(develop inductively; big idea emerges at C)*.
   A. Abraham makes the worship of God his priority (vv. 3–10).
   B. God intervenes and acknowledges Abraham's obedience (vv. 11–14).
   C. God returns to reaffirm His blessing and promise (vv. 15–19).
   D. Worshiping God and not your kids requires the conviction that God will provide (vv. 8, 14).

Specific details also lend more credibility to this sermon and hold a listener's interest. Without the specific images, the introduction becomes bland. It would sound something like this: "When a child enters your life, your life begins to revolve around your child. You do everything you can to help your child succeed. You arrange your schedule around your child, and you spend whatever it takes to give your child opportunities to play sports, take music lessons, and participate in educational trips." The image is true, but not compelling.

The closing illustration from *Forrest Gump* is another case in point. While listeners do not need to know the name of the school, talking about the Greenbough County Central School makes the illustration more concrete. Specific details engage listeners.

Interview

Steve, where have you preached this particular sermon?

I developed it and preached it a couple of years ago on Father's Day at Dry Creek Bible Church, the congregation I serve in south central Montana.

What was the response?

One guy said something like, "I hated that sermon." But I knew what he was saying by the twinkle in his eye. He meant, "That was painful, because God convicted me about worshiping him instead of my kids."

Does preaching Old Testament narratives come naturally for you?

No! God's taken me on quite a journey. I've always had a heart for Bible exposition. In fact, my heroes have been preachers like John MacArthur Jr., Maynard Mathewson (my father), John Piper, Haddon Robinson, George Rutenbar, Charles Swindoll, and Warren Wiersbe. When I tried to do exposition in Old Testament narratives, though, I found out that the traditional sermon forms used by expositors didn't fit the stories. It's taken me several years to make the adjustment. Some of my heroes have been influential in helping me make the shift. I'm still learning, but preaching Old Testament narratives comes much more naturally than it did for me ten years ago, or five years ago, or even three years ago.

You ended up reading the entire story in your sermon on Genesis 22:1–19. Do you always read the whole story?

It depends. This is one of the tough decisions expositors have to make. How much of the story should I read from the text, and how much of it should I paraphrase? When preaching longer stories, I usually summarize much of the material in my own words. I read only particular sections or statements in the text. The length of the story in Genesis 22:1–19, though, allowed me to read the entire story during the course of the sermon. However, I tried to intersperse comments and transitions that helped the sermon flow like a story.

Are your sermons primarily inductive or deductive when you preach from narrative?

They are almost always inductive. Stories work inductively, so I try to preach them inductively.

Do you preach without notes?

Yes. When I first started preaching, I brought a full manuscript into the pulpit. Gradually, I weaned myself away from a manuscript and then from abbreviated notes. About three years ago, I started preaching entirely without notes, and I've never gone back.

How do you remember everything?

I'm amazed at how the human mind remembers details. Listen to a guy tell a fishing story. Or listen to a woman relate a story about a close scrape with a Doberman while she's out jogging. These folks don't need notes. The human mind has an amazing capacity to remember details. When I preach Genesis 22:1–19, I worry more about forgetting the *Forrest Gump* story than about the details. Once I get into the story, the details spill out on their own. Of course, I have to get familiar with the material to remember it. I don't try to memorize, but I read through my sermon manuscript several times, especially at night. I read once in a *Reader's Digest* article that what you go over in the evening is what you'll remember in the morning. I also go through a couple of dry runs from the platform.

Does it help to write notes in the margins of your Bible?

If you intend to preach without notes, this ends up working against you. Believe me, I've tried it. Scribbling notes in the margins erases the very advantage you gain by preaching without notes—connection to your audience. I make a couple of exceptions, though. I always write out the big idea at the top of the page that has the text I'm preaching. That keeps me on track. Also, if I want to talk about a particular item from the text—a word, a phrase, an event, or a character— I will sometimes underline it or circle it in my Bible. If I don't trust myself to remember the *Forrest Gump* story, I may write "Gump" in the margin at the end of Genesis 22. These minor notations will not hinder eye contact, but I discipline myself not to stuff the margins with notes.

Since you used an illustration from Forrest Gump, how do you feel about quoting scenes from Hollywood movies or lyrics from popular songs?

It's necessary to confront the ideas to which people are exposed and then challenge them with biblical truth. This is the genius of Bible exposition. One line of thinking says that by quoting movies or songs, a preacher encourages people to watch them or listen to them. I don't buy that. I was aware that several people in my congregation watched *Forrest Gump*. I had heard about the scene I described, so I rented the movie to get my facts straight. In my sermons, I have quoted lyrics from John Lennon and Jewel Kilcher. I never do this to appear contemporary. I do this to help people evaluate cultural messages by biblical standards. I may say, "Jewel got this right. This lines up with what the Bible says." Or I may say, "Jewel got it wrong here. Don't buy into this idea, because it's the opposite of what this Bible story teaches."

Speaking of culture, how do you keep your finger on your culture's pulse?

I subscribe to *Time* magazine and *Sports Illustrated*. I also peruse my wife's issues of *Good Housekeeping*. I ask people in my congregation to share copies of their magazines when they finish reading them. This cuts down on the cost of subscribing to everything. I read book reviews and movie reviews. Once a month or so, I'll visit a place like Barnes & Noble and see which books are selling. I take time to skim through magazines I ordinarily don't read. I discover what music is hot and what video games kids are buying. I walk around with a legal pad or a three-by-five card and take notes. In fact, some people think I'm a store employee and ask me for help! Most of all, I spend time with people and pay attention to what is influencing them.

Your sermon contains only a few brief references to Jesus Christ. Is it legitimate to preach an Old Testament narrative without showing how it points forward to Christ?

I've wrestled with this issue quite a bit recently as I've worked through *Preaching Christ from the Old Testament* by Sidney Greidanus.[1] In his book Greidanus compares the christological approach of Martin Luther with the theocentric approach of John Calvin. While the view of Greidanus falls somewhere between the two,[2] my view is closer to Calvin's. Based on Calvin's understanding of the Triune God, his God-centered sermons were implicitly Christ-centered.[3] But because of (1) his insistence on unfolding the mind of the author in a passage of Scripture and (2) his focus on the sovereignty and glory of God as his interpretive center, Calvin did not see the need to make every Old Testament sermon explicitly Christ-centered. He preached what was in the passage. Even Bryan Chapell, a preaching professor from the Reformed tradition, says, "A sermon remains expository and Christ-centered not because it leapfrogs to Golgotha, but because it locates the intent of the passage within the scope of God's redemptive work."[4] In fact, Chapell suggests that sometimes a Christ-centered sermon may not even mention Jesus. The issue is, does a sermon demonstrate the relationship of the passage preached to the overall war between the seed of the woman and Satan.[5]

Sometimes, though, my sermons from Old Testament narratives will point explicitly to Jesus Christ. A few stories I recently preached from Judges seemed incomplete without moving to the Gospel. At other times, a story may communicate a theological idea that needs further explanation in light of the new covenant. Believe me, I am passionate about preaching Jesus Christ! The people who have heard me preach the whole counsel of God on a weekly basis know my passion to exalt Christ. When I add this to the fact that my preaching occurs in the context of Christ-centered worship services, I don't feel pressured to show how every Old Testament story I preach points forward to Jesus. Often, such an approach does not pay sufficient attention to a story's specific message nor to the legitimate ethical demands that flow from it.

---

1. Sidney Greidanus, *Preaching Christ from the Old Testament* (Grand Rapids: Eerdmans, 1999).

2. Ibid., 227.

3. Ibid., 147.

4. Bryan Chapell, *Christ-Centered Preaching: Redeeming the Expository Sermon* (Grand Rapids: Baker, 1994), 296.

5. Ibid., 295.

17

✾ ✾ ✾ ✾ ✾

THE CRIPPLE'S STORY

✾ ✾ ✾ ✾ ✾

A Sermon by Donald Sunukjian on 2 Samuel 9

Foreword

My daughter, Anna, tells me she's ready to trade in her beginner-model flute for an open-hole flute. An open-hole flute produces a better quality sound; however, it also magnifies the risk of distorting the sound if the flutist mishandles it. The flutist's fingertips must cover the holes on the keys.

Similarly, preachers who select a first-person narrative form to preach an Old Testament story step up to an instrument that can increase the quality of their presentation. However, they also run the risk of distorting the presentation if they misuse this instrument. Don Sunukjian provides a model of how to use the first-person narrative form creatively and accurately to preach an expository sermon from an Old Testament story. He uses this form in the following sermon on 2 Samuel 9.

Sunukjian currently teaches preaching at Biola University's Talbot School of Theology. Previously, he pastored churches in Arizona and Texas, and he also taught preaching at Dallas Theological Seminary. He earned Th.M. and Th.D. degrees at Dallas Theological Seminary. He also earned a Ph.D. in communication from the University of California at Los Angeles (UCLA). Sunukjian has written the commentary on the book of Amos in *The Bible Knowledge Commentary.*

In his manuscript, Sunukjian includes notes to himself about gestures, expressions, and physical movements. He italicizes these notes and puts them in parentheses. He also uses bold print to highlight the statements in which he hints at his big idea.

Sermon Manuscript

(The speaker enters on crutches, looking around, peering down hallways, admiring the majestic building he's in.)

I still don't know my way around the palace. You ought to see all the rooms. And it's kind of hard to get around *(motioning toward his mangled feet).*

This is the house of David, King David. It's the finest in the land. Imported wood *(touching, caressing).* Silk tapestries *(motioning).*

(The speaker seats himself on a piano bench.)

My name is Mephibosheth. I love it here. My wife and I and our small son have a suite of rooms on the second floor. We've been here about three months now.

Why do I live here? That's a good question.

I'm not a visiting dignitary; I'm not an ambassador assigned to this country or anything like that. I'm not a court official; I have no administrative functions here. I'm not a relative either, though I admit David treats me like a son, and has become a grandfather to my boy, Mica.

Why *do* I live here? I will tell you, for it's an amazing story.

My father was killed when I was very young. My memories are vague, for I was five years old. I remember playing in front of the house on my father's estate when a horseman came riding into the yard. I remember the furious beat of hooves, the lather on the horse, the shout from the rider to my baby-sitter in the house: "Take the boy and run. The Philistines are coming! The King and the Prince are dead. Israel is defeated and every man flees!" And then he was off to warn others.

I remember the baby-sitter giving a cry, grabbing her shawl, a little bit of bread and cheese, and grabbing me by the hand—"We must run! Hurry! Fast! We must run!"

We left everything on the spot, and we ran. From the sound of things, the Philistines were barely a mile away. I remember the war shouts as they overran one estate after another. We heard the sounds of futile resistance by the owners, and then men screaming as they died.

We ran and we ran. We ran all that afternoon and into the night. When it was dark, we slipped into a field to catch our breath and hopefully to sleep. But the Philistines continued to pillage into the night, and the sounds came close again. So we got up to run once more.

We ran into the darkness—I don't know how long. We were trying to reach the river to cross over into a corner province in the north, where we did not think they would follow.

But I couldn't go on—my side ached, my lungs were bursting. I remember falling to the ground.

The baby-sitter said, "Come."

"I can't."

"They will kill us."

"I can't," and I started to cry.

She picked me up and began to carry me as she ran. But I was pretty big; five years old can be a heavy load to carry. For a while her fear gave her strength, but as the night wore on, I noticed her eyes began to glaze with exhaustion. Her steps began to stagger. And suddenly, without warning, she collapsed.

I don't remember exactly . . . but I remember her pitching forward, with me in her arms. I remember my legs beneath me *(bending forward)* and her heavy weight falling on me, and then I remember—*(two snaps of the fingers to indicate breaking bones)!*

Something was broken! I screamed. I screamed for her to get off me, but she wasn't moving. I cried and struggled, and eventually got out from under her. I remember screaming into the night for someone to come—and then I remember nothing else.

Several days later I awoke in the house of a man named Makir who lived far on the other side of the river we were trying to reach. I learned we had been found the next morning by others who were fleeing. They had taken us with them the next couple days and had brought us across the river and into safety.

I must have been in shock from the pain, for I remember nothing of all that. I only know that when I woke, my ankles and feet were mangled and numb . . . and I knew that I would never walk again.

That tells you how I got to be this way. But that doesn't tell you who I am.

My father who was killed in that battle was not an ordinary soldier. He was Prince Jonathan. King Saul was my grandfather. In the course of time, if all had gone well, I would have been king of this land after my father Jonathan.

But after the battle, all was in chaos. King Saul was dead. My father was dead. Two of my father's brothers, my uncles, were dead. The Philistines controlled our land and were seizing everything for themselves.

It took a few weeks before we could assess the situation, before the remnant of Israel's government began to appear in exile. It came together by bits and pieces, and it wasn't much.

One of my uncles had survived—Ishbosheth *(shakes head)*. Out of the strength and grandeur of Saul's house, out of the glorious manhood of Jonathan and my uncles, who should survive—Ishbosheth, the most incompetent! He had neither the heart or the head to rule. Left to himself, he was all right, but in a position where he was expected to lead, he could not do it.

Fortunately, Abner also lived and made it across the river. Abner was the commander of the army, a bull of a man—strong, stalwart, muscular, and a leader—ready mind, strength of will, a man who could give orders.

For all practical purposes Abner took over the government in exile. Ishbosheth was the figurehead. Abner was loyal to him and served him as he served my grandfather. But essentially Abner was the power, the one who made things happen.

Those were difficult days, but I was not too involved. I was a boy. I was crippled. And it was obvious that whatever course the kingdom took, it would take it without me. I was shunted aside; I was not to have any part of the kingship.

Well, that soon became of no matter, for it was not long before the kingship was gone from our family. For, after seven years, when I was twelve, the whole land turned from us to David.

And that's the way it's been for the fifteen years since then—David.

How did David and I get together?

I had never met David until three months ago when we moved here.

My early opinion before I knew him was bitter. From what I'd been told, he and my father Jonathan knew each other once. When they were young, they were best friends. They fought side by side. But something must have happened, for by the time I was born David was an outlaw and was considered a traitor.

There were two explanations for this. Some said that my grandfather King Saul had an insane jealousy of David and had tried to kill him—that he had an irrational hatred of David, and that David had to flee to protect himself.

Others said my grandfather saw through David and knew that beneath the surface David was treacherously scheming to take the kingship for himself and away from my father Jonathan.

I was inclined to believe the latter explanation—that David was a scheming traitor—for a couple of reasons. One, at the time of the battle in which my father was killed, David was living with the enemy in Philistia. According to reports he had even volunteered to help the Philistines in the battle but was turned down. Two, soon after the battle and Israel's defeat, while we were trying to regroup in the north, David moved back into the southern section of our land and had himself crowned king of the southern tribes.

So my early opinion of him was negative. And this opinion seemed to be confirmed seven years later when I was twelve. At that time, Abner our leader had gone south to negotiate a consolidation of our northern part of the kingdom with David's southern part. While there, he was tricked into a secret meeting and killed by one of David's generals. A few days later Ishbosheth was assassinated in the north.

I heard the assassins were executed by David, but who knows whether this was genuine justice or whether David was simply silencing his henchmen after they had done this dirty work. "Dead men tell no tales."

In either case, with Abner and Ishbosheth dead, David became king of all the land, and that's the way it's been for the last fifteen years.

And I have to admit, regardless of what I thought about David, it's been good for the kingdom. There's been a great expansion of territory, an unbroken string of victories, stability, prosperity. There's even been talk of a dynasty, a dynasty founded by David. **Supposedly, David has had a dream in which God has promised that David's sons would rule after him—a dynasty. And there's even a promise of some Great Son in the future.**

During all these events I was left in that far northern province, apparently forgotten. Makir was kind—I married his daughter, we had a small son. I did what I could to make myself useful—some bookkeeping for Makir, a little carpentry. I'm not good, but I appreciate fine wood *(glances around palace)*.

And that brings me up to about three months ago, which is when it happened. One day Ziba showed up with the message, "David wants to see you."

I hadn't seen Ziba for about ten years. Ziba used to manage the estate for my father and grandfather. He too had fled across the river but had returned when things stabilized under David. He was living near our old home area, and from what I had heard, he was doing okay for himself.

He said David wants to see me . . . That sounded ominous. Why does David want to see me? *(Light dawns!)* He's going to kill me! To establish a dynasty requires the elimination of all rivals. I'm the last living member of Saul's line. With Jonathan, my uncles, and Ishbosheth dead, I'm the last one who could make a claim to the throne and take the lost inheritance. By getting rid of me, the last potential enemy, David makes his dynasty secure.

I didn't want to see David, but the wagon was waiting to take me there. I had no choice. I could have asked for Makir to help, but that simply would have brought retaliation against him for interfering. I kissed my wife good-bye. Neither of us thought we would see the other again.

On the way there in the wagon I asked Ziba, "How did David hear about me?"

"One day he sent word for me to come to the palace. When I got there, he asked if any of Jonathan's descendants were still living. I told him about you."

"Why? Why not keep your mouth shut?"

"Because I was afraid he'd find out anyway and then punish me for not telling him. Besides, he said his intentions toward you were good."

"Fool! What possible reason could he have for doing good to me? He has everything to gain by my death . . . I'm going to my execution."

We rode in silence until we came to Jerusalem. *(Gaping awe!)* I had heard about the new capital David had built, but this was unbelievable. What an impregnable fortress! And the palace—never had I seen such a place!

I was taken inside and told to "sit here" in some waiting room while Ziba went through some doors. He came back in just a few minutes and directed me through the doors.

I went through the doors into a great room. At the other end, someone was sitting. It was obviously David. As I hobbled toward him, he watched me in silence, with penetrating gaze.

I thought, "He's going to kill me. I'm a threat to his kingdom, to the stability of his dynasty. But if he's going to kill me, I'm going to make it as hard on him as I can. I'm not going to give him the satisfaction of appearing rebellious."

So with great difficulty *(kneeling)* I got on my knees and bowed to indicate that he was my King.

I heard a thunderous voice. "Mephibosheth!"

With my head still bowed, I said, "I am your loyal servant."

Then I heard, "Don't be afraid."

I looked up . . . his eyes were smiling and his face seemed kind. He told me, "Rise, and sit by me on the seat."

"Your father," he continued, "was my dearest friend. When we were young, we both knew that the kingship would be taken from Saul's house and that I was to rule. At that time your father made me swear that when this happened I would never harm him. He made me vow that as God blessed me and I was established as king, I would never raise my hand against any of his descendants.

"Thirty years ago I made a covenant with your father, a solemn promise, that when that time came I would act kindly to any of his descendants.

"I have sought you out and brought you here in order to fulfill my promise. I am restoring to you all of the land and estate of your father and grandfather. The farmlands, the cattle, the orchards, the buildings—they are all yours. All the revenues that the estate produces are yours. All of its operations are in your hands. Ziba will return to your service as foreman as he was for your father and grandfather. His sons and servants will work the land and turn over the revenues to you.

"You will have an entirely free hand. You may come and go as you please, for whatever your business requires. But I want you to bring your wife and boy here to the palace and be part of my family."

That was three months ago. Today I am a wealthy man and a member of David's family.

Here was a King who owed me nothing. But he determined to seek me out and lift me up.

What was I to him? I could offer him nothing. In fact, in his eyes I was a potential enemy. I was hostile to his rule.

But he brought me to his palace, restored the inheritance I had lost, and made me part of his family. And I have shared the laughter and love of his house ever since.

I've got to go now. Thank you for letting me tell my story.

(Gets up and exits, pausing every few steps to say another of the following sentences.)

You know that dream David had—where sons of his sons would rule until there comes some "Great Son of David"? I wonder if there will ever be a Son of David who will be anything like his father? *(Steps)*

Do you think there will ever be a Son of David who will seek out an enemy and lift him up, who will restore the inheritance that was lost? *(Steps)*

Would he take a cripple and make him a son of the king?

If he would, I hope you get to meet him.

(Exit)

Afterword

Stories work by indirection. Don Sunukjian retains this sense of indirection when he preaches the story of David's kindness to Mephibosheth. He doesn't return at the end to say, "For those of you who might have missed the point, let me tell you what it is." Instead, the sermon resembles a dot-to-dot picture. Sunukjian places the dots in a sequence so that when listeners draw lines between them, they see the picture emerge. He does this at the end of the sermon by having Mephibosheth provide some hints that listeners cannot miss. The questions Mephibosheth asks as he leaves the platform lead the hearers to say, "Yes! Jesus Christ is the Son of David who seeks out his enemies, lifts them up, and restores their lost inheritance!" At that moment, the listeners have identified the sermon's big idea.

The whole sermon answers the question, *Why does Mephibosheth live here?* This question is the sermon's subject. The answer, or complement is, *Because David's kindness compelled him to seek out an enemy, lift him up, and restore his lost inheritance.* Of course, Sunukjian's intent is to point people to Jesus Christ, the Son of David who performed the ultimate act of kindness in seeking out his enemies, lifting them up, and restoring their lost inheritance. Sunukjian never asks, "What has Jesus done for you?" Yet, this is the question he attempts to answer through the telling of this story.

Even though this sermon is pure story, it works because Sunukjian has organized his thoughts clearly. Following is the outline on which the sermon is based.

> Introduction: Mephibosheth raises the question, "Why do I live here?"
> I. Act 1: Mephibosheth tells how he ended up crippled.
>   A. He describes the battle that forced him to flee.
>   B. He describes how his baby-sitter fell on him.
>   C. He describes how he reached safety in Makir's house.
> II. Act 2: Mephibosheth reveals his identity.
>   A. He identifies his father as Prince Jonathan and his grandfather as King Saul.
>   B. He describes how the kingship shifted away from his family.
> III. Act 3: Mephibosheth relates how he ended up in David's palace.
>   A. He admits his early bitterness towards David.
>   B. He tells about David's request to see him.
>   C. He describes David's affirmation of loyal love at their meeting.
> Conclusion: Mephibosheth anticipates the rule of a Son of David who will seek out an enemy, lift him up, and restore his lost inheritance.

Good storytellers know how to use transitions. While Sunukjian's transitions are lean, they are effective. To move from act 1 to act 2, Sunukjian simply says, "That tells you how I got to be this way. But that doesn't tell you who I am." Sunukjian transitions from act 2 to act 3 by shifting the spotlight to David. He says, "For, after seven years, when I was twelve, the whole land turned from us to David. . . . And that's the way it's been for the fifteen years since then—David. . . . How did David and I get together?" To move from act 3 to the conclusion, Sunukjian simply uses chronology. He says, "That was three months ago. Today I am a wealthy man. . . ."

You may have noticed that Sunukjian does not use any formal illustrations, nor does he bring the story into the twenty-first century. He doesn't need to. He relies on painting vivid scenes. To do this, he uses concrete terms. Instead of telling us that Jonathan's baby-sitter got really tired, Mephibosheth tells us that "her eyes began to glaze with exhaustion. Her steps began to stagger." Words like "glaze" and "stagger" flash clear, vivid images onto the screen of our minds. Good communicators also use descriptions that appeal to our senses. We can feel "the furious beat of hooves," we can see "the lather on the horse," and we can hear the "shout from the rider" to Jonathan's baby-sitter.

By the time Mephibosheth hobbles off the platform, listeners are thinking about Jesus—not about Don Sunukjian or Mephibosheth. Listeners leave with a profound sense of the kindness that Jesus, the Son of David, has shown to them.

Interview

Don, where have you preached this particular sermon?

I prepared this sermon during my first pastorate as I was preaching through the books of Samuel. After I came to 2 Samuel 9 and studied it, I decided to develop a sermon using a first-person narrative form.

What was the response?

As I was leaving the platform, I heard a new Christian seated in the front say, "Fantastic!" He had gotten the point, and he appreciated the artful way in which the sermon communicated it. Later responses from other listeners were along the lines of, "Thanks for showing us the truth in a creative way."

What do you find most difficult about preaching Old Testament narratives as compared to preaching other literary genres in the Bible?

The most difficult task is to determine the theological truth, the true spiritual point intended by the author. Old Testament narratives are not just stories, they are theology. Scripture says that God reveals himself though his words and deeds. So I must ask, What is the revelatory truth in this story? What is the timeless statement that God is making through this account? Too often, we simply tell the story and then give "four practical lessons for daily life."

What's wrong with finding "four practical lessons" from the text?

It's doubtful the original author thought in terms of "four practical lessons." Instead, his mind was preoccupied with the single, central theological truth revealed by the event. The morals we draw from the text are usually derived from small peripheral statements that were never intended to stand on their own as timeless truths. Further, in our sermons these morals are usually unconnected to each other. They emerge as miscellaneous, disconnected observations. The sermon thus lacks a central and powerful focus. In the past, this is what the best evangelical preachers have done because that's all they knew. Fortunately, we're getting more good commentaries that orient us to theology of the text.

Speaking of commentaries, what commentaries or books have helped you the most in preaching biblical narrative?

Brevard Childs's commentary, *The Book of Exodus*, was eye opening. This was my first exposure to a commentary which understood that narrative communicates theology. Allen Ross, an evangelical, does a good job identifying the theology communicated by the text in *Creation and Blessing*, his commentary on Genesis. J. P. Fokkelman's four-volume series, *Narrative Art and Poetry in the Books of Samuel*, has helped me tremendously, too. I am currently reading through it again in my devotional time. In the New Testament Gospels,

Darrell Bock's recent two-volume set, *Luke*, in the Baker Exegetical Commentary series is also excellent.

Do you study the Hebrew text or consult Hebrew tools when preparing your sermons?

Yes. I use an interlinear Hebrew text, along with BDB [*Hebrew and English Lexicon of the Old Testament* by Francis Brown, S. A. Driver, and C. A. Briggs] and Bruce Einspahr's *Index to Brown, Driver, and Briggs Hebrew Lexicon* (Chicago: Moody, 1976). Then, I use the best exegetical commentaries available. These resources help me pick up on literary clues—such as chiasmus or the repetition of key words—that point me to the theology of the text.

Could you give us an example of how using the Hebrew Bible and tools helped you understand the text?

The other day, I was studying the text of 1 Samuel 15 and noticed how the term "voice" threads itself through the story. It appears in verses 1, 14, 19, 20, 22, and 24. If I had not used the Hebrew text, I would have missed the reference in verse 14 when Samuel says, "What then is the voice of sheep in my ears? What is this voice of cattle that I hear?" The major English translations simply render this as "bleating" or "lowing." This literary clue is important, because the meaning of the story turns on the word "voice." In the end, God rejects Saul for listening to the "voice" of the people instead of listening to the "voice" of God.

Are your sermons primarily inductive or deductive when you preach from narrative?

Either. It just depends on what's best for the passage. In an inductive sermon, the speaker asks a question and then lets the unfolding message answer it. This sustains the listener's interest. But deductive sermons can also work well as long as listeners come up with their own questions after hearing the deductive truth stated early. If they have questions such as, "Is that really true?" or "Does that have a bearing on my life?" their interest can be similarly sustained. Though they know "your" truth, they wonder if you will answer "their" questions.

Do you preach without notes?

Yes, almost always.

How do you remember everything when you preach without notes?

First, I make sure I have a clear outline so that the broad strokes of the sermon stay easily in my own head. Next, I write out a sermon manuscript. To the extent that I sweat over the wording in my preparation, that wording will tend to stick in my mind. Finally, I mentally rehearse the sermon as many times as possible. If I'm not sitting on the platform during the worship service, I will review my manuscript, or at least the broad strokes of the message, in the last few minutes before I go up. Hopefully, as I go up to preach, the sermon is fresh in my mind. Though I don't take up any manuscript or any notes, I find that 80 to 85 percent of what I've written comes through in my preaching.

What are the challenges you face in preaching a first-person narrative?

As I mentioned earlier, the main challenge is to communicate the author's theological point rather than simply performing a drama with a moral tacked on at the end. As in any narrative literature, our first task is to pin down the theology that the story communicates. A second challenge is to decide which character(s) will convey the events of the story. You can use a main character or a minor character who is a witness to the events in the story. You can even use someone who is not mentioned in the story but would have been present. A third challenge is how to communicate the application. How will the listeners perceive the relevance of the story for their lives? Finally, it's important not to use this form too often just because it is interesting and captivating for the listener. Don't use it when another form will get across the truth more effectively.

How often do you use the first-person narrative form?

Once every five months or so. I had to learn not to do it more often.

Please elaborate on application. How can you put application in a character's mouth without it sounding awkward or trite?

Sometimes, you can have the character say, "What I did was no different than when you. . . ." Then you describe the modern issue. Or you can use a more subtle way to get the listener to think of application, such as a linguistic clue. I did this in my sermon on David and Mephibosheth. I used the expression "Son of David" to get people thinking forward to Jesus' willingness to seek out his enemies, lift them up, and restore their inheritance. This approach requires you to drop in little clues throughout the sermon. For example, I referred to David's dream in order to point people to the future. If I'm preaching to an audience that is not biblically literate, I may have someone read a New Testament passage beforehand that identifies Jesus as the Son of David. A third way of doing application is evangelistically. If the events of the narrative lend themselves to salvation, the character can explain the Gospel. For example, a Christmas shepherd could reflect on how his lambs died in the temple sacrifices to postpone sin, but this "Lamb" will die to take away sin.

Do you ever use a costume or props when you preach a first-person narrative?

No. There's an obvious audience-interest value in doing that. But I don't have any drama training, and I don't want to wear a bathrobe! The main reason I don't put on a costume, however, is because it might cause the listener to think, "Our pastor is acting, and maybe this happened a long time ago, but it doesn't happen today." Twenty-first century garb says, "Our pastor is still preaching." Preaching in your normal attire also allows you to use language and events of the twenty-first century. This gives a contemporary feel to the message. Though I don't dress in costume, I'm very likely to use a prop if it fits the message. For example, when I'm preaching from Pilate's perspective, I typically use a bowl of water and a towel. If I'm Jonah, I'm sitting on an elevated platform, overlooking Ninevah from a hill, waiting for God to destroy it.

Good preachers exegete their culture as well as the text. How do you stay in touch with our changing culture?

I read a newspaper every day and *Newsweek* every week. I also read *Reader's Digest*, as well as a half-dozen other publications to which our family subscribes. I also listen to the news as I drive to work. I like to take men out to breakfast and lunch to find out what's going on in their world. I made this a regular routine in my pastoral ministries. Finally, having five children helps! I listen to them to stay in touch with the younger generation.

18

✿✿✿✿✿

THE HIGH COST OF LAMB

✿✿✿✿✿

A Sermon by Paul Borden
on 2 Samuel 11–12

Foreword

If someone compiled a list of the top ten Bible stories used by preachers, the story in 2 Samuel 11–12 would stand near the top. Preachers gravitate to the David-Bathsheba story. However, not every sermon handles this story well. Paul Borden's sermon is a happy exception. It embodies what a sermon from an Old Testament narrative should be like.

Paul Borden has had a distinguished career as a player-coach in the field of Old Testament narrative preaching. As a player, he has served as preaching pastor at Bear Valley Church in Denver, Colorado. As a coach, he taught preaching with Haddon Robinson at Denver Seminary. Borden also served as academic dean and vice president of Denver Seminary. Currently, Borden serves as a church growth consultant for the American Baptist Churches of the West. He earned a Th.M. degree at Dallas Theological Seminary and a

Ph.D. in higher education administration from the University of Denver. He contributed a chapter on preaching Old Testament narrative, titled "Is There Really One Big Idea in That Story?" in *The Big Idea of Biblical Preaching*.

Sermon Manuscript

Most of us remember the great sins of history. We recall that Brutus killed Caesar, that Henry VIII killed Thomas More so he could marry Anne Boleyn, and that Benedict Arnold betrayed his country. We remember the assassination of Abraham Lincoln by John Wilkes Booth, the kidnapping of the Lindbergh baby, and the serial killers of our own time. Somehow these major events seem to stick in our minds. They are the sins we remember.

I find that when I talk to people both in and outside the church, they also remember the great sins of the Bible. They remember that Adam and Eve disobeyed God, and God put a curse on the earth. I must admit that every time I have to mow my lawn I get angry that Adam sinned! We remember how Aaron created the golden calf and how Israel celebrated a drunken orgy around that idol. We think of Belshazzar's feast—the night he took the vessels that had been seized from the temple in Jerusalem and then basically blasphemed God. We think of Peter's denial and Judas's betrayal. But when it comes to the great sins of the Bible, there is one that gets remembered the most. I want to talk to you about this event.

About a year before this event occurred, David and his commander in chief, Joab, had begun to fight a major war that almost cost them the nation. In fact, when you read Psalm 60, David describes the nation like a boxer that is up against the ropes and has taken too many blows. We are not sure whether he is going to stand or even win the match. You see, Israel had fought a two-front war. Joab had taken half of the army and gone one direction, and David had taken the other half and gone the other direction. Because of God and because of the ability of Joab and David as generals, Israel came out victorious. Winter set in, and the fighting stopped. In those days, armies did not fight in the winter. Then spring came. David said to Joab, "We have some mopping up operations to do. I want you to take the army out and begin to finish the battle we really won last fall."

One day, after hard work running the affairs of state, David went up to the roof of the palace. Perhaps, as other kings, he had gardens up there. It would be cool, a place to rest and to relax. And since the palace was built on a high part of the city, he could look two or three blocks all around the palace and see the homes where people lived. As David walked along the roof that night, he looked down into a courtyard and saw by the cistern a beautiful woman taking a bath. He liked what he saw, and so he sent to find out who the woman was.

When word came back that she was Bathsheba, David knew her. After all, Uriah, her husband, was one of the leading men in his army. Uriah and Bathsheba probably had been at state dinners. They had attended palace parties. David had probably seen Bathsheba close up, not only at a distance. So he called for her. That night she came and snuck into the palace, and David and Bathsheba slept together. She went home early in the morning and nothing happened for several months, until one day when a messenger arrived at the palace with a personal message for David's eyes only. When David opened the message, he learned that Bathsheba was pregnant and that she had not slept with anyone else because her husband had been away fighting a war.

I imagine that when David read that message, his heart turned to stone. You see, he understood that under the law of Israel both he and Bathsheba were to be executed. They had committed a capital offense—adultery.

David sent word to Joab who was out mopping up the battle left over from the year before, and he said, "Send Uriah back and let him bring a report of what's been happening on the battlefield."

So Uriah came back to the palace and gave David his report. That night, David said, "Uriah, would you please stay until I can compose a message for your commander. I'll send you back tomorrow." Of course, David hoped that Uriah would go down and sleep with his wife. Several months later, when the baby was born, they could pin that child on her husband, Uriah. But Uriah didn't sleep with his wife that night. In fact, he slept with the servants. The next morning when David asked why, he said, "Well, I can't go home and enjoy my marriage bed when my men are sleeping in tents."

So David said, "Uriah, you need to stay another day. I need to gather more data to send back to Joab." And that night he threw a banquet at the palace. He made sure that the wine flowed freely, he made sure that the servants constantly filled Uriah's glass. Uriah became drunk that night, and of course, David hoped that in that drunken state he'd go home and sleep with his wife. But Uriah did not. So the next morning, Uriah received a message to take back to his commander in chief. He didn't realize it, but this message literally carried his own death warrant. For you see, David had given Joab instructions to plan a strategy in battle that no wise general would ever plan. When he returned to the battle, Uriah was to take a handful of men and lead an attack against the city they were trying to take. He was to go in close to the wall with the support group behind them. What a poor military strategy! As the warriors came close to the wall, people standing on the wall could shoot arrows, throw spears, and even drop rocks. They could easily kill the defenseless men who were down at the base of the wall.

Joab went ahead with the plan, and Uriah and the other soldiers were killed. So Joab wrote back to David and told him what had happened. David sent a reply back and said, "That's the way it is in war. Sometimes you live, sometimes you die."

The period of mourning ended for Bathsheba, and David took her into his harem. She lived in the palace, and a few months later the baby was born. David probably assumed he had covered over the problem of the adultery. Even though a few servants could probably count the months on their fingers and not make it to nine, David figured that the sin had been covered.

One day Nathan the prophet asked for an audience with King David. And as he stood before the king, he said, "I have a story to tell you. In our land there is a very rich farmer. He has flocks and herds and more money than he knows what to do with. One day a guest came to visit him and stayed for dinner. Instead of taking one of his own sheep and killing it for dinner, the rich man went down the road to the place of a poor farmer who had only one sheep. In fact, this sheep had become the household pet. The rich farmer took that sheep, tore it away from the poor man, took it back and killed it, and served it to his guest."

When David heard that, he stood up from his throne and said, "That man has shown no pity. He must be destroyed, and he must pay."

Nathan looked at David and said, "David, that's you. You're the man. What you did to Uriah and with Bathsheba is exactly what I've been talking about." David's sin was exposed by Nathan that night.

But I would submit to you, that behind this event which changed the life of David, and behind all the sins that went with it—the sins of treachery and lying and murder and adultery—behind all these sins there was a greater sin. In fact, it is the sin that you and I are tempted to commit. Often we look at the story of David and Bathsheba and say, "That has no relevance to me. I've never committed adultery. I've thought about murder, but I don't think I will carry it out."

God said to David, "Your life will be changed because behind the murder, behind the adultery, behind the lying, there's a greater sin." In fact, if you look at 2 Samuel, everything David does from chapters one through ten turns to gold. And everything he does from chapters thirteen through the end of the book turns to dust because of what happened in 2 Samuel 11–12.

In fact, we have to ask why was this sin so different, because David had committed great sins before this. In 1 Samuel, David had lied, and because of his lie, all the priests except one had been killed. David said, "It was my fault." Also in 1 Samuel, David had left the land when God had told him to stay, and for sixteen months he lived by his own wits as a liar and a con man. God punished him, but not like he did after 2 Samuel chapters 11–12. You see, behind the murder, behind the adultery, behind the lying, behind the treachery there was a greater sin that David committed.

To see what that sin is, I would like you to turn with me to 2 Samuel 12:9. This is what Nathan says to David: *"Why did you despise the word of the LORD by doing what is evil in his eyes? You struck down Uriah the Hittite with the sword and took his wife to be your own. You killed him with the sword of the Ammonites; now, therefore, the sword will never depart from your house, because you despised me and took the wife of Uriah the Hittite to be your own. This is what the LORD says: 'Out of your own household I am going to bring calamity upon you. Before your very eyes I will take your wives and give them to one who is close to you, and he will lie with your wives in broad daylight. You did it in secret, but I will do this thing in broad daylight before all Israel.'"*

First, notice that Nathan didn't separate the sins. He didn't see it as the sin of murder and the sin of adultery and the sin of lying and the sin of treachery. He said, "It's just one big package."

Second, notice that he says, "In committing this package of sins you despised me. You despised my word. Because of that, your children will kill each other. Your own son will plan a coup and will kill many of your best men. And your own son will take your wives and your concubines, and he'll put them in a tent on the palace roof. And one by one he'll go in and sleep with them, because you despised me and you despised my word."

That's an interesting statement. Here's David who wrote many of the Psalms and who wrote the Word of God himself. How did David despise God and his Word? Look with me at verse 7: *Then Nathan said to David, "You are the man! This is what the LORD, the*

God of Israel, says: 'I anointed you king over Israel, and I delivered you from the hand of Saul. I gave your master's house to you, and your master's wives into your arms. I gave you the house of Israel and Judah. And if all of this had been too little, I would have given you even more.'"

Notice what God is saying: "David, I took you and made you king. David, I gave you might. David, I gave you an army. David, I even gave you a harem. I gave you everything. And you know what, David? You weren't happy with what I gave you. You wanted what I hadn't given you, and you went after it ruthlessly. David, do you despise my grace? Do you despise my grace? To go after that which is not yours, that which I haven't given you to make it your own, it will change your life."

Have you ever gone to a wedding in the summertime? You are standing there at the reception. The bride and groom are up front, and people are laughing and talking and having a good time. Somebody from a distance has come to the wedding, someone you don't know. As this well-groomed man or beautifully dressed lady walks into the room, you notice this person is dressed in white. The man has on a white suit and white shoes and white tie. Or the lady has on a nice white dress and white shoes. Everyone turns as they walk through the room. And as they go by you, you notice that right on the back of the suit coat or on the back of the dress is a big black spot. When you go home, what do you talk about? You don't talk about how great the tie looked. You don't talk about how great the dress looked. All you focus on is, "Didn't they know they had that black spot? What did they do, did they rub up against something? Why didn't somebody tell them?" All you can talk about is that black spot.

That's often the way life is. We don't talk about who we are and what we have. Sometimes, all we ever think about are the black spots. We talk about what we don't have. We forget all the things God has given us and just focus on what we don't have. Commercials reinforce these feelings of inadequacy. Every Christmas, Radio Shack tells you that if you don't buy your child that thousand-dollar computer, she's not going to make it in life.

When our first son was born, he was over ten pounds. When I first saw this hunk of a child, my first thought was, "I've got to feed him for the next eighteen years!" My second thought was, "Ten pounds . . . he's going to be a quarterback. He's going to hit some home runs. He's going to score the winning basket." I couldn't wait for the day that my son said, "Dad I want to play Little League. Dad I want to go to football practice. Dad I want to play basketball." But after one year of Little League, he said, "Dad, I think I want to play the trumpet." Then our daughter came along, eight pounds, long and thin. And I thought, "Gymnast, volleyball, basketball player." But she decided to be in the color guard. If it hadn't been for a wise mother, I would have missed the gifts and talents God gave my children. Because he didn't give them the gifts and talents I wanted, all I could focus on were the black spots. What they didn't do, what they couldn't do, what they didn't want to do. I'll never forget the night I stood on the floor of Mile High Stadium in Denver. It was my son's senior year. He played and won the state championship for band, and I had tears in my eyes. I was so proud of my son, but I almost missed it.

You see, God in his grace often gives us good gifts. But because we focus on the black spots, because we're taught to be dissatisfied, because we're taught to be competitive, we often only want what it is that we don't have. The Scripture tells us to be satisfied with what we have. I don't know if you have thought about what that means, but imagine taking all the stuff you own—your house, your cars, your clothing, your ranch, your machinery, your toys, your television sets, your appliances—and putting it all out on a big field and drawing a circle around it. God says, "Whatever's inside the circle, be content with it." Now that doesn't mean you can't acquire things outside the circle if you have the means to secure them. But it means you don't spend your life saying, "I want a house like they have. I want a car like they have. I want my ranch to be like that person's ranch. I want to have the implements they have. I want to wear the clothes they wear."

If that's what we focus on, the day will come when we ignore the grace of God and we will go after that which God in his grace has not given us. David's life was changed. God said, "I've given you a kingdom, I've given you might, I've given you power, I've even given you wives. If you had wanted more, I would have given it to you. But David, you went after that which was not yours to have." Friends, when you commit that sin, God says, "It despises my grace."

Now after hearing this, some of you are thinking, "Oh, I feel so bad. Paul you've done a good job making me feel guilty. What do I do about it?" I want you to notice what David did. Look with me, in verse 13, at what happens when Nathan finishes speaking: *Then David said to Nathan, "I have sinned against the LORD." Nathan replied, "The LORD has taken away your sin. You are not going to die. But because by doing this you have made the enemies of the*

LORD *show utter contempt, the son born to you will die."* In other words, he's saying, "David there must be payment, and the payment will be that the baby will die. But even though you committed adultery and premeditated murder—both capital offenses—you won't die."

Now I don't know why God did that. I think some of it had to do with David's response. Every time in Scripture when God confronts him, David doesn't make excuses. David doesn't say, "I'm sorry God. Let me tell you about my background. Let me tell you about my upbringing. Let me tell you about how abused I was as a child. Let me tell you that I'm codependent." David never did that. Every time God says, "David, you're wrong," David replies, "God, you're right. I am wrong. Forgive me." When we take that position, that's when God can be merciful. David said, "God, I throw myself into your hands. You're right, I'm wrong." God said to David, "When you take that approach, I will be merciful. You will not die."

Several years ago, I was in California and was going to speak at a church. The pastor of the church at that time was on the board of Denver Seminary. I really wanted a day to myself, so I took some time off before I met with this pastor on Saturday. On Saturday evening, while we were having a conversation, he asked me about some things I had done. I answered him, but I didn't want him to know that I had just taken the day off. On Sunday afternoon, when I got on the plane and was flying back to Denver, a thought struck me: "Paul, when this pastor asked you if you'd done this, this and this, you said yes when really you hadn't. That's a lie."

I thought, "Now wait a minute, God. Seminary professors don't lie. I didn't lie. I mean, I didn't tell him everything, but I didn't lie."

And God said, "Yes, you lied." And for about the next month, every morning when I woke up, God said, "When you met with that man you lied to him."

"Oh no, God, I didn't lie. Will you get it straight?! I just didn't tell him everything."

"No, Paul, you lied to him."

Finally, I couldn't stand it any more. One morning I walked into my office, waited until he'd be in his office, and I picked up the phone. I got Tom on the line and said, "Tom, do you remember when I was at your house about a month ago."

He said, "Yes."

"Do you remember on Saturday night you asked me this, this, and this?"

He said, "Yes."

"Remember I told you this, this, and this. Well, I lied. I did something else."

Tom said, "Oh, okay, good."

I said, "What do you mean?"

He said, "It's nice to know somebody else lies. I forgive you."

I hung up the phone and I never felt so good. That's what God wants! God is looking for men and women who will come to him and admit they have forgotten his grace. God is looking for men and women who will say, "God, you are right, I'm wrong."

David was forgiven, but in the process he learned a hard lesson. David and Bathsheba's baby got sick. David began to weep and pray and fast. He was praying that somehow God would spare the baby. When the baby died, the servants were so afraid that they said, "David is in such an emotional, fragile condition that we can't tell him his baby died." But when David heard the news, he got up, washed his face, quit praying, quit crying, and asked for something to eat. The servants said, "This doesn't compute. Why now, since the baby died, are you acting normal?"

Notice David's response in chapter 12, verse 22: *He answered, "While the child was still alive, I fasted and wept. I thought, 'Who knows? The LORD may be gracious to me and let the child live.' But now that he is dead, why should I fast? Can I bring him back again? I will go to him, but he will not return to me." Then David comforted his wife Bathsheba, and he went to her and lay with her. She gave birth to a son, and they named him Solomon. The LORD loved him; and because the LORD loved him, he sent word through Nathan the prophet to name him Jedidiah.*

Notice David's statement, "I prayed and asked God to be gracious and let the child live." And when God wasn't gracious, when the child died, David said, "That's okay; I've come to learn that I can accept the grace of God. When God gives me good gifts, I'll accept them. And when God doesn't give me a good gift, that's okay too." David learned to trust the gracious gifts of God.

When I pastored a church in Trenton, New Jersey, I made friends with a man who is still my friend today. He had only two years of college, but before I got to Trenton, he got a job with IBM. He started out at the bottom. But as IBM was growing, he progressed through the ranks. After I left Trenton, I still kept in touch. Often I asked him, "Bill, how is it going?" He'd tell me about this promotion and that promotion and about how he liked his work. One day, he told me that he had now reached a new level in the company. He was proud that he had reached this level even though he didn't have a college degree. Six months later I was visiting Bill, and I asked him how his new position was going. He said, "Oh, I don't have that anymore."

I asked, "Why not?"

He said, "Well, Paul, when I got this new promotion, I didn't realize that they wanted more than extra hours. They wanted my soul. They wanted me there on Saturdays, Sundays, and at nights. Oh, they paid me well, but they wanted me to give my soul to the company. So about three months ago, I went into my boss and said, 'Is it possible for me to go back to the position I had before this promotion?' My boss thought I was crazy, and he said, 'Don't you realize that if you go back to that position you'll never be promoted again? Oh, you'll have job security, but you'll never be promoted again.' I said, 'Yes I understand that. I enjoy working for IBM, but I also enjoy my family. I enjoy my daughter. I'm also involved in our church, and I have commitments and responsibilities there. I'm not going to sacrifice my family or my commitment to Jesus Christ and the church so I can make more money with IBM.' My boss said, 'I don't understand it, but I'll work it out.' So about two months ago I went back to my old position. Now, I put in my forty hours and I come home. I have time for my family, I have time to be involved in the church, and I have time to be what God wants me to be."

That's a man who understands the grace of God. God in his grace had given him a family. God had given him responsibilities in the church. God had given him a good job. He was not so dissatisfied with his lot in life that somehow he had to sell his soul to the corporation.

David's life was changed when he sinned by taking Bathsheba as his wife and killing her husband, because he despised the grace of God to go after that which was not his. The good news is that God forgave him. And David learned that when the baby died, God saw fit at that point not to be gracious. But it was okay with David. He would focus on the good gifts God had given him.

There's a military general who served his God well. He served his commander in chief well, and he served his nation well. In the midst of war, his chief executive said, "Would you come back and give us intelligence reports?" Then, when this general did it, his commander in chief told him to take some R and R.

But he refused. He said, "I can't." And when the chief executive asked him why he couldn't take some R and R, this is what the general said: "The ark and Israel and Judah are staying in tents, and my master Joab and my lord's men are camped in open fields. How could I go to my house to eat and drink and lie with my wife? As surely as you live, I will not do such a thing."

If anyone understood the grace of God, it was Uriah. He was no summer soldier. He had seen men die. He had seen men wounded. But he understood that when God called him to be involved in battle, that was his job. He knew that he could not go back and enjoy that which was not his to enjoy. And it cost him his life. But in 2 Samuel 11–12, in God's eyes, the hero is Uriah. He was a man who understood that he needed to be happy with what God in his grace had given him at that time in his life, and not to go after that which was not his to have. David failed. Uriah was the hero.

Afterword

In this sermon, Paul Borden does more than retell the story. However, he doesn't do anything less. He retells the story well, painting vivid pictures that help listeners see the various scenes. He also weaves in modern illustrations and images. The "black spot" image sticks in listeners' minds and helps them remember how they often look at what's missing in their lives. Towards the end of the sermon, the story about the IBM worker provides a tangible example of what the text looks like when fleshed out in a believer's life. Even though the listeners' circumstances differ from the illustration, enough connections exist to help listeners figure out how to apply the truth to their unique situation.

The sermon unfolds inductively. That is, Borden shapes the sermon so that the big idea surfaces at the end. The big idea of the sermon is, *Believers must learn to accept what the grace of God has given them and what the grace of God has not.* Borden outlines the sermon like this:

Introduction
I. God punishes David severely for committing a sin greater than murder and adultery (11:1–12:12).
II. God forgives David because he faces his sin head-on (12:13).
III. (*Big idea*) David learns to accept what the grace of God gives him and what the grace of God does not (12:14–25).
Conclusion

When you go back and read Borden's introduction, you find that it simply introduces the first move in the sermon—David's sin of adultery and murder. It does not tip off readers that the sermon will eventually talk about learning to accept God's grace. This is typical of an introduction to an inductive sermon. It may introduce only the first move, not even the subject of the sermon.

One of Borden's most strategic decisions is to return to Uriah at the end of the sermon to contrast his conduct with David's. Borden could have commented on the contrast between Uriah and David at the moment in the story when Uriah refused to enjoy the company of his wife. He could have said, "Now you'll notice that Uriah is handling things exactly the opposite of how David handled them." Instead, Borden saves this comparison between the two men for the end of the story. This makes the comparison more dramatic. In the end, although David is the story's main character, Uriah emerges as the hero.

Preachers who work with large blocks of text have to strike a balance between summarizing some parts of the story and reading other parts directly from the text. Because the story Borden preaches covers two chapters, he tells much of it in his own words. Then, he asks the reader to look at key statements in the text.

Interview

Paul, what do you find most difficult about preaching Old Testament narratives as compared to other literary genres in the Bible?

To be honest, I find it easier than preaching some other literary genres because I've been preaching Bible stories for quite a few years. When I first started, it was more difficult. The difficulty was making a consistent theological transfer from the Old Testament context and God's expectations then to New Testament church issues today. The challenge is to find the eternal theological principle in the Old Testament story rather than using the story to illustrate a New Testament theological truth. There are theological constructs in Old Testament narratives that you may not get in the New Testament Epistles.

Could you give an example of a theological construct that appears in an Old Testament narrative but not in the New Testament?

Yes. In 2 Samuel 1–4, David is on hold. He still doesn't have the whole nation on board as far as his kingship is concerned. These chapters provide an interesting study on when to use power and when not to use power. David takes advantage of events but doesn't force events. In chapters 5–10, once he becomes king, he moves like a knife through butter. He exercises power in line with his authority as king. I don't know any place else in Scripture where there's such a study on when to use and not to use power.

What other difficulties do you face in making a consistent theological transfer from the Old Testament story to New Testament theology?

In some areas of life, God works much differently. For example, in Deuteronomy 28–30, God basically says, "Obey and I'll bless you; disobey and I'll crush you." It's just the opposite in the New Testament. God attracts people through suffering rather than prosperity. So I have to wrestle with how to preach a theological message that says, "When people obey, God blesses them richly; when they disobey, God will crush them." I cannot simply say, "If you do x, y, and z, here's what God will do for you." You can't say, "Obey God, and you will come out of the fiery furnace alive."

Where have you preached this sermon on 2 Samuel 11–12?

I've used it in several contexts, especially in Bible conferences. I use it a lot at men's retreats.

What kind of response have you received?

The one comment I consistently get relates to the whole idea of despising God's grace. People apply this in a lot of different directions. Some will say, "I didn't realize God's grace in giving me this family or my wife." Others apply it in terms of ministry. They've learned to look at more than the black spots of life. The story in 2 Samuel 11–12 has been used to put people on a horrible guilt trip, but this sermon gives people hope.

Do you use Hebrew or consult Hebrew tools when preparing your sermons?

No, I don't read the Hebrew text; but I use the best commentaries based on the Hebrew text. In a sense, then, I'm trusting their work. God has given the church a number of teachers with skills in Hebrew exegesis. Unfortunately, not all of them give useful data. They tend to focus on issues of history and grammar, but they don't always look at the flow of the narrative and how it communicates theology.

Are your sermons primarily inductive or deductive when you preach from narrative?

They are almost always inductive. In fact, 98 percent of the sermons I preach, period, are inductive. You almost have to preach inductively in narrative because that's how stories usually communicate.

Do you preach without notes?

Yes, I preach without notes, and I preach without a pulpit.

How do you remember everything when you preach without notes?

First, I develop the sermon based on plot. Plot is a memory aid for me. If I know how I will develop the disequilibrium and move to reversal, I don't need notes. I remember Haddon Robinson standing in front of our homiletics class, holding up some connected Tinkertoys as an illustration, and saying, "For every sermon, you should create an abstract design. You should say, 'This is what I want to do first, second, etc.'" He used the connected Tinkertoys to illustrate the movement from one thought unit to the next. Second, the biggest key is to write, write, write. The more you write, the more you remember. I tend to write extended outlines rather than full manuscripts. The key is, I prepare my exegetical and homiletical outlines in complete sentences. If you don't put your outline points in complete sentences, you will not think in complete thoughts. Finally, I preach a new sermon out loud by myself a minimum of three times. I have never memorized a sermon. That's not my purpose. Rather, the repeated reading causes my mind to retain what I have prepared.

Your sermon is creative. How do you stimulate your creativity?

I am a firm believer in working on the creative cycle. This means doing my exegetical work and my thinking well ahead of time. Then I take time to reflect. I need the lag time for my mind to work. So I counsel preachers to work one or two weeks ahead. I did this when I served as preaching pastor at Bear Valley Church in Denver. Also, you need a courage to break paradigms. Break paradigms with the mentors you respect highly, not necessarily because they were wrong but because something else may fit you better. You are a different person.

As a preacher committed to exegeting your audience as well as the text, how do you stay in touch with our changing culture?

I've come out of the closet when it comes to the media. I watch television. I go to movies, read novels, read *Sports Illustrated* and *Newsweek*, and read books by people who interpret what's going on in our culture. For example, I recently read *Deep Change* by Robert Quinn who teaches at the University of Michigan Business School. He argues that organizations in the twenty-first century have one of two choices: slow painful death or deep painful change. You have to read, watch, and then come back and reflect. My wife and I recently watched a Broadway show, *Tap Dogs*, and left saying, "We went to a Gen X play." They took an old medium, tap dancing, and communicated through a Gen X format.

Do you ever use the first-person narrative form when preaching an Old Testament narrative?

Yes. I've done a lot of first-person narratives in my years of preaching. In fact, my wife Teresa and I recently did the story of David and Abigail as a first-person narrative. However, I have to say that I prefer third-person sermons. I take the role of the storyteller, somewhat like Mark Twain did. That means I can jump back and forth between characters and even jump in and out of first person. It gives me more flexibility. When I do brief application at end of a third-person sermon, it's not such a sharp jolt as in a first-person sermon.

What other challenges make first-person narratives demanding?

First, it takes more preparation. I always do a plot line and a full manuscript when I do a first-person narrative. Second, it's a challenge to cover parts of the story in a way that is legitimate for the character who is telling the story. Third, I have to find humor in the sermon that is not anachronistic. It's so easy to jump to the twenty-first century to be funny rather than finding the legitimate humor in the story. I'm talking about an approach that resembles a production of Shakespeare's *Julius Caesar* in which a clock rings rather than strikes. It may get some laughs, but it really detracts from the story. Fourth, it's more difficult to share application from the viewpoint of a character in the story without sounding corny.

How often do you use the first-person narrative form?

I used to tell my homiletics students that four times a year is stretching it. Probably a couple of times provides the optimum effect without overdoing it.

Do you ever use a costume or props when you preach a first-person narrative?

I have done everything from no props to complete costumes. If you use a costume, you better make sure you work on it so it looks authentic. Your costume does not need to be elaborate. Twice, I've done angels and used a white baptismal robe and bare feet. These costumes were simple yet effective. On the other hand, I did a sermon as King David with a full robe and crown. I rented this at a costume rental place whose market consisted of people in theatrical productions. Just make sure your costume doesn't get in the way.

What books have helped you the most in preaching biblical narrative?

On the preaching side of the task, I've learned a lot from Eugene Lowry's work *The Homiletical Plot*, and from his subsequent book, *Doing Time in the Pulpit*. These books help preachers develop a narrative, plot-based style of preaching. This style works the best in expository sermons from Old Testament narratives.

19

❀ ❀ ❀ ❀ ❀

Our Fathers Who Are on Earth

❀ ❀ ❀ ❀ ❀

A Sermon by Haddon Robinson
on 2 Samuel 13–18

Foreword

High school band directors rarely attain notoriety, but Lawrence Fogelberg became an exception. I remember Mr. Fogelberg as a guest conductor at some of the band festivals I attended as a trumpet player in the Morton (Ill.) High School band. Occasionally, Mr. Fogelberg served as a judge at our district and state band competitions. But his fame stems from his role as a father. His son Dan paid tribute to him by writing a song. In the lyrics to "The Leader of the Band," Dan Fogelberg says of his father:

> The leader of the band is tired and his eyes are growing old,
> but his blood runs through my instrument and his heart is in my soul.
> My life has been a poor attempt to imitate the man;
> I'm just a living legacy to the leader of the band.

Unfortunately, not all father-child relationships play out so well. Few of King David's children had reasons to deliver a stirring tribute to "the leader of the land." Instead, King David had reason to deliver a stirring lament for a son he lost due to his failure as a father.

In a sermon that covers the sweep of 2 Samuel 13–18, Haddon Robinson captures the emotion of David's lament in 2 Samuel 18:33 as well as the events leading up to it. Robinson heightens the impact of this sermon by skillfully using a first-person narrative form. In the following sermon, he tells the story as King David.

Robinson is considered the dean of evangelical preachers. He currently serves as the Harold John Ockenga Distinguished Professor of Preaching at Gordon-Conwell Theological Seminary. In 1996, a Baylor University survey named him as one of the twelve most effective preachers in the English speaking world. Robinson's textbook, *Biblical Preaching: The Development and Delivery of Expository Messages*, has sold over 200,000 copies. Prior to his appointment at Gordon-Conwell Theological Seminary, Robinson taught preaching for nineteen years at Dallas Theological Seminary and served as president of Denver Conservative Baptist Seminary for eleven years. Robinson graduated from Dallas Theological Seminary with a Th.M. degree. He then earned an M.A. in sociology and speech from Southern Methodist University. Eventually, he received a Ph.D. in communication from the University of Illinois.

Sermon Manuscript

My name is David Jessison. Most folks know me simply as David. No one ever calls me Dave. I have been looking forward to this opportunity to speak to you. I have been assured that you will be a friendly audience.

When I accepted the invitation to be here, I was asked to speak to you about being a father. On that subject, I really do not have much that I can tell you. I say that with both embarrassment and grief. You see, I have been a success in almost everything I did. I made my mark in the military. In fact, when I was just a teenager I enlisted in the Israeli army and helped to win a strategic battle against our enemy the Philistines. Throughout my younger years, I won significant battles against troops that outnumbered us and almost overwhelmed us. Later I commanded an army of over 250,000 soldiers. I think it is fair to say that because of my leadership, Israel became the most dominant nation in western Asia.

But I wasn't simply a general. I had to be a statesman. I molded Israel into a nation and elevated it to its greatest power. When I came to the throne the nation was sand. When I left it was marble. Frankly, after my predecessor Saul, the country was near chaos. After my forty years as king, Israel was in her glory. For example, I instituted law courts, developed commerce with surrounding nations, appointed a superintendent of agriculture, and contributed to the arts and the culture of the nation. I organized the Levites and singers in the tabernacle. I feel I am boasting, but I do not mean to do so. Let me simply point out that historians have described my era as "the golden age of Israel."

Although a great deal has been written about my success as a soldier and a statesman, it doesn't really tell you about what I am on the inside. Believe it or not, I have the soul of a poet. I have been a singer and a musician. As a lad I learned to play on the rubaba, a rather crude musical instrument of only one or two strings. That could not hold the music in my heart. Later in my life I invented new, more elaborate instruments for my music. My music captured the many colors in my life. You know some of the songs I have composed. You have them there in the book before you. No, not the hymnbook. The Bible. I wrote as least seventy-three of what you call "psalms." You can see how those hymns express a whole range of human emotions. Some are alive with joy. Others express my struggles and doubts. Some I wrote only for myself. Others I wrote to help my people sing praise to God.

What I am trying to say in all this is that most people in my time and since have considered me a brilliant success. While some people write history and others read it, I made it. That's what God enabled me to do. Yet, what I must confess to you this morning is that I was a failure as a father.

I don't want to bore you with family history, but perhaps it could be of some help to you. At a crucial period of my life, I had an affair. It didn't seem like much when it began, but it escalated and got out of hand. In trying to cover it up, it led to deceit and later murder. Even though God forgave me for what I did, the whole thing had a dreadful effect on my family.

One of my sons, Amnon, forced himself upon his half sister, Tamar. When he had intercourse with her, he pushed her out of his life as though she were garbage. Incest and rejection devastated her. Her full brother, Absalom, came to hate Amnon, and he determined to avenge her shame. I don't need to go into the whole story, but he waited two years until at a feast he threw at harvest time he murdered Amnon. Maybe that wouldn't have happened if I had acted to punish Amnon myself. But after my own sin, I found rebuke of my sons very, very difficult.

Absalom rebelled against me. He determined to steal my throne. He had what it took to do it. He was a handsome man, strikingly handsome. He had a flowing head of hair that was the envy of men and an attraction for women. He was a charmer. He stole the hearts of the people. He promised them anything they wanted. He flattered them. He excited their imaginations. He had uncanny ability. He was one of those men who was born to be king.

He got so many people to follow him that I had to leave the capital with my army and allow Absalom and his followers to take over the city. Absalom would not rest, though, until I was destroyed and out of his way. We were headed for battle, and everyone knew it.

However the battle went, though, I knew that I could not win. If Absalom lost, he would be slain or else taken captive in disgrace. On the other hand if he defeated my forces then I would be dethroned and probably killed, and all of my hopes for our nation would be shattered. Worst of all, though, I felt I had brought this day of doom on myself.

My associates didn't share my feelings for Absalom. They looked at him as a traitor, and I'm sure they felt he was a spoiled darling of an aging king. They wouldn't let me go to the battle. They said I was too valuable to the cause. I suspect that they also felt I was too old for battle. Perhaps my generals suspected I was unstable. They knew how much I loved Absalom. I appreciated their loyalty, but they couldn't understand the anguish that filled my heart.

So they went off to the battle and left me behind. It was absolute agony to have to wait. The last words I uttered as my men departed were, "Deal gently for my sake with the young man," and "Beware that none touch the young man Absalom." I wanted to do anything I could to protect him.

The fighting itself took place in the forest of Ephraim. During the battle a tragic accident took place. My son Absalom was riding through the thick stand of trees and his head caught in the branches of one of those trees. His mule went out from under him, and he hung there suspended between heaven and earth. He was helpless. I was told later that one of the generals found him there and put three darts through my son's heart. He might as well have driven them through mine.

Of course, I didn't know what had happened. I waited eagerly for news. Two separate messengers came to bring me a communiqué. The first told me that my troops had won the strategic conflict. When I asked, "Is it well with the young man Absalom?" he avoided my question. He was too polite or he was too afraid, I guess, to cause me pain.

The second messenger, a Cushite, told me everything. The battle was won, but my son was lost. As the king, I suppose I should have been elated. After all, my kingdom was saved. The enemy was defeated. But as a father, I was devastated. The victory meant nothing. I was plunged into grief. I went up to a room over the gateway and sobbed, "O my son, Absalom, my son, my son Absalom! Would that I could have died instead of you, O Absalom, my son, my son!" I couldn't stop. I had lost my son. It was the worst moment of my life.

I can imagine how some of you are thinking. "Old man, your grief and shame were far too late." You would be right, and I couldn't blame you. But let me tell you what I have learned too late, and perhaps you can learn from me.

One thing you might learn from my experience is that children need the presence of a father. I have come to realize that our children need our personal influence. I should have known that. The most important passage in the sacred law of God declared, "Hear, O Israel: The LORD our God, the LORD is one. Love the LORD your God with all your heart and with all your soul and with all your strength. These commandments that I give you today are to be on your hearts. Impress them on your children. Talk about them when you sit at home and when you walk along the road, when you lie down and when you get up." How can you do that unless you are with them? You need to take advantage of those special moments when nothing is happening and everything is happening. A daughter or son needs the presence of a father.

Quite honestly, when Absalom was growing up, I didn't take much time with him. You see, I had a complicated family situation. I had seven wives, and in addition had concubines. I know that the law spoke against that, but that's what kings did in my time. It was a way to establish alliances. It was part of the surrounding culture. I ended up with twenty children—nineteen boys and one girl. I had all these family relationships, and I was responsible for all of them and those children beside. It was an impossible situation! No matter how much I loved my son, Absalom, I could only give him a tiny slice of my time.

That's not all. I was busy. I was busy about important matters. I had an army to direct, and I supervised a personal force of about five hundred men. Look, let's face it. I had battles to fight, treaties to negotiate, a government to organize, and a nation to govern.

Given my schedule, I couldn't take time or make time for a growing boy. I gave the responsibility to others. Yet, I could have found the time. I was in charge of my life. I should have taken the time. When Absalom was a boy, he never came to me with a broken toy; as a result, when he was a man he never came to me with a broken heart.

Look, permit me to tell you something. Time is your enemy, but it is disguised as your friend. The family is as old as creation. Before there were nations, there was the family. But *your* family is fleeting. A father has to get what he has with his children fast. You think that you'll have them forever. After all, they were there yesterday. They are there today. They will be there tomorrow. But you only have them as they are right now. Time is our enemy because we are preoccupied with ourselves. If your major concerns are your job, your opportunities, then time has gotten in its blows before you know it, and some opportunities with your children will never return.

Busyness is an escape route. I know busy. Sometimes people in your culture ask, "Can a woman combine a career with being a mother?" That's not a bad question for a man to ask himself. If you fail to ask it as I did, your son or daughter may have a broken life and you may end up with a broken heart. However you do it, give your children a place in your schedule. Children need a father's time.

But that's not enough. Merely spending time with your children is not enough. A child needs a father's example. I failed to provide that for Absalom. At a crucial time in my life and in Absalom's life, I let him down. I had an affair with Bathsheba. I tried to cover it up by having her husband—a man by the name of Uriah—killed in battle. Bathsheba had a baby as a result of our adultery. I spent a year in open, deliberate disobedience to God. Absalom couldn't have helped but know. I spent a year or more off in the far country. Absalom followed me. I returned to God and received his forgiveness, but Absalom didn't bother to return. He stayed out there in the far country.

That passage in the law that talks about spending time with your children also says something else. Something more basic. It says that what you give your heart to is what your children live with. Children need the example of a father. If you expect your children to follow your God, you have to follow him yourself. Family living seldom rises higher than family devotion. Children need to see a model of what we value. "You shall love the LORD your God with all your heart, with all your soul, and with all your strength." I lived for a short time in rebellion against the Father of the universe. I was in no position to guide my children to God.

I've rambled on long enough. I don't have much to tell you about being a good father. Maybe my experience can be of some help to you. Put first things first. Don't be a slave to a date book. Put a time in that date book to do something important with your children. Spend time with them. I know how valuable your time is. Why not give some of it to your son or daughter?

But if you're going to give your children a close association in your life, then you better give them something to model. If you're caught up in the values of your culture, your children may be better off not being around you. What you love is what you model, and what you model determines how your children respond. If you have a love for God and his Word, they need to be close to you. If you have an honest devotion to God, your children will pick it up—if they can walk along with you. Just be.

That afternoon when I learned that Absalom had been killed was the worst day of my life. As successful as I was in my public life, I had failed my son. I went to the room over the gate of the city and wept like a woman in mourning. "O my son Absalom! My son, my son Absalom! If only I had died instead of you—O Absalom, my son, my son!" I meant that. I would have gladly died for him. What I failed to do was live for him. I found that much more difficult.

Afterword

Haddon Robinson's sermon offers two lessons from King David's failure as a father. The danger with this kind of approach is that the preacher will extract lessons from peripheral items in the story. This sermon avoids that mistake because Robinson built it on careful exegesis. Basically, he looked at the events of 2 Samuel 13–18 and asked the question, *Why did Absalom rebel against David?* This question becomes the subject of an idea. The answer or complement is, *David didn't provide a good relationship or a good role model as a father.*

Robinson gains further exegetical support for this idea by turning to Deuteronomy 6:4–9, a central passage in the Mosaic law. Books like Samuel trace Israel's success or failure at keeping the law given through Moses. So Robinson explores how David failed to flesh out the commands in Deuteronomy 6:4–9 in his family life. The exegetical idea, then, is: *Absalom rebelled against David because David failed to provide a good relationship and a good role model as a father.*

When Robinson states this as a homiletical or preaching idea, he states it in positive terms: *Children need a father's presence and a father's example.*

Robinson's sermon flows smoothly because his thoughts flow smoothly. Thoughts flow smoothly when a preacher takes time to outline them. Even first-person narratives need a sermon outline to organize the progression of thought. The outline for this sermon looks something like this:

Introduction
A. David introduces himself and offers a disclaimer about his failure as a father.
B. David reviews his success as a soldier and a statesman.
I. David reviews his family history that led to his failure as a father.
A. He mentions his affair, which had a dreadful effect on his family.
B. He relates his failure to rebuke his son, Amnon, for raping Tamar.
C. He describes his grief over Absalom's rebellion and eventual death.
II. David shares what he learned from his failure as a father.
A. Children need a father's personal influence (or presence).
B. Children need a father's example.
Conclusion
A. David shares some application ideas.
B. David laments his failure to live for his son.

In the sermon, Robinson uses language skillfully. He crafts statements that leap into the minds of listeners. For example, he says, "When Absalom was a boy he never came to me with a broken toy; as a result, when he was a man he never came to me with a broken heart." Then he observes, "Time is your enemy, but it is disguised as your friend." As Robinson speaks the words of David, he uses common, earthy language, yet it never descends into profane, trite slang. The sermon's language also captures David's pathos or emotion. Robinson accomplishes this through statements like, "One of the generals found him there and put three darts through my son's heart. He might as well have driven them through mine."

Interview

Haddon, where have you preached this particular sermon?

I developed it for use at a Promise Keeper's conference in Dallas at which I was invited to speak.

What was the response?

God used it in a very singular way. A good friend of mine had doubts about how a first-person narrative would work in that setting, but he told me later that when I started preaching, the whole stadium became quiet. Men sat down and stopped going out to the concession stands. I think the sermon was effective because it was a first-person narrative, while all of the other sermons delivered at this Promise Keeper's conference used a traditional form.

What do you find most difficult about preaching Old Testament narratives as compared to other literary genres in the Bible?

I think it's more difficult to understand what the idea is behind a narrative. You're never quite sure that you've nailed it, especially when the author does not give you many editorial clues.

What are the challenges you face in preaching a first-person narrative?

One of the main challenges is how to apply the text if you're playing the part of David or Nathan or somebody else. Also, it's harder to show people where you are in the Bible. If you're telling your own story in the first person, you have a harder time pointing out that you're dealing with verse 18.

How often do you counsel your students to use the first-person narrative form?

I'd say about five times a year. If you use the form more frequently, it loses its effectiveness. Always ask, Is this the best way to get across the truth to the audience?

Do you ever use a costume or props when you preach a first-person narrative?

Usually I don't. I have used a costume a couple of times, but never a full costume. When I preached a Christmas sermon as Joseph, I used a carpenter's belt, but not a full gown. I occasionally use props to help the audience concentrate. When I preached a sermon as King Herod, I used a scepter. It was not a large scepter, but I talked about it and used it to help me gesture. I've used a shepherd's crook and even a slingshot when I preached the narrative in 1 Samuel 17. But I didn't use the slingshot to act out the event.

How do you handle application when using a first-person form?

You have to place the major application in the thrust of the narrative itself as opposed to giving people several modern application images. You rely on the overlap of the Bible character's experience with a modern person's experience. The circumstances are different, but there's a similar tension. Good playwrights do this. They will create a play that took place in the 1800s, but if they do a good job, the audience will identify with the tension the central character faces. In a first-person narrative, application has to be more subtle. It's much harder for a Bible character to say, "If I was a housewife, I would do such and such."

Do you ever step out of character at the end of a first-person narrative and give application as a twenty-first-century preacher?

On occasion, when I've preached this first-person narrative on David I have stepped out of character at the end of the sermon and offered specific application. I've paused and said, "Let's leave David for a moment." Then, I have encouraged fathers to put their children in their appointment books. I've asked fathers to tell their children "I love you." I've challenged grandparents to model loving God for their grandchildren.

Do you use Hebrew or consult Hebrew tools when preparing your sermons?

Yes. I'm not as skilled as I'd like to be, though. When I'm dealing with particular words and phrases, I look them up in a lexicon. I wish I could get the flow of the text as well as I can when I read the Greek New Testament, but I offset this limitation by comparing several English translations. It's amazing how much you can learn about the Bible when you read it in a number of different translations. Then I look at the best critical commentaries that work in the Hebrew text. I also look at Jewish commentaries. Sometimes, they get a grasp of what's going on in a way that English commentaries don't.

Are your sermons primarily inductive or deductive when you preach from narrative?

They are almost always inductive. It's the nature of stories to move towards resolution. A good story unfolds and doesn't resolve itself until the end. You could preach a deductive sermon from a narrative, though, if you arranged it like a movie that shows a murder in the opening scene. Then, the rest of the movie shows why or by whom.

Do you preach without notes?

Yes, I always preach without notes.

How do you remember everything?

I find that well-designed sermons remember themselves like a good joke remembers itself. When you hear a good joke, you don't need to pull out a three-by-five card to write it down. The details remember themselves.

How do you stay in touch with our changing culture?

I read news magazines and I look at the *New York Times* book reviews. When I'm on a plane, I'll pick up popular publications like *People* magazine. I always ask, What's going on here? I do the same when I watch television, particularly the commercials. I ask, What's going on here? What message is the commercial or show trying to get across? If I come across magazines geared for younger generations, I look at their topics and how they develop them.

How do you stimulate your ability to produce creative, descriptive wording?

I have worked at this for a number of years, so the process is much more natural. I am conscious of looking for hard nouns and vivid verbs. I shy away from adjectives and adverbs. Also, when I'm reading a novel or a well-written book, I pay attention to the way concepts are worded. I'm currently reading Tim Stafford's novel *The Stamp of Glory.* When I read authors like Stafford or Philip Yancey, I ask myself, "How did he get this point across so well?" Some of this seeps into your soul.

20

❀❀❀❀❀

WHAT DO YOU DO
WHEN THE ROOF CAVES IN?

❀❀❀❀❀

A Sermon by Alice Mathews
on Isaiah 7:1–14

Foreword

The Wal-Mart store in Bozeman, Montana seems an unlikely place to run into screen stars. Yet friends of mine have turned into an aisle and bumped into folks such as Meg Ryan, Dennis Quaid, and Michael Keaton—entertainment personalities who choose to make Montana a part-time home.

Similarly, the prophetic literature in the Old Testament may seem like an unlikely place to encounter stories, but preachers will find quite a few narratives embedded among the poetic oracles, hymns, parables, and laments in the Old Testament prophets. While studying the virgin birth prophecy in Isaiah 7, Alice Mathews discovered a compelling story. She developed the following sermon from this story contained in Isaiah 7:1–14.

Mathews currently serves as the Lois W. Bennett Distinguished Associate Professor of Educational and Women's Ministries at Gordon-Conwell Theological Seminary. She is also a cohost with Haddon Robinson and Mart De-Haan of the *Discover the Word* daily radio program produced by RBC Ministries. Other ministry experiences include serving as a pastor's wife and as a missionary with her husband Randall in France and Austria with the Conservative Baptist Foreign Mission Society. She has also held administrative positions with Denver Seminary and the Seminary of the East. After earning an undergraduate degree in piano and Bible from Bob Jones University, Mathews earned an M.A. in clinical psychology from Michigan State University and a Ph.D. in religion and social change from the University of Denver. She is the author of *A Woman God Can Lead.*

Sermon Manuscript

What kind of week have you had? Pretty good? Pretty bad? Somewhat stressful? Just plain fun? Most of us move through each week with a mixture of the pretty good and the pretty bad, the somewhat stressful and the just plain fun. Life usually comes at us that way: It's a mixed bag.

What is it that causes stress? We can often identify what causes us stress because it's the thing that wakes us up at 3 A.M. and keeps us from going back to sleep. Or it's what keeps us from focusing productively on the things we know we need to do. We all experience stress to some degree. Stress comes from that nagging concern, that gnawing worry that takes its toll on our sleep, on our concentration, and sometimes on our relationships.

Then there are also those times when life seems to give us a pounding with both fists. We feel pummeled by the worst things that can happen.

In 1994, my husband Randall and I were faced with a major decision. We had settled into retirement in Denver, Colorado, when I received a job offer from a seminary on the East Coast. We wrestled with the fact that accepting the job would mean selling our Denver house and moving far from all that was familiar to us—our friends, our family, and our church. We had lived in Denver for fourteen years, but the situation in Philadelphia seemed to be God's next step for us. So we talked. We prayed. We took two months to make the decision to move east.

We put our house on the market, and eight days later we had a contract on it—so fast that we had to move into temporary housing for two months before the major move east. Moving is stressful. If you've done it, you know what it involves. But a job change is also stressful. I found myself wondering if I'd be able to do what I was being hired to do. Would I meet the expectations of people we hardly knew?

We organized our lives from the big move east. And in the midst of the move came the phone call from France telling us that our only son had just been killed by a drunk driver. With our stateside daughters, we immediately made the long journey to France to deal with the horrible aftermath of a grisly accident.

To say that the roof had caved in on top of us feels like an understatement. The move was very stressful. The imminent job change was highly stressful. Now came the ultimate stress: the death of our only son.

I know as I stand here this morning that I am not alone in facing this level of stress. Many of you have stood at a graveside, overwhelmed by the stress of deep loss. We all live with small stresses every day, and times come when we're raked and harrowed with the pain of major stress. How do we handle such times? Where do we turn? How do we manage?

Back in 1978, two stress researchers named Pearlin and Schooler published the results of a broad research project on how people handle stress. They found that Americans tend to handle stress in one of three different ways.

Some people handle stress by changing the situation. If you're stressed by debt, you change the situation by cutting your spending to the bone until your debts are paid off. If you're stressed by a stubborn habit in your life, you practice saying no to it until the habit is altered. You do what you have to do to change any situation that causes you stress. The problem is that it's not always possible to change the situation. Some situations are beyond our control. How, for example, do you change the situation of an incurable illness or the loss of someone you love deeply?

A second way that some people handle stress is that they manage their emotions about the stressful situation. Managing our emotions means that we try to talk ourselves out of feelings we're experiencing. We try to convince ourselves that we're not angry when we are. We deny that anything is bugging us and we paste on a happy face. That's the way we try to manage our emotions about situations that cause us stress. The problem with this option is that it's very hard to maintain, and it's also not effective. It's really a bad choice, though many of us use it to cope with stress.

The third way people cope with stress, according to the researchers, is by changing the meaning of the stressful situation.

What do the researchers mean by that? What is it to change the meaning of a situation?

There's an intriguing story buried in Isaiah 7 that gives us a case study in major stress. The story is about a king named Ahaz who ruled the tiny kingdom of Judah, made up of two Israelite tribes, Judah and Benjamin. A couple hundred years earlier ten of the twelve tribes of Israel had split off as a separate nation, and the two tribes in the south became the nation of Judah, with Ahaz as its king at the time of our story.

As the narrative opens in Isaiah 7, Ahaz faces a desperate situation: two kings—Rezin from Syria and Pekah from the northern ten tribes known as Israel—have joined hands to overpower Judah. In fact, they have marched up to take Judah's capital, Jerusalem.

In Isaiah 7:2 we read, *So the hearts of Ahaz and his people were shaken, as the trees of the forest are shaken by the wind.* That's stress with a capital S. Little Judah was besieged by two much more powerful nations. The situation looked hopeless, and Ahaz had no resources with which to change the situation. He faced major stress. In fact, he was quaking in his royal sandals.

God, however, was not blind to the situation. In Isaiah 7:3–6 we see God speaking to the prophet Isaiah with a message to be delivered to the terrified king. God said to Isaiah, *"Go out, you and your son, to meet Ahaz at the end of the aqueduct of the Upper Pool, on the road to the Washerman's Field. Say to [Ahaz], 'Be careful, keep calm, and don't be afraid. Do not lose heart because of these two smoldering stubs of firewood. . . . [It's true they] have plotted your ruin, saying, 'Let us invade Judah; let us tear it apart and divide it among ourselves, and make the son of Tabeel king over it.'"*

If you think about it, it almost sounds as if God is counseling Ahaz to manage his emotions about the situation. He said, "Be careful, keep calm, and don't be afraid." Imagine how you'd feel if you had been Ahaz that day. Perhaps you'd hear him saying, "Yeah, sure, keep calm!? You can say that, but you're not about to be torn apart and divided between two cruel conquerors! This is a CRISIS. It's not time for managing my emotions about the situation!"

But this wasn't all God said to the king that day through the prophet Isaiah. He went on (in Isaiah 7:7–9): *Yet this is what the Sovereign LORD says, "It will not take place, it will not happen, for the head of Aram [Syria] is Damascus, and the head of Damascus is only Rezin. Within sixty-five years Ephraim [Israel's northern ten tribes] will be too shattered to be a people. The head of Ephraim is Samaria, and the head of Samaria is only [Pekah]. If you do not stand firm in your faith, you will not stand at all."*

That was good news for the king. God offered Ahaz an opportunity to change the meaning of this major stress in his life: he could know that Rezin and Pekah would not triumph over him. In effect, God told Ahaz, "Get some perspective on this situation, Ahaz! Your enemies aren't as powerful as they look! But Ahaz, there is one condition: if you don't stand firm in your faith, you won't stand at all."

The Bible doesn't tell us what Ahaz said or did that day, but from what follows we can make a good guess. The narrator tells us in verses 10–12, *Again the LORD spoke to Ahaz, "Ask the LORD your God for a sign, whether in the deepest depths or in the highest heights." But Ahaz said, "I will not ask; I will not put the LORD to the test."*

Note what happened here. God offered Ahaz a chance to name his terms, any terms, for proof that what he had been told was true. But Ahaz refused! Of course, he couched his refusal in pious language, saying, "I won't put the Lord to the test." But his pious language masked his lack of faith.

What followed shows us an interesting side of Isaiah who is now furious with the king for refusing God's offer. You can hear the prophet's anger in verses 13 and 14 as he responds to the faithless king: *Hear now, you house of David! Is it not enough to try the patience of men? Will you try the patience of my God also? Therefore the Lord himself will give you a sign: The virgin will be with child and will give birth to a son, and will call him Immanuel.*

All right, Ahaz. If you won't ask for a sign, you'll get one anyhow: "A virgin will be with child and will give birth to a son, and will call him Immanuel." God's sign to a quaking king was a miracle, the miracle of Immanuel—God with us. Ahaz faced a stressful situation, one he could not change by his own power. It was a situation so stressful that he couldn't manage his emotions about it either. God offered him the opportunity to change the meaning of the situation: GOD is here. God is with us. Immanuel.

What difference should Immanuel have made for Ahaz? Did he believe the Sovereign Lord that Rezin and Pekah were really nothing to worry about? It didn't look like that. But God had changed the meaning of the situation. He told Ahaz, "There's NOTHING to worry about. So get things into perspective. GOD is with you. What more do you need?"

You can't always change your situation, but Immanuel makes it possible for you to change the meaning of your situation—any situation. How does this work?

A central truth of the Bible is that the sovereign Lord, the creator of the heavens and earth, has power beyond all principalities and powers, and he uses that power for his purposes on behalf of his people.

We see this in God's deliverance of Israel out of Egypt against impossible odds.

We see it in God's intervention as Joshua fought against the five kings of the Amorites. God caused the sun to stand still in the heavens so Joshua could finish the battle.

We see it in God's help when David went out against the giant Goliath with only a slingshot and faith in the Lord.

Ahaz must have known his people's history—that the God who is greater than the surging Red Sea, even greater than the sun and moon in the heavens, and certainly greater than the great giant the Philistines could put up against Israel—that God was with Ahaz. Would that enable this king to change the meaning of his situation?

God had told Ahaz, "If you don't stand firm in your faith, you won't stand at all." Ahaz missed the meaning of the sign, and he missed the opportunity to change the meaning of his situation.

If any of us missed God's sign to Ahaz in Isaiah 7:14, none of us as followers of Jesus Christ could miss it when we read the same words again in Matthew 1:23. Here the gospel writer quotes Isaiah's prophecy verbatim in reporting the angel's conversation with Joseph about Mary's pregnancy: *Behold, a virgin shall be with child, and bear a Son, and they will call His name Immanuel, which is translated 'God with us.'*

Seven hundred years after Ahaz, Isaiah's prophecy was fulfilled in the birth of another baby, the Lord Jesus Christ. Once again the people of God were under great stress. Rome occupied and ruled their land, often with arbitrary cruelty. It had been four hundred years since the people had heard the voice of God's prophet in the land. Religion had become a series of empty legalisms and many of the leaders were corrupt.

What could it have meant to the first-century Jews that a baby was born, a baby named Immanuel—God with us? Could that new Word from God change the meaning of their situation?

From John 1:11, we learn that this baby *came unto his own, but his own received him not.*

His own—they knew the history of their people and the miracles of their God.

His own—they knew the Scriptures.

His own—they knew Isaiah 7:14.

But they did not receive him. They missed the opportunity to change the meaning of their situation.

You and I face stressful situations at the turn of the century and of the millennium. Is there a word of hope and promise for us as there was for a faithless king or a faithless people more than two thousand years ago? The gospel writer John wrote that *He [Jesus Christ, the Word] came to his own and his own did not receive him, . . . BUT as many as received him, to them he gave the right to become children of God, even to those who believe in his name.* If you and I have been joined to the family of God by faith, this promise is for US: God is with US.

Immanuel, God with us, can change the meaning of every situation if we respond in faith. That hasn't changed over the centuries. God had told Ahaz, "If you do not stand firm in your faith, you will not stand at all." First-century Jews like the seeking Pharisee Nicodemus learned from Jesus' lips that eternal life from the eternal God could not be his apart from faith in the Christ who was sent into the world as Immanuel, God with us.

Faith in the savior of the world—Immanuel, God with us—is still the prerequisite today. If we do not stand firm in our faith, we will not stand at all. When stress pummels us and we find ourselves down for the count—when everything looks hopeless—then faith in the promise of Immanuel can make the important difference.

The fact that God is with us doesn't necessarily change the situation, but it does change the meaning of the situation. No situation is ever the same if you believe that God is with you in it. But it's not enough to say, "God is with US." We must each remind ourselves that God is with ME.

Israel's greatest king, David, knew stress:

- He lost a child in death.
- Another son rebelled against him and enlisted others in a rebellion.
- He was betrayed by a close friend.
- He was chased by a jealous king and treated as an outlaw for ten long years.

Yet this king—dogged by severe stresses during much of his life—wrote a great affirmation: "The Lord is MY shepherd . . . Yes, though I walk through the valley of the shadow of death, I will fear no evil, FOR THOU ART WITH ME."

Do you believe it? Do you really believe it? God is with US. God is with ME. Whatever you go through, you can know the promise. But you must make it personal: God is with ME. The promise of God's presence changes the meaning of every stressful situation. And that reality changes the meaning of all of life. It's a fact that makes a radical difference in the living of our days.

Afterword

Suppose Alice Mathews had started her sermon by saying, "Please turn with me to Isaiah 7 and look at an interesting story about an Israelite king named Ahaz." Few listeners would have been compelled to continue listening. Instead, Mathews forms an attention grabbing introduction out of the issue dealt with in the story. When she asks listeners about their week and about the cause of stress in their lives, she creates an interest factor that compels listeners to think about the story in Isaiah 7 rather than about the roast in the oven or the football game on network television.

Specificity lends credibility to her supporting material. When she refers to research on how people handle stress, she cites the researchers by name rather than by prefacing their conclusions with a bland description like "Studies suggest that . . ." She also mentions the year when the research took place. Few, if any, listeners will check the sources you mention, but mentioning the sources verifies the credibility of your citation.

Mathews's sermon develops inductively. In other words, she end-loads rather than front-loads the big idea. The sermon unfolds in three movements. The first movement tells the story in Isaiah 7:1–14 and explores how Ahaz had the opportunity to change the meaning of his stressful situation. Then, since the Gospel of Matthew draws a connection between this story and the birth of Jesus, the second movement explores how God's people living seven hundred years after Isaiah had the opportunity to change the meaning of their stress because of the birth of Jesus. Finally, the third movement provides a full statement of the big idea and directs it to a modern audience. The sermon's big idea is, *God with us can change the meaning of any stressful situation if we respond in faith.* The outline of Mathews's sermon looks like this:

Introduction
A. We all have to live with stressful situations in life.
B. Sometimes, stress even pummels us with what seems like a knock-out punch.

   C. Stress researchers (Pearlin and Schooler) found that people cope with stress in one of three ways:
     1. Some people change the situation causing them stress.
     2. Other people manage their emotions about the stressful situation.
     3. Still others change the meaning of the situation.

  I. Ahaz faced a stressful situation and had the opportunity to change its meaning.
    A. Ahaz was under terrible stress (7:1–2).
    B. God was concerned about Ahaz's stress and sent a message through Isaiah (7:3–9).
    C. But Ahaz refused God's message, God's sign, and the hope it could bring (7:10–14).

 II. Seven hundred years later, God's people again had the opportunity to change the meaning of their stress under the tyranny of Rome.
    A. Jesus' birth brought God's people the possibility of hope (Matt. 1:23).
    B. But their lack of faith caused them to miss the opportunity to change the meaning of their situation.

III. (*Big idea*) God with us can change the meaning of any stressful situation if we respond in faith.
    A. Application: No situation remains the same when you believe God is in it with you.
    B. Example: David changed the meaning of his stress by affirming God's presence (Ps. 23).
   Conclusion: You need to make the promise of Immanuel personal (God is with me).

Mathews tells the story by reading it a section at a time and then commenting on it. However, she does this without violating the flow of the story. She weaves in her comments so that her sermon feels like a story, not just a running commentary.

Interview

Alice, what piqued your interest in Old Testament narratives?

A few years ago, I started teaching a Bible class of two-hundred-fifty women every Wednesday at a large church in Denver. During the six years prior to my ministry, the senior pastor had taught this group of ladies from didactic literature. Since he had already covered a lot of the New Testament Epistles, I began looking for stories of women in Scripture that could help women living in modern times. For the first year, I focused on women in the Old Testament—their choices and the results of those choices. I had always been taught that you cannot determine doctrine from biblical narrative, but I found this idea to be untrue.

What circumstances led you to prepare a sermon from this story in Isaiah 7?

A few years ago, I was asked to speak at a Christmas party for all of the Conservative Baptist missionaries in Colorado. The organizers wanted a sermon-length, biblical exposition—not something light. As I was reading through the various Christmas narratives, I was arrested by the statement in Matthew 1:23 that Jesus' birth fulfilled Isaiah's prophecy in Isaiah 7:14. I went back to Isaiah 7 to see the context, and the next thing I knew, I was hooked on the narrative. It is a tragic yet wonderful story. By the way, the story doesn't stop with Isaiah 7:14. It goes on into chapter eight. However, the entire story was a bit larger than I wanted to cover in one sermon.

Have you preached this sermon anywhere else?

Yes. I've used it in chapel at Gordon-Conwell Theological Seminary and Denver Seminary. I also preached it at a large Evangelical Free church in Madison, Wisconsin in their three morning services. I even preached it to the staff at Radio Bible Class when they asked me to speak in their weekly chapel.

How have people responded to the sermon?

The first time I preached it, the person who organized the Christmas party took copious notes. He said, "I'm going to preach this story myself." In every setting I've delivered it, people have responded positively because it's a practical kind of message. Listeners have been encouraged to hear that Christians have resources to help us change the meaning of our stress.

Why are Bible stories a good choice for preachers?

As Haddon Robinson says, "A story sneaks under our defenses like a stealth bomber." Haddon, Mart DeHaan, and I have just finished four years working through Jesus' parables on the *Discover the Word* radio broadcasts. I realize more than ever that when Jesus chose stories to communicate truth, he chose something that has a power most people do not realize. Stories get truth to our emotions before our minds can veto the truth. That's why I am sold on working with biblical narrative. The two books I have written for women [now published as one volume titled *A Woman God Can Lead*] deal exclusively with the stories of women in the Scriptures.

What do you find most difficult about preaching Old Testament narratives as compared to other literary genres in the Bible?

If I were working with a didactic passage, I would look for different things, like a sequence or progression of thought. I don't have that aid when I work with narrative. I have to deal with how the plot unfolds and how the characters develop. I must pay attention to these features to discover the meaning of the story. For example, several years ago I was working on a narrative message about Leah and her relationship with Rachel. I wanted to focus on Leah's difficulties as an unloved wife. If she had stopped having children after the fourth one, I had a neat message. But what she said about her fifth, sixth, and seventh babies messed up my nice idea! When I interpret a story, I must deal with people's choices, actions, and the decisions they have made. The sermon must be faithful to the text.

What books have helped you the most in preaching Biblical narrative?

Robert Alter's book *The Art of Biblical Narrative* really opened my mind to the power of narrative. Like I said earlier, studying Jesus' parables have helped me see how stories communicate truth.

Do you use Hebrew or consult Hebrew tools when preparing your sermons?

Although I have studied Greek, I have not studied Hebrew. Thankfully, my daughter graduated from Denver Seminary in Hebrew and has taught it. So I use Old Testament experts around me, like her, to guide me. I have learned to use the basic Hebrew tools such as a lexicon.

Are your sermons primarily inductive or deductive when you preach from narrative?

They are almost invariably inductive. It seems to me that narrative lends itself to discovery. If you don't tip your hand at the front end of the sermon, the audience goes along for the ride.

Do you preach without notes?

Yes, I do now. I didn't always preach without notes, but once you learn to do it, you never go back. The benefit is your contact with the audience. In the past, when I preached with a manuscript in front of me, it may have been smoother. But smoother is not always better. There are times, especially with younger audiences, when people want a sense of the humanness of the speaker. They're not looking for the perfect orator but someone with whom they can connect.

How do you remember everything when you preach without notes?

The key is to simplify your outline and prepare a manuscript. The sermon has to make sense and flow or you can't remember it.

How do you stay in touch with our changing culture?

My work is in the area of what's going on in our culture with women, so that's where I focus. This is only a single slice of culture, but it cuts across all generations. Because I am interested in sociology, my antennae are always out for cultural trends and shifts. I may pick up on these by reading a magazine article or by listening to people talk.

Your sermon is creative. How do you stimulate your creativity?

When I am preparing a sermon on a narrative, I really soak in the narrative and its context. I work inductively. I let the story get hold of me and then I think about it a lot. As I think about the story, my mind will make connections with material I've read or studied. For example, after I had spent a significant amount of time studying and thinking about Isaiah 7, I realized the connection with my studies in stress management. I didn't start with my stress management studies and then go looking for a story to fit them. It wasn't until the story took shape that I prepared the sermon's introduction.

Do you ever use the first-person narrative form when you preach Bible stories?

Yes. I've done several shorter ones—about eleven and a half minutes each—on the *Discover the Word* radio program. A couple of years ago, I was invited to speak to a Salvation Army group on a college campus. I delivered a first-person narrative sermon on John 12, the story of Mary anointing Jesus at Bethany. I told the story as Mary.

What are the challenges you face in preaching a first-person narrative?

Am I even going to pull this off convincingly? Can I be this person? It's one thing to stand outside the character, but it's another thing to tell the story from a character's viewpoint. It's a challenge to create a believable narrative without compromising the person telling her story. It's hard to figure out how to get important background pieces into this, so that the person doesn't sound egotistical. I want the character to tell the story in a way that is faithful to the biblical text and that gives the listener the relevant information and application.

APPENDIX A

❀ ❀ ❀ ❀ ❀

ADVANCED PLOT ANALYSIS

❀ ❀ ❀ ❀ ❀

This appendix may initially frighten you. It deals with the dreaded *H* word—"Hebrew." However, like the Abominable Snowman in the story of Rudolph the Red-Nosed Reindeer, Hebrew turns out to be a dependable friend rather than a dreaded enemy. Studying Old Testament narratives in the Hebrew Bible will pay big dividends to those willing to use the Hebrew text in plot analysis.

Logically, the exegetical steps described in this appendix should happen before those in chapter 3. The plot analysis steps in chapter 3 flow out of the plot analysis steps in this appendix. However, I initially withheld this material to avoid scaring you off if you do not study the text in Hebrew or if you find Hebrew intimidating. Let me make it clear: while Hebrew gives you an edge, you can still do solid exegetical work in Old Testament narrative literature without it.

If you have never learned Biblical Hebrew and do not intend to learn it now, feel free to skip this appendix. I don't want you to get stressed out by a Hebrew exegesis blizzard. However, you might skim this chapter to understand what studies in the Hebrew text can contribute. You may even decide it's worth learning. Also, the chapter may shed light on some of the concepts that the more in-depth commentaries discuss. But if you start to get bogged down, move on.

Getting Your Hebrew up to Speed

Let me offer a word to readers who find Hebrew intimidating or have let their Hebrew skills wane. Perhaps you passed Hebrew courses in seminary by the skin of your teeth. You have not cracked your Hebrew Bible since your last exam in a grammar or exegesis course. You have long since forgotten what a *dagesh forte* or a jussive verb is. I still encourage you to resuscitate your Hebrew skills. You don't have to operate at the skill level of your seminary Hebrew professors to use it. As you may recall, the easiest portions of the Hebrew Bible to read are the stories. The syntax is not complex. You probably started reading the text with portions of Genesis or with the book of Ruth.

Besides, there are better tools available today. With a computer program like Logos or Hermeneutika's *Bibleworks*, you can look at a chapter or a verse of Hebrew text and immediately identify its form. In the *Bibleworks* program that I use, placing my cursor on a Hebrew term will immediately parse it. But isn't this as naughty as using an interlinear? Your Hebrew professors had a good reason for scolding you when you consulted an interlinear. They wanted you to learn to figure out on your own that a verb is a Hiphil imperfect rather than a Qal perfect. But once you finish a seminary course, any tool that helps you move more quickly is fair game. It's better to use Hebrew in ministry with the aid of an interlinear or a computer program than to avoid Hebrew and not use an interlinear. The more you work with the language, the less you will have to rely on the crutches. Perhaps you will need to spend some time in the grammar you used in seminary, possibly Lambdin's or Weingreen's.[1] Believe me when I tell you it's worth the effort. You may want to purchase a more recent grammar by the likes of Page Kelley, C. L. Seow, Allen Ross, or Ethelyn Simon.[2] Simon's book, *The First Hebrew Primer: The Adult Beginner's Path to Biblical Hebrew,* may be the most user-friendly grammar on the market. Menahem Mansoor's grammar and a second volume of readings from Genesis both have companion audiocassettes that help learners with pronunciation.[3] Bryan Rocine's recent grammar teaches textlinguistic concepts from its start.[4]

1. Thomas O. Lambdin, *Introduction to Biblical Hebrew* (New York: Charles Scribner's Sons, 1971); Jacob Weingreen, *A Practical Grammar for Classical Hebrew,* 2d ed. (Oxford: Clarendon, 1959).

2. Page H. Kelley, *Biblical Hebrew: An Introductory Grammar* (Grand Rapids: Eerdmans, 1992); Choon Leong Seow, *A Grammar for Biblical Hebrew* (Nashville: Abingdon, 1987); Allen P. Ross, *Introducing Biblical Hebrew* (Grand Rapids: Baker, 2001); Ethelyn Simon, Irene Resnikoff, and Linda Motzkin, *The First Hebrew Primer: The Adult Beginner's Path to Biblical Hebrew,* 3d ed., rev. (Oakland, Calif.: EKS, 1992).

3. Menahem Mansoor, *Biblical Hebrew Step by Step,* 2d ed. (Grand Rapids: Baker, 1980); idem., *Biblical Hebrew Step by Step,* vol. 2: *Readings from the Book of Genesis,* 3d ed. (Grand Rapids: Baker, 1984). The companion audiocassettes for the two volumes are also published by Baker.

4. Bryan M. Rocine, *Learning Biblical Hebrew: A New Approach Using Discourse Analysis* (Macon, GA: Smyth & Helwys, 2000).

This appendix will explore the value of textlinguistic analysis in Old Testament narrative literature. Rocine's grammar allows you to learn these concepts and brush up on your Hebrew at the same time.

If you're not convinced you can learn Hebrew well enough to use it, keep reading this chapter. The type of analysis I propose does not involve tacking obscure labels onto clauses and verbs. Though there is a place for microanalysis, I intend to show you how to move quickly through the Hebrew text and distinguish between the main storyline and background statements.

If you would like to learn Hebrew but do not live close to a Bible college or seminary, check the external education departments of these institutions. Some of them may offer correspondence or on-line programs. Perhaps you can find an area pastor who knows Hebrew and would be willing to tutor you.

If you are a seminary or Bible college student who is serious about preaching, invest the time and energy it takes to learn Hebrew. While we desperately need preachers who can speak to their culture, we do not gain an edge by shaving hours from the biblical languages and replacing them with classes on relating to people. My cousin, Ed Stroup, is an emergency room doctor in Spokane, Washington. A major part of his success stems from his ability to relate to people. His gentle, even-keeled personality contributes to his excellence as a physician. But when he attended the University of Washington medical school, he didn't acquire his abilities to relate to patients by taking more "practical" courses in place of courses on anatomy, physiology, and pharmacology.

Is it too much to ask someone who plans to invest his or her life in teaching a particular document to learn the language in which that document was written? My plea is, take the time to learn or relearn Hebrew. The investment will enrich your preaching of Old Testament narratives. Let me show you how.

The Wonderful World of Text Linguistics

Several years ago, literary scholars advanced our understanding of how Old Testament narratives work. Now, Old Testament scholars working in the field of text linguistics are helping exegetes make remarkable advances. Text linguistics, or discourse analysis, is a subdiscipline of general linguistics.[5] Walter Bodine explains the larger discipline: "Linguistics is the study of language as language, in contrast to the study of any specific language. The term 'general linguistics' comprehends all of the varied theoretical positions of linguists."[6] As

---

5. I use the expressions "discourse analysis" and "text linguistics" interchangeably. Bodine observes, "What has been called 'discourse analysis' in the United States has more often been known as 'text linguistics' in Europe" (Walter R. Bodine, introduction to *Discourse Analysis of Biblical Literature: What It Is and What It Offers,* ed. Walter R. Bodine, Society of Biblical Literature Semeia Series [Atlanta: Scholars Press, 1995], 2).

6. Walter R. Bodine, "Linguistics and Biblical Studies," in *The Anchor Bible Dictionary,* ed. David Noel Freeman, vol. 4 (New York: Doubleday, 1992), 327.

related to biblical studies, general linguistics would include aspects such as phonology (the sound system of a language), morphology (the study of forms or the smallest meaningful units of a language), syntax (the study of the structure of such units as phrases, clauses, and larger combinations), semantics (the study of the expression of meaning in language), discourse analysis (the linguistic study of units that are larger than the sentence), historical/comparative linguistics (the study of language development over time and the systematic comparison of related languages), and graphemics (the study of writing systems).[7]

As a subdiscipline of general linguistics, discourse analysis (or text linguistics) focuses on blocks larger than the sentence, traditionally the largest unit of syntactical analysis.[8] Several evangelical Old Testament scholars who have done work in this discipline have been associated with the Summer Institute of Linguistics (SIL), the school behind the Wycliffe Bible Translators.

Discourse analysts work their way through a text clause by clause, observing the verb forms and their position in each clause. To engage in this kind of analysis, exegetes must brush up on the notations that describe verbal forms and their positioning in a clause (see table A.1).

Table A.1
Notations Used in Discourse Analysis

qatal	perfect
yiqtol	imperfect
qᵉtol	imperative
qotel	participle
wayyiqtol	preterite or imperfect with *waw* consecutive
weqatal	*waw* (ו) plus perfect
NC	verbless noun (nominal) clause
w	marks the presence of a *waw* (ו)
0	marks the absence of a *waw* (ו)
x	indicates pre-verb material; something else in the clause "fronts" the verb

For example, a construction such as וְהִיא שָׁלְחָה (Gen. 38:25) would be described as *w* + x + *qatal*. This notes that a perfect *(qatal)* verb is preceded by something, in this case a pronoun. The *w* marks the presence of *waw* (ו) be-

7. Bodine, introduction to *Discourse Analysis*, 3–4.
8. Ibid., 1–5. See also Bodine, "Linguistics and Biblical Studies," 330. Evangelicals have written two readable introductions to general linguistics for Bible students: Peter Cotterell and Max Turner, *Linguistics and Biblical Interpretation* (Downers Grove, Ill.: InterVarsity, 1989); and Moisés Silva, *God, Language, and Scripture: Reading the Bible in the Light of General Linguistics* (Grand Rapids: Zondervan, 1990).

fore the pronoun. However, if the construction lacked the *waw* (ו) and read as הִיא שָׁלְחָה, then the notation would appear as 0 + x + *qatal.* A form like וְשִׁחֵת (Gen. 38:9) would simply be described as *w* + *qatal* or else as *weqatal.*[9]

So what's the payoff? Basically, discourse analysis will yield two results. First, it will help interpreters discover which clauses in the story carry the main storyline and which clauses contain background information that is subsidiary to the main line. Second, it will help interpreters discover which sections of the text are "marked" or emphasized.

Plot Lines in a Story

The starting point for textlinguistic analysis is the consensus among scholars that *"wayyiqtol* [preterite] clauses are the structures of choice in Biblical Hebrew for presenting chronologically successive events."[10] In a study of 11,359 nonquotational clauses (narration as opposed to characters' speech) taken from the Pentateuch, 1–2 Samuel, and the book of Jonah, Robert Bergen and his associates found that 50.7 percent of them began with a *wayyiqtol* form.[11] The main line or foreground of a story is advanced by these *wayyiqtol* forms. On the other hand, the subsidiary line or background is built by *qatal* (perfect) forms.[12] Van Wolde explains:

> In Biblical narratives a distinction can be made between the clauses presenting continuity in a text, and interrupting clauses, indicating a change in situation. Their difference can be described as "sequential" versus "non-sequential," or as "foreground clauses" versus "background clauses."
>
> The sequenced series of verbal clauses are indicated by *wayyiqtol* forms presented by the narrator (thus in a narrator's text). They refer to single, sequential actions or events advancing the plot and present the information as fore-

9. For the full range of possibilities, see A. F. Den Exter Blokland, "Clause Analysis in Biblical Hebrew Narrative—An Explanation and a Manual for Compilation," *Trinity Journal* 11 (spring 1990): 87–89.

10. Robert D. Bergen, "Evil Spirits and Eccentric Grammar: A Study of the Relationship between Text and Meaning in Hebrew Narrative," in *Biblical Hebrew and Discourse Linguistics,* ed. Robert D. Bergen (Dallas: Summer Institute of Linguistics; Winona Lake, Ind.: Eisenbrauns, 1994), 325. John H. Sailhamer describes *wayyiqtol* verbal patterns as providing "the effect of sequence in time" (*The Pentateuch as Narrative* [Grand Rapids: Zondervan, 1992], 13). See also Alviero Niccacci, "Analysis of Biblical Narrative," in *Biblical Hebrew and Discourse Linguistics,* ed. Robert D. Bergen (Dallas: Summer Institute of Linguistics; Winona Lake, Ind.: Eisenbrauns, 1994), 176–79.

11. Bergen, "Evil Spirits and Eccentric Grammar," 326, 334. The reason for excluding speech (quotational) clauses in this analysis is the embedding of speech clauses in nonspeech (nonquotational) clauses. In other words, speech clauses do not advance the storyline, although the introduction of a speech clause does advance it (such as "And he said").

12. See Christo H. J. van der Merwe, "An Overview of Hebrew Narrative Syntax," in *Narrative Syntax and the Hebrew Bible: Papers of the Tilburg Conference 1996,* ed. Ellen van Wolde, Biblical Interpretation Series, ed. R. Alan Culpepper and Rolf Rendtorff, vol. 29 (Leiden: Brill, 1997), 10, 12.

grounded material, whereas the word-order VSO [verb-subject-object] puts the new information (expressed in the verb) in a fronted position. . . . An interruption in this chain of actions or events is indicated by the non-sequential verb forms, of which the (x-)qatal, w^ex-qatal, and (x-)qotel forms are the most frequently used, as well as by a word-order in which the verb is not fronted but the subject, object or adverb. Thus the verb form and the word-order are the devices used in Biblical Hebrew to mark the transition from the foreground (sequentiality) to the background (nonsequentiality).[13]

Bryan Rocine provides a helpful illustration of the difference between the mainline and the secondary line of a story. Think of the narrative as a video. "The mainline forms keep the video playing. The off-the-line [background] forms slow or even freeze the video for commentary, often at the points of greatest emphasis."[14] David Dawson concurs, noting that "material in non-mainline clauses adds to the narrative, not by moving it forward, but by contributing background information and creating a setting for the narrative."[15]

Based on the research of scholars like Robert Longacre, Robert Bergen, Francis I. Andersen, John Sailhamer, Alviero Niccacci, Christo H. J. van der Merwe, and Nicolai Winther-Nielsen, I propose a simplified approach to analyzing plot lines in Old Testament narratives. Once exegetes learn this approach, they can expand or modify it based on further research in the field.

The approach I propose begins by going through the story and separating nonspeech (nonquotational) clauses from speech (quotational) clauses. A speech clause is something a character says. The interpreter will deal with the speech sections later. First, the interpreter takes each nonquotational clause and identifies it either as main line (foreground) or secondary line (background).[16]

Main Line (Foreground)

As noted above, the main line (foreground, storyline, sequence of events) is advanced by *wayyiqtol* forms. Thus, any clause containing a *wayyiqtol* form advances the main line of the narrative. For example, Genesis 38 unfolds with a series of *wayyiqtol* forms. Fifteen occur in sequence until the first "interruption" of the main line at the end of verse five with a *weqatal* construction. A *wayyiqtol* form in verse six returns the reader to the main line or foreground. Longacre describes the

13. Ellen van Wolde, "Linguistic Motivation and Biblical Exegesis," in *Narrative Syntax and the Hebrew Bible: Papers of the Tilburg Conference 1996*, ed. Ellen van Wolde, Biblical Interpretation Series, ed. R. Alan Culpepper and Rolf Rendtorff, vol. 29 (Leiden: Brill, 1997), 39.

14. Rocine, *Learning Biblical Hebrew*, 53.

15. David Allen Dawson, *Text-Linguistics and Biblical Hebrew* (Sheffield: Sheffield Academic Press, 1994), 126. Dawson likens mainline clauses to "bones" and off-line [background] clauses to "joints."

16. See Alviero Niccacci, "Basic Facts and Theory of the Biblical Hebrew Verb System in Prose," in *Narrative Syntax and the Hebrew Bible: Papers of the Tilburg Conference 1996*, ed. Ellen van Wolde, Biblical Interpretation Series, ed. R. Alan Culpepper and Rolf Rendtorff, vol. 29 (Leiden: Brill, 1997), 188 n. 59, 197.

function of the main storyline: "Such a primary storyline ideally encodes a series of punctiliar consecutive 'happenings': whether actions, motions, cognitive events, contingencies (things that happen to people), or speech acts."[17]

Here are a couple of additional details. First, *wayyiqtol* forms are always clause-initial. That is, they occur first in the clause. They are not preceded or fronted by a subject (noun or pronoun) or a particle (conjunctive or subjunctive).[18] Furthermore, *wayyiqtol* forms are not negated in Hebrew narrative literature. Thus, it appears that a negated *qatal* (perfect) form can function like a *wayyiqtol* form and signal the main storyline.[19] Third, the *wayyiqtol* form וַיְהִי (from the root הָיָה, "be, happen") often functions as a transition marker. In such a case, the clause it begins is a secondary line or an off-line in the story rather than a mainline.[20] Its function is to introduce a reference to time or to introduce a new scene or episode.[21] Occasionally, וַיְהִי functions as an ordinary *wayyiqtol* verb form and begins a mainline clause. In these instances, it has the meaning "became."[22] Finally, an isolated *weqatal* form functions on the mainline of a narrative just like a *wayyiqtol* form. This is discussed below.

Secondary Line (Background)

Basically, all other types of clauses serve as a secondary or subsidiary lines to the main storyline. At this level, scholars have made various proposals, some of which get quite complicated. Below, I have summarized the main constructions used to indicate secondary line or background information.

x + qatal

Hebrew scholars, including those who are text linguists, recognize that the normal pattern in a clause is verb-subject-object (VSO).[23] When the verb in

---

17. Robert E. Longacre, "*Weqatal* Forms in Biblical Hebrew Prose," in *Biblical Hebrew and Discourse Linguistics,* ed. Robert D. Bergen (Dallas: Summer Institute of Linguistics; Winona Lake, Ind.: Eisenbrauns, 1994), 67.

18. Robert E. Longacre observes, "Since preterites occur only in verb-initial clauses, the preposing of a noun (whether the subject or the object) precludes the use of a preterite and makes necessary recourse to the perfect" ("Discourse Perspective on the Hebrew Verb: Affirmation and Restatement," in *Linguistics and Biblical Hebrew,* ed. Walter R. Bodine [Winona Lake, Ind.: Eisenbrauns, 1992], 178).

19. Longacre now grants this, amending his previous view that a לֹא + *qatal* form is "off the storyline by reason of its irrealis status (i.e., it tells what *didn't* happen rather than what happened)" ("*Weqatal* Forms in Biblical Hebrew Prose," 68).

20. Rocine, *Learning Biblical Hebrew,* 52.

21. Christo H. J. van der Merwe, Jackie A. Naude, and Jan H. Kroeze, *A Biblical Hebrew Reference Grammar* (Sheffield: Sheffield Academic Press, 2000), 332–33.

22. Ibid., 333.

23. Barry L. Bandstra explains, "Biblical Hebrew is a verb-first language. When an explicit subject is present, the expected and most frequent order of constituents in narrative verbal clauses is V-S-O. When the subject is implicit in the verbal form, the order is V-O" (Bandstra, "Word Order and Emphasis in Biblical Hebrew Narrative," in *Linguistics and Biblical Hebrew,* ed. Walter R. Bodine [Winona Lake, Ind.: Eisenbrauns, 1992], 115).

Biblical Hebrew is preceded by any other constituent (noun, adverb, etc.), marked word order occurs.[24] That is, the writer is emphasizing either the subject or the object of the verb. Sometimes *qatal* is fronted by an object. For example, in Genesis 20:16, the construction אָמַר וּלְשָׂרָה ("And to Sarah he said") indicates a change of topic.[25] Sometimes *qatal* is fronted by a subject. Van der Merwe cites an example: "In Gene[sis] 20:4 God is already addressing Abimilech and the X-V word order cannot be to mark primarily a changed topic; it is rather to discontinue the series of events in order to provide some background information."[26] Longacre describes an x + *qatal* clause as presenting a "participant-oriented action." He explains, "The noun is highlighted and the verb is demoted."[27] Adverbs can also front *qatal* forms. An example is the construction יָצָא וְאַחַר ("And afterwards [he] came out") in Genesis 38:30. The purpose here is to place emphasis on the timing.

Niccacci suggests that x + *qatal* forms provide either "antecedent" information or "background" information. By antecedent information, Niccacci refers to "all the data that an author wishes to communicate to his reader in order to make him understand the following story."[28] Background information operates "inside the story" and conveys "secondary details, descriptions, or reflections."[29] Genesis 3:1 provides an example of an x + *qatal* clause providing antecedent information. On the other hand, the final two of three quotation formulas in Genesis 3:14–17 are backgrounded through *w* + x + *qatal* structures.[30]

Other Marked Constructions

Longacre refers to four other constructions as "backgrounded activities" that he sees as separate from the primary storyline advanced by *wayyiqtol*

24. Christo H. J. van der Merwe, "Discourse Linguistics and Biblical Hebrew Grammar," in *Biblical Hebrew and Discourse Linguistics,* ed. Robert D. Bergen (Dallas: Summer Institute of Linguistics; Winona Lake, Ind.: Eisenbrauns, 1994), 43 n. 34.

25. Ibid., 30–31.

26. Ibid., 31.

27. Longacre, "*Weqatal* Forms in Biblical Hebrew Prose," 67. "In a given language some events are backgrounded relative to others, especially if such events are more participant oriented than action oriented, if the events portrayed are not strictly sequential, or if some events are regarded either as preparatory to what is reported on the primary storyline or as resultant on such primary events. . . . Characteristically, the secondary tense has a past or perfective meaning, while the meaning of the primary storyline is punctiliar consecutive events in the story world" (ibid.).

28. Alviero Niccacci, "Analysis of Biblical Narrative," 181.

29. Ibid.

30. Ibid., 194–95. Similarly, John H. Sailhamer provides helpful examples in his commentary on Genesis. For example, in Genesis 3:1 he points out that the *w* + x + *qatal* clause structure of הָיָה וְהַנָּחָשׁ ("Now the serpent was") indicates that a new narrative section has begun and gives the background information for what follows (what Niccacci calls "antecedent" information) ("Genesis," in *The Expositor's Bible Commentary,* ed. Frank E. Gaebelein, vol. 2 [Grand Rapids: Zondervan, 1990], 50 n. 1). On the other hand, in Genesis 42:23 the *w* + x + *qatal* clause structure of יָדְעוּ לֹא וְהֵם ("And they did not know") provides background in the form of "a comment to the reader" (ibid., 247 n. 23).

forms and the secondary storyline (consisting of actions that are either partic-ipant-oriented or backgrounded) signified by x + *qatal* constructions.[31] First, a noun + imperfect (x + *yiqtol*) construction describes a continued activity in past time. Second, a *hinneh* + participle (x + *qotel*) form provides even more attention with an explicitly durative form preceded by an attention calling particle. Third, a participle can appear on its own (0 + *qotel*) with an explic-itly durative force. Fourth, a participle can be fronted by a noun (x + *qotel*).

A Nominal Verbless Clause

According to Longacre, nominal verbless clauses, along with *hayah* (הָיָה) clauses and *yesh* (יֵשׁ) clauses, provide setting. He explains, "Such clauses offer necessary detail as to participants, props, and circumstances without which a story cannot be adequately staged—or restaged at crucial junctions—and with-out which the reader might not understand what is reported as transpiring."[32]

Of course, background or secondary line constructions can work together as in Genesis 1:1–2 where the four clauses that provide antecedent informa-tion (background that precedes the story) contain various forms.

1	0 + x + *qatal*
2a	w + x + *qatal*
2b	Nominal verbless clause (noun clause without a verb)
2c	w + x + *qotel*

Weqatal Forms

Robert Longacre has provided one of the most plausible analyses of *weqatal* forms in Hebrew narrative. He notes two main functions. First, a string of *weqatal* forms in nonquotational sections of a Biblical Hebrew nar-rative signals a "how-it-was-done procedural discourse."[33] For example, Gen-esis 29:3 uses four *weqatal* forms to describe the four steps that shepherds would typically take to water flocks from a well. This sets up the account of Jacob's significant deed for Rachel of single-handedly removing the rock from the well—a task normally completed when several shepherds were present.[34] Second, "an isolated *weqatal* in the narrative framework marks a climactic or at least a pivotal event."[35] For example, in Judges 3:20–23, a long string of *wayyiqtol* forms describes Ehud's assassination of King Eglon. However, the

---

31. Longacre, "Discourse Perspective on the Hebrew Verb," 179–80.

32. Ibid. See also Niccacci, "Basic Facts and Theory," 194–95.

33. Longacre, "*Weqatal* Forms in Biblical Hebrew Prose," 57, 95.

34. For several additional examples and a fuller discussion of the Genesis 29:3 example, see ibid., 57–66.

35. Ibid., 71, 95. Tal Goldfajn argues, "Wayyiqtol and weqatal seem to be saying 'after that' where 'that' refers back to the last event narrated. In the case of the weqatal form it is mainly an 'after that' of future events . . . while the 'after that' of the wayyiqtol form refers to past events" (*Word Order and Time in Biblical Hebrew Narrative*, Oxford Theological Mono-graphs [Oxford: Clarendon, 1998], 143).

final act of bolting the door is reported with a *weqatal* form. Longacre takes this as a case of special marking.[36] Rocine considers an isolated *weqatal* a "surrogate mainline" since it advances the action like a *wayyiqtol* form does.[37] Longacre also argues that the *weqatal* form of the verb *hayah* (וְהָיָה) marks significant background or important events to follow.[38] For example, the action of the "battle" between David and Goliath in 1 Samuel 17:48–49 unfolds through a series of *wayyiqtol* forms. However, the first clause begins with וְהָיָה.[39] The clause indicates that the Philistine took the initiative to attack David. Most English versions (NIV, NKJV, NASB) translate it as a temporal clause.

Clauses Beginning with a Conjunction or Relative Pronoun

Forms such as כִּי (causal conjunction), כַּאֲשֶׁר (comparative conjunction), and אֲשֶׁר (relative pronoun) are grammatically subordinate to the main clause that precedes them. Because *wayyiqtol* forms are clause initial, any conjunctions or relative pronouns must be followed by *qatal* forms.[40] By virtue of their function and the verb form they contain, such clauses supply backgrounded rather than foregrounded information. Niccacci comments:

> Main and dependent sentences are identified not only by the absence or presence, respectively, of subordinating conjunctions such as *ki*, *'asher*, *l*^e*ma'an*, etc. They are also identified by the place of the finite verb: first place in main sentences, second place in subordinate sentences. When subordinating conjunctions are present, the subordination is both grammatical and syntactic; otherwise, it is syntactic only but no less real.[41]

Rocine's Discourse Profile Scheme for Historical Narrative

Bryan Rocine has created a helpful "discourse profile scheme" that ranks the degrees to which a construction slows down the forward progress of historical narrative.[42] This appears in table A.2. Rocine adapted this scheme from Robert Longacre, a pioneer in the field of textlinguistic analysis of Hebrew narrative.

The scheme indicates that *wayyiqtol* forms, as well as isolated *weqatal* forms, carry the mainline of the narrative. Notice the ranking of off-the-line forms. This ranking is not in order of importance. Rocine explains, "The

---

36. For a fuller discussion of this example and several others, see Longacre "*Weqatal* Forms in Biblical Hebrew Prose," 71–84.
37. Rocine, *Learning Biblical Hebrew*, 212–13.
38. Ibid., 84.
39. For further examples, see ibid., 84–91.
40. Ibid., 68.
41. Niccacci, "Basic Facts and Theory," 198.
42. Rocine, *Learning Biblical Hebrew*, 53, 424.

lower a verb form is in the profile, the farther away it is from the mainline and the more it tends to retard the forward progress of the mainline."[43]

Table A.2
Rocine's Discourse Profile Scheme for Historical Narrative

Mainline	1a. *Wayyiqtol*
	1b. Pivotal/climactic event on the mainline: Isolated *Weqatal*

Off-the-line:
2. Topicalization: X-*qatal*
   3. Embedded Direct Speech
      4. Relative past background: *Qatal* in a dependent clause
         5. Relative non-past background: *Yiqtol* in a dependent clause
            6. Background activities: Participle
               7. Embedded Procedural Discourse
                  8. Transition marker: *Wayyiqtol* of היה
                     9. Scene setting: Verbless clause
                        10. Irrealis scene setting: Negation of any verb by לא

Direct Speech

While the quotation formulas (used to introduce direct speech) in *wayyiqtol* forms advance the main line of the narrative, the actual quotation does not advance it "no matter how long and complex the direct speech is."[44] These quotations are "embedded" in the storyline.

What about doing textlinguistic analysis of direct speech? Unless a quotation consists of several sentences, doing textlinguistic analysis becomes the kind of microanalysis that will not help most preachers. Bandstra notes that "compared to narrative discourse, it [spoken discourse] allows greater flexibility. Nonverbal clauses are more frequent, as well as single words or fragmentary dialogue."[45] Therefore, the flexibility of direct speech makes it harder to pin down conclusions. The frequent brevity of direct speech makes such a quest unnecessary.

However, for those interpreters who are interested, preliminary analysis by textlinguists shows that the main line of communication in a direct speech is

43. Ibid., 53. Rocine's profile scheme contains at least one term that has not been discussed in this appendix. By "topicalizaton," Rocine refers to the shift in focus or topic which takes place when a *qatal* verb is fronted by a subject or an object (23).
44. Niccacci, "Analysis of Biblical Narrative," 180. For a thorough study of the "quotative frame," that is, the report that introduces the quotation, see Cynthia L. Miller, *The Representation of Speech in Biblical Hebrew Narrative: A Linguistic Analysis,* Harvard Semitic Monographs, ed. Peter Machinist, no. 55 (Atlanta: Scholars Press, 1996). For a more concise discussion, see Cynthia L. Miller, "Introducing Direct Discourse in Biblical Hebrew Narrative," in *Biblical Hebrew and Discourse Linguistics,* ed. Robert D. Bergen (Dallas: Summer Institute of Linguistics; Winona Lake, Ind.: Eisenbrauns, 1994), 199–241.
45. Bandstra, "Word Order and Emphasis in Biblical Hebrew Narrative," 119.

initiated by *qatal* forms (0 + *qatal*) for past action, simple nominal clauses (SNC) for present, and x + *yiqtol* forms (followed by *weqatal* forms) for future action.[46] Subsidiary lines of communication that break into the main line of direct speech are indicated by the same forms that break into the main line of narrative or nonquotational material: x + *qatal* for the past, simple nominal clauses (SNC) for the present, and x + *yiqtol* for the future (see tables A.3 and A.4).

Table A.3
The Main Line of Communication in Old Testament Stories

Temporal Axis	Narrative	Direct Speech
Past	*wayyiqtol*	*qatal*
Present		SNC
Future		*weqatal*[a]

a. X-*yiqtol* is the initial verb form. However, a chain of *weqatal* constitutes the mainline of communication.

Table A.4
The Subsidiary Line of Communication in Old Testament Stories

Temporal Axis	Narrative	Direct Speech
Past	X-*qatal*	X-*qatal*
Present	SNC	SNC
Future	X-*yiqtol*	X-*yiqtol*

To look at this from another angle, chains of *weqatal* forms in direct speech function like chains of *wayyiqtol* forms in narrative (nonquotational) materials. They advance the main line of communication.[47] For example, David's declaration to Goliath in 1 Samuel 17:46 begins with an *X-yiqtol* form and then proceeds with a series of *weqatal* forms:

This day Yahweh <u>will deliver</u> *(X-yiqtol)* you into my hand, and I <u>will strike</u> *(weqatal)* you and <u>remove</u> *(weqatal)* your head from you. And I <u>will give</u> *(weqatal)* the dead bodies of the army of the Philistines this day to the birds of the sky and the wild beasts of the earth, and all the earth <u>will know</u> *(weqatal)* that there is a God in Israel.[48]

46. For this analysis, see Niccacci, "Analysis of Biblical Narrative," 176–77. See also Niccacci, "Basic Facts and Theory of the Biblical Hebrew Verb System in Prose," 182–87.
47. Niccacci, "Analysis of Biblical Narrative," 178.
48. Author's translation. The verb forms are underlined for convenience. The initial X-*yiqtol* forms consists of the verb יַסְגֶּרְךָ fronted by the temporal construction הַיּוֹם הַזֶּה.

Interpreters interested in textlinguistic analysis of direct speech should also consult the discussion in Bryan Rocine's Hebrew grammar. He classifies the type of material in direct speech into four categories: predictive narrative, instructional discourse, hortatory discourse, and historical narrative.[49] Then, throughout his grammar, he describes how each of the four types distinguishes between mainline and off-the-line clauses. He notes that while historical narrative can be found inside direct speech, it acts a bit differently in this setting.[50]

Marked Text

In addition to helping interpreters distinguish between main and secondary plot lines, discourse analysis also helps interpreters spot sections of marked or emphasized text. I've studied photographs of the Dead Sea Scrolls, which contain the oldest existing Hebrew manuscripts of the Old Testament. The copyists did not use indentation, underlining, italics, or different font sizes to single out sections of text. In the Psalms I studied, they did put the name Yahweh in an older script, presumably out of reverence for the divine name. Otherwise, without special effects and with limited space, the writers of Hebrew Scripture had to highlight sections of a story through other means. Discourse analysis can ferret out these highlighted sections.

Robert Bergen has provided one of the most helpful discussions in his article on the "eccentric grammar" of 1 Samuel 16:13–23. He writes,

> Since written language is a medium for the transference of facts, ideas, beliefs, and attitudes, it follows that a writer will drop some hints within a text to assist the reader in the task of figuring out which parts are more important than others. In other words, language texts are both semantically and grammatically contoured. The creator of a text *intends* some of the materials to be interpreted as more important than others.
>
> One means that authors often use to mark semantically noteworthy materials is with statistically rare . . . features, such as rare spellings, odd lexical items, irregular clause structures, and other higher-level deviations from established norms within a given genre. . . . Writers often encode one portion of a text as more important than others through the use of these statistically unusual features, so by identifying them a text analyst may predict with some degree of accuracy those portions of a text that the writer intended to be most important. Portions of a text identifiable by this means are considered to be "grammatically marked."[51]

Bergen has developed a form of analysis that he describes as "clause-level contour analysis." Basically, he uses a computer program and chart to analyze

49. Rocine, *Learning Biblical Hebrew,* 62–63.
50. Idem.
51. Bergen, "Evil Spirits and Eccentric Grammar," 321–22.

the non-speech (nonquotational) clauses in a narrative. This chart tracks the verb form and the structure of each clause. Each clause receives a "value," and a quick comparison of clause values points out emphasized clauses or clusters of clauses. This raises a critical question: Would an ancient reader have perceived what modern interpreters comprehend through such sophisticated analyses made possible by modern computer technology? Bergen answers affirmatively. For example, when clause-level contour analysis discovers a statistically rare form, he notes,

> The magnitude of statistical deviation is great enough to suggest that the clause would have caught the attention of a fluent speaker of Biblical Hebrew. Because the grammatical pattern differed so significantly from the established norms, the auditor's brain would have had to perform additional tasks in its efforts to cope with this clause structure. The increased effort expended in the process would have had the practical effect of causing information in that clause to be highlighted.[52]

Recording the Data

What I propose for preachers is a two-stage process for doing discourse analysis. First, they will produce a linear chart that tracks verb form and placement in each nonquotational clause. This chart, a simplified version of Bergen's chart, will help exegetes immediately see the places where the text is marked. Second, the exegete will produce a "text layout" in English (but based on the Hebrew text) which puts main line clauses at the margin and then indents subordinate or secondary line clauses. Direct speech is also indented and placed in italics.[53]

Verb Form and Placement Chart

I suggest preparing a "Verb Form and Placement" chart with the following fields: *reference, verb, pre-verb material,* and *description.* This chart can be handwritten or done on a word processor. In a word processing program, such as Wordperfect or Microsoft Word, you can place the material in an actual chart or in a series of columns (fields) formed by simple tab stops. The reference field simply lists the verse number. The verb field then records the actual Hebrew verbal forms found in the nonquotational clauses. On a handwritten chart, the exegete can quickly write the form in consonants. In a word processing document, the Hebrew text can be easily imported from Logos or Hermeneutika's *Bibleworks.* From the *Bibleworks* program, I can copy sections of Hebrew text into the bottom of the Wordperfect document where my

---

52. Ibid., 326.
53. This is a modification of the approach suggested in Robert B. Chisholm Jr., *From Exegesis to Exposition: A Practical Guide to Using Biblical Hebrew* (Grand Rapids: Baker, 1998), 135–42.

chart is located. Then it is easy to cut and paste the verb forms into the chart. The pre-verb material field includes any pre-verb materials in cases like x + *qatal* forms. This material, when present, can be included in the same manner described for the verb field. Finally, the description field puts the construction in a "code" (see table A.5). When the chart is complete, the final field or column can be scanned quite quickly, and the exegete can spot the structure of the narrative clauses and see marked sections almost immediately. As an example, I have charted Genesis 38 (see table A.6). Exegetes can, of course, modify or tailor this approach to reflect refinements from further research or to accommodate further data.

Table A.5
Codes for Use in a Verb Form and Placement Chart

WI	*wayyiqtol*	x	pre-verb material
I	*yiqtol*	w	*waw* (וֹ)
P	*qatal*	x + P	x + *qatal*
Pt	*qotel* (participle)	wP	*weqatal*
If	*qetol* (infinitive)	*	form of *hayah* (הָיָה)

Table A.6
A Verb Form and Placement Chart of Genesis 38

Reference	Verb Form	Pre-Verb Material	Description
38:1	וַיְהִי		WI*
38:1	וַיֵּרֶד		WI
38:1	וַיֵּט		WI
38:2	וַיַּרְא		WI
38:2	וַיִּקָּחֶהָ		WI
38:2	וַיָּבֹא		WI
38:3	וַתַּהַר		WI
38:3	וַתֵּלֶד		WI
38:3	וַיִּקְרָא		WI
38:4	וַתַּהַר		WI
38:4	וַתֵּלֶד		WI
38:4	וַתִּקְרָא		WI
38:5	וַתֹּסֶף		WI

Reference	Verb Form	Pre-Verb Material	Description
38:5	וַתֵּלֶד		WI
38:5	וַתִּקְרָא		WI
38:5	וְהָיָה		wP*
38:5	בְלִדְתָּהּ		If
38:6	וַיִּקַּח		WI
38:7	וַיְהִי		WI*
38:7	וַיְמִתֵהוּ		WI
38:8	וַיֹּאמֶר		WI
38:9	וַיֵּדַע		WI
38:9	יִהְיֶה	כִּי לֹא לוֹ	0+x+I*
38:9	וְהָיָה		wP*
38:9	בָא	אִם־	0+x+P
38:9	וְשִׁחֵת		wP
38:9	נְתָן	לְבִלְתִּי	x+If
38:10	וַיֵּרַע		WI
38:10	עָשָׂה	אֲשֶׁר	0+x+P
38:10	וַיָּמֶת		WI
38:11	וַיֹּאמֶר		WI
38:11	אָמַר	כִּי	0+x+P
38:11	וַתֵּלֶךְ		WI
38:11	וַתֵּשֶׁב		WI
38:12	וַיִּרְבּוּ		WI
38:12	וַתָּמָת		WI
38:12	וַיִּנָּחֶם		WI
38:12	וַיַּעַל		WI
38:13	וַיֻּגַּד		WI
38:13	לֵאמֹר		If
38:14	וַתָּסַר		WI
38:14	וַתְּכַס		WI

Reference	Verb Form	Pre-Verb Material	Description
38:14	וַתִּתְעַלָּף		WI
38:14	וַתֵּשֶׁב		WI
38:14	רָאֲתָה	כִּי	0+x+P
38:14	גָדַל	כִּי־	0+x+P
38:14	נִתְּנָה	וְהִוא לֹא־	w+x+P
38:15	וַיִּרְאֶהָ		WI
38:15	וַיַּחְשְׁבֶהָ		WI
38:15	כִסְּתָה	כִּי	0+x+P
38:16	וַיֵּט		WI
38:16	וַיֹּאמֶר		WI
38:16	יָדַע	כִּי לֹא	0+x+P
38:16	וַתֹּאמֶר		WI
38:17	וַיֹּאמֶר		WI
38:17	וַתֹּאמֶר		WI
38:18	וַיֹּאמֶר		WI
38:18	וַתֹּאמֶר		WI
38:18	וַיִּתֶּן		WI
38:18	וַיָּבֹא		WI
38:18	וַתַּהַר		WI
38:19	וַתָּקָם		WI
38:19	וַתֵּלֶךְ		WI
38:19	וַתָּסַר		WI
38:19	וַתִּלְבַּשׁ		WI
38:20	וַיִּשְׁלַח		WI
38:20	לָקַחַת		If
38:20	מְצָאָהּ	וְלֹא	w+x+P (=WI)
38:21	וַיִּשְׁאַל		WI
38:21	לֵאמֹר		If
38:21	וַיֹּאמְרוּ		WI

Reference	Verb Form	Pre-Verb Material	Description
38:22	וַיָּשָׁב		WI
38:22	וַיֹּאמֶר		WI
38:23	וַיֹּאמֶר		WI
38:24	וַיְהִי		WI*
38:24	וַיֻּגַּד		WI
38:24	לֵאמֹר		If
38:24	וַיֹּאמֶר		WI
38:25	מוּצֵאת	הִוא	x+Pt
38:25	שָׁלְחָה	וְהִיא	w+x+P
38:25	לֵאמֹר		If
38:25	וַתֹּאמֶר		WI
38:26	וַיַּכֵּר		WI
38:26	וַיֹּאמֶר		WI
38:26	יָסַף	וְלֹא־	w+x+P (=WI)
38:27	וַיְהִי		WI*
38:27	לְדִתָּהּ		If
38:28	וַיְהִי		WI*
38:28	בְלִדְתָּהּ		If
38:28	וַיִּתֶּן		WI
38:28	וַתִּקַּח		WI
38:28	וַתִּקְשֹׁר		WI
38:28	לֵאמֹר		If
38:29	וַיְהִי		WI*
38:29	כְּמֵשִׁיב		If
38:29	יָצָא	וְהִנֵּה	w+x+P
38:29	וַתֹּאמֶר		WI
38:29	וַיִּקְרָא		WI
38:30	יָצָא	וְאַחַר	w+x+P
38:30	וַיִּקְרָא		WI

244 ✿✿✿

Exactly how does this chart help an exegete? The chart makes it easy to spot where various forms interrupt the string of *wayyiqtol* forms and where the story moves from main line to secondary line. The first variation from the *wayyiqtol* string comes in verse five where a וְהָיָה form marks significant background. An infinitive construct form carries the action in this backgrounded clause.

Scanning down through the forms, an exegete will notice that verse 9 is highly marked. The conjunction כִּי introduces a clause containing an imperfect verb fronted by both the negative לֹא particle and the preposition with suffix לוֹ, stressing that the offspring resulting from a union between Onan and Tamar would not be considered an heir of Onan's. The next clause begins with another וְהָיָה form, supplying another piece of significant background: Onan refused to impregnate Tamar.

Likewise, the grammar in verse 14 is significant. The string of *wayyiqtol* forms is interrupted by two כִּי clauses. The first one is causal, explaining that Tamar set up shop as a cult prostitute because of what she observed or saw. The second one introduces a clause that specifies the content of Tamar's observation. This is followed by a *w + x + qatal* clause that fronts the pronoun "she." The clause provides a key piece of background information: she (Tamar) had not been given to Judah's third son, Shelah.

Finally, the grammar of verse 25 calls for attention. The main line of the narrative moves from Judah's declaration in verse 24 (וַיֹּאמֶר) to Tamar's declaration in verse 25 (וַתֹּאמֶר). Two backgrounded clauses supply insight into Tamar's declaration. First, the x + *qotel* form (הִוא מוּצֵאת) emphasizes the durative nature of Tamar's experience ("She was being brought out"). Second, a *w + x + qatal* clause stresses Tamar's role. *She* sent a message to her father-in-law. In verses 20 and 26, the negated perfects seem to function like *wayyiqtol* forms and advance the main storyline.

In his clause contour analysis, Bergen notes infrequent or rare roots as well as verb occurrence in infrequent stems. For our purposes, a program such as Logos or Hermeneutika's *Bibleworks* will indicate the number of times a root appears in the Hebrew Bible. Another option is to use the data provided in *A Reader's Hebrew-English Lexicon of the Old Testament* by Armstrong, Busby, and Carr.[54] This tool goes through the Old Testament chapter by chapter and lists terms that appear less than fifty times. After each term, a number is given in parentheses indicating how many times the word appears in the Old Testament. For verbs, three numbers appear. The first indicates how many times the particular verb occurs in the book (such as Genesis or Judges) in the given stem (Qal, Niphal, etc.). The second indicates how many times the verb oc-

54. Douglas L. Busby, Terry A. Armstrong, and Cyril F. Carr, *A Reader's Hebrew-English Lexicon of the Old Testament* (Grand Rapids: Zondervan, 1989).

curs in the entire Old Testament in the given stem. The third indicates how many times the verb occurs in all stems in the entire Old Testament.

Text Layout

After preparing the kind of chart described above, the exegete should proceed to stage two: a layout that arranges the text in a format reflecting the main lines and secondary lines of the story. This has the advantage of showing nominal ("verbless") clauses as well as speech clauses. While this could be done in Hebrew, it will probably be best to do it in English. The product will be easier to read, and the manipulation of Hebrew text gets a bit tricky in some word processing programs because of the switch from left justification to right justification. My suggestion is to copy the English text from Logos or *Bibleworks* into a word processing document.

Moving clause by clause, place the main line clauses containing *wayyiqtol* forms at the left margin. Indent all other clauses one tab stop to show that they belong to a secondary line within the narrative. Also indent speech clauses one tab stop and italicize them. I recommend underlining all the verbal forms in the nonquotational clauses. Brief comments can be placed in parentheses to the right of the clause in question. As an example, I have produced a text layout of Genesis 38 (see table A.7). This layout is based on the New King James Version. It is usually easier to use a more literal version like the New King James Version or the New American Standard Bible. Of course, an exegete can also provide a personal translation of the text.

Table A.7
Text Layout of Genesis 38

1	It came to pass at that time	
	that Judah departed from his brothers,	
	and visited a certain Adullamite whose name *was* Hirah.	
2	And Judah saw there a daughter of a certain Canaanite whose name *was* Shua,	
	and he married her	
	and went in to her.	
3	So she conceived	
	and bore a son,	
	and he called his name Er.	
4	She conceived again	
	and bore a son,	
	and she called his name Onan.	
5	And she conceived yet again	
	and bore a son,	
	and called his name Shelah.	
	He was at Chezib	*(weqatal* of verb *hayah)*
	when she bore him.	(infinitive constr.)
6	Then Judah took a wife for Er his firstborn,	
	and her name *was* Tamar.	(nominal clause)
7	But [it came to pass]	

Er, Judah's firstborn, was wicked in the sight of the LORD,   (nominal clause)
and the LORD <u>killed</u> him.

8   And Judah <u>said</u> to Onan,

"Go in to your brother's wife and marry her, and raise up an heir to your
    brother."

9   But Onan <u>knew</u>

that the heir <u>would</u> not <u>be</u> his;   (0+x+*yiqtol*)
and it <u>came to pass</u>,   (*weqatal* of verb *hayah*)
when he <u>went in</u> to his brother's wife,   (0+x+*qatal*)
that he <u>emitted</u> on the ground,   (*weqatal*)
lest he <u>should give</u> an heir to his brother.   (neg. particle + infinitive)

10 And the thing which he <u>did displeased</u> the LORD;   (x + *qatal* is the subject)
therefore He <u>killed</u> him also.

11 Then Judah <u>said</u> to Tamar his daughter-in-law,

"Remain a widow in your father's house till my son Shelah is grown."
For he <u>said</u>,   (כִּי + *qatal*)
"Lest he also die as his brothers did."
And Tamar <u>went</u>
and <u>dwelt</u> in her father's house.

12 Now in the process of time [lit. "the days <u>became many</u>"]
the daughter of Shua, Judah's wife, <u>died</u>;
and Judah <u>was comforted</u>,
and <u>went up</u> to his sheepshearers at Timnah,
he and his friend Hirah the Adullamite.

13 And it was <u>told</u> Tamar,

<u>saying</u>,
"Look, your father-in-law is going up to Timnah to shear his sheep."

14 So she <u>took off</u> her widow's garments,
<u>covered</u> *herself* with a veil
and <u>wrapped</u> herself,
and <u>sat</u> in an open place
which *was* on the way to Timnah;

for she <u>saw</u>   (causal כִּי + *qatal*)
that Shelah <u>was grown</u>,   (כִּי + *qatal*)
and she <u>was</u> not <u>given</u> to him as a wife.   (*w* + x + *qatal*)

15 When Judah <u>saw</u> her,
he <u>thought</u> she *was* a harlot,

because she <u>had covered</u> her face.   (causal כִּי + *qatal*)

16 Then he <u>turned</u> to her by the way,
and <u>said</u>,

"Please let me come in to you";
for he <u>did</u> not <u>know</u> that she *was* his daughter-in-law.   (causal כִּי + *qatal*)
So she <u>said</u>,
"What will you give me, that you may come in to me?"

17 And he <u>said</u>,

"I will send you a young goat from the flock."
And she <u>said</u>,
"Will you give me a pledge till you send it?"

18 Then he <u>said</u>,

"What pledge shall I give you?"
So she <u>said</u>,
"Your signet and cord, and your staff that is in your hand."

Then he <u>gave</u> *them* to her,
and <u>went in</u> to her,
and she <u>conceived</u> by him.

19 So she <u>arose</u>
and <u>went away</u>,
and <u>laid aside</u> her veil
and <u>put on</u> the garments of her widowhood.

20 And Judah <u>sent</u> the young goat by the hand of his friend the Adullamite,
to <u>receive</u> *his* pledge from the woman's hand,
but he <u>did</u> not <u>find</u> her.   (*w* + neg.+ *qatal*; in place of *wayyiqtol*)

21 Then he <u>asked</u> the men of that place,
<u>saying</u>,
"Where is the harlot who was openly by the roadside?"
And they <u>said</u>,
"There was no harlot in this place."

22 And he <u>returned</u> to Judah
and <u>said</u>,
"I cannot find her. Also, the men of the place said there was no harlot in this place."

23 Then Judah <u>said</u>,
"Let her take them for herself, lest we be shamed; for I sent this young goat and you have not found her."

24 And it <u>came to pass</u>, about three months after,
that Judah <u>was told</u>,
<u>saying</u>,
"Tamar your daughter-in-law has played the harlot; furthermore she is with child by harlotry."
So Judah <u>said</u>,
"Bring her out and let her be burned!"

25 When she *was* <u>brought out</u>,   (x + participle)
she <u>sent</u> to her father-in-law,   (*w* + x + *qatal*)
<u>saying</u>,
"By the man to whom these belong, I am with child."
And she <u>said</u>,
"Please determine whose these are—the signet and cord, and staff."

26 So Judah <u>acknowledged</u> *them*
and <u>said</u>,
"She has been more righteous than I, because I did not give her to Shelah my son."
And he never <u>knew</u> her again.   (*w* + neg.+ *qatal*; in place of *wayyiqtol*)

27 Now it <u>came to pass</u>,
at the time for <u>giving birth</u>,   (infinitive)
that behold, twins *were* in her womb. (*hinneh* + nominal clause)

28 And <u>so it was</u>,
when she was <u>giving birth</u>,   (infinitive)
that *the one* <u>put out</u> *his* hand;
and the midwife <u>took</u> a scarlet *thread*
and <u>bound</u> it on his hand,
<u>saying</u>,
"This one came out first."

29 Then it <u>happened</u>,
as he <u>drew back</u> his hand,   (infinitive)

that his brother <u>came out</u> unexpectedly; (*w + hinneh + qatal*)
and she <u>said</u>,
  "How did you break through? This breach be upon you!"
Therefore his name <u>was called</u> Perez.
30 Afterward his brother <u>came out</u> (*w + x + qatal*)
  who had the scarlet *thread* on his hand.
And his name <u>was called</u> Zerah.

Joshua 1 provides another interesting example. When placed in chart form, the main line of Joshua 1 is relatively easy to track (see table A.8).

Table A.8
A Verb Form and Placement Chart of Joshua 1

Reference	Verb Form	Pre-Verb Material	Description
1:1a	וַיְהִי		WI*
1:1b	וַיֹּאמֶר		WI
1:1c	לֵאמֹר		If
1:10a	וַיְצַו		WI
1:10b	לֵאמֹר		If
1:12a	אָמַר	וְלָרֹאוּבֵנִי וְלַגָּדִי וְלַחֲצִי שֵׁבֶט הַמְנַשֶּׁה	w + x + P
1:12b	לֵאמֹר		If
1:16a	וַיַּעֲנוּ		WI
1:16b	לֵאמֹר		If

Basically, the chapter consists of four speeches. After an initial וַיְהִי form, the pattern of the nonquotational material into which these speeches are embedded consists of a *wayyiqtol* form followed by the infinitive form לֵאמֹר. This pattern occurs at three of four points where nonquotational material introduces quotational material. The clear variation is in the announcement of the third speech in 12a, where a perfect verb preceded by pre-slot material (three prepositional phrases, each preceded by a *waw*) occurs instead of a *wayyiqtol* form. Then the infinitive form לֵאמֹר occurs as usual. While this marks or highlights the recipients of the address, it also marks this material as subsidiary to the main storyline. This does not imply the subsequent speech is less important, but rather distinguishes the section in 1:12–15 from 1:16–18. The "answer" in verse 16, then, comes in response to Joshua's "order" to the whole nation in 1:10–11, not simply the words to the Transjordan tribes in 1:12–15.

❀❀❀ 249

Before proceeding, we should note that identifying plot lines (grounding) and marked sections of text can help interpreters either confirm or establish their conclusions about the plot shape of a text. Nicolai Winther-Nielsen, for example, uses his discourse analysis of Joshua 3–4 as the basis for establishing the chapters' "superstructure," what I call plot shape (see table A.9).[55]

Table A.9
The Superstructure of Joshua 3–4

Extent	Content	Superstructure
3:1	March to Jordan	Exposition
3:2–5	Preparatory orders for crossing	Inciting incident
3:6–13	Orders for crossing	Mounting tension
3:14–17	Crossing into water	Climax
4:1–10	Orders for stone collection	Interpeak tension
4:11–14	Crossing in front of people	Lessening tension
4:15–18	Crossing out of water	Resolution
4:19–24	Arrival at Gilgal	Conclusion

Joshua 3:14–17 provides an example of how textlinguistic analysis provides insight in the story's pace. As noted in table A.9, this episode constitutes the first peak in the climax of Joshua 3–4. Table A.10 is a chart of the verb structure of Joshua 3:14–17, which happens to be entirely nonquotational material. I have chosen not to chart participial forms when they have a nominal or an adjectival function. Thus, I have not charted three occurrences of נֹשְׂאֵי ("who bore") in verses 15 and 17 because they have an adjectival function. However, I have charted this same form in verse 14 where it has a verbal function. Likewise, I have not charted the two occurrences of הַיֹּרְדִים ("which were flowing down") in verse 16 because they have an adjectival function.

Table A.10
A Verb Form and Placement Chart of Joshua 3:14–17

Reference	Verb Form	Pre-Verb Material	Description
3:14	וַיְהִי		WI*
3:14	בִּנְסֹעַ		If
3:14	לַעֲבֹר		If

55. Nicolai Winther-Nielsen, "The Miraculous Grammar of Joshua 3–4," in *Biblical Hebrew and Discourse Linguistics*, ed. Robert D. Bergen (Dallas: Summer Institute of Linguistics; Winona Lake, Ind.: Eisenbrauns, 1994), 308.

Reference	Verb Form	Pre-Verb Material	Description
3:14	נֹשְׂאֵי	וְהַכֹּהֲנִים	w + x + Pt
3:15	כְּבוֹא		w + If
3:15	נִטְבְּלוּ	וְרַגְלֵי . . .	w + x + P
3:15	מָלֵא	וְהַיַּרְדֵּן	w + x + P
3:16	וַיַּעַמְדוּ		WI
3:16	קָמוּ		P
3:16	הַרְחֵק		If
3:16	תַּמּוּ	וְהַיֹּרְדִים . . .	w + x + P
3:16	נִכְרָתוּ		P
3:16	עָבְרוּ	וְהָעָם	w + x + P
3:17	וַיַּעַמְדוּ		WI
3:17	הָכֵן		If
3:17	עֹבְרִים	וְכָל־יִשְׂרָאֵל	w + x + Pt
3:17	תַּמּוּ	עַד אֲשֶׁר־	0 + x + P
3:17	לַעֲבֹר		If

Table A.11 is a text layout of the same passage, based on the NKJV.

Table A.11
Text Layout of Joshua 3:14–17

14 So it <u>was</u>,
    when the people <u>set out</u> from their camp
    to <u>cross over</u> the Jordan,
    with the priests <u>bearing</u> the ark of the covenant before the people,
15   and as those who bore the ark <u>came</u> to the Jordan,
    and the feet of the priests who bore the ark <u>dipped</u> in the edge of the water
    (for the Jordan <u>overflows</u> all its banks during the whole time of harvest),
16 that the waters which came down from upstream <u>stood</u> *still,*
    and <u>rose</u> in a heap very far away at Adam, the city that *is* beside Zaretan.
    So the waters that went down into the Sea of the Arabah, the Salt Sea, <u>failed</u>,
    and <u>were cut off</u>;
    and the people <u>crossed over</u> opposite Jericho.
17 Then the priests who bore the ark of the covenant of the LORD <u>stood</u>
    firm on dry ground in the midst of the Jordan;
    and all Israel <u>crossed over</u> on dry ground,
    until all the people <u>had crossed completely over</u> the Jordan.

This discourse analysis of Joshua 3:14–17 helps an interpreter analyze the pace of the story. After an initial וַיְהִי to mark the beginning of the episode (another וַיְהִי form begins a new episode in 4:1), the next six clauses are backgrounded, halting the main line of the action until a *wayyiqtol* form (וַיַּעַמְדוּ) finally appears at the beginning of verse 16. Winther-Nielsen describes the effect of the "miraculous syntax" of the episode: "Several temporal descriptive clauses *in slow motion* describe how the waters suddenly stopped when the feet of the priests were dipped into the water."[56] "And after this major event [indicated by the *wayyiqtol* form וַיַּעַמְדוּ], the story stops completely."[57] Basically, the *wayyiqtol* form is restated by a clause-initial *qatal* (0 + *qatal*). Further backgrounded clauses then provide additional specifics. Finally, another *wayyiqtol* form appears in verse 17 and it, too, is followed by further backgrounded clauses that reiterate what has already been narrated. David Howard makes a similar analysis about the effect of the syntax in 3:14–17 on the pace of the narrative:

> Here the narrative slows to a crawl, so that the reader can savor the wonder of the miracle and view it from as many different perspectives as possible. The author, by writing in this way, affirms God's greatness and power and intervention on his people's behalf. The point is not so much that the people were able to cross over the Jordan, but the *manner* in which they were able to cross: by a glorious and mighty miracle of God.[58]

For Further Reading

If you want to learn more about textlinguistic analysis of Old Testament narratives, you will benefit from a couple sources to which I have already referred. I recommend starting with the work edited by Robert Bergen, *Biblical Hebrew and Discourse Linguistics*. Begin by reading Bergen's own chapter "Evil Spirits and Eccentric Grammar: A Study of the Relationship between Text and Meaning in Hebrew Narrative." Then, read the chapters by van der Merwe, Longacre, Niccacci (two chapters), and Winther-Nielsen. These will provide a good introduction to textlinguistic analysis of Hebrew Narratives.

I also highly recommend Bryan Rocine's grammar *Learning Biblical Hebrew: A New Approach Using Discourse Analysis*. As noted previously, this grammar incorporates the basic concepts of textlinguistic analysis into the study of elementary Hebrew grammar. You can brush up on your Hebrew grammar and learn textlinguistic analysis at the same time.

---

56. Winther-Nielsen, "The Miraculous Grammar of Joshua 3–4," 308 (emphasis added).
57. Ibid., 310.
58. David M. Howard Jr., *Joshua*, New American Commentary, ed. E. Ray Clendenen, vol. 5 (Nashville: Broadman and Holman, 1998), 129.

Chiasmus

Interpreters who work in the Hebrew Bible may also incorporate the search for chiasmus or chiastic structure in their analysis of a story's plot. In chiastic structure, "the same language and style elements are repeated in the second part in reverse order—last matching first and first matching last."[59] Thus, a chiastic pattern is diagrammed as follows:

Sometimes, there is a lone element at the center, on which the pattern turns. In this case, the pattern would be diagrammed as follows:

Israeli scholar Yitzhak Avishur finds that all examples of chiasmus in the Hebrew Bible should be classified into four categories:[60]

1. Chiasmus in a *verse* of prose or poetry.
2. Chiasmus in a *paragraph* of prose and in a *stanza* or *strophe* in poetry.
3. Chiasmus in an *entire work* in prose (a story or a speech) and in poetry (a poem or a speech).
4. Chiasmus in a *literary division* (a cycle of stories, a series of chapters, or a whole biblical book).

What is the value of identifying a chiastic structure? Writers used chiastic structure to limit the boundaries of a section.[61] When a lone item stands at the center of a chiasm, the writer makes it the focal point or turning point.[62]

59. Yitzhak Avishur, *Studies in Biblical Narrative: Style, Structure, and the Ancient Near Eastern Literary Background* (Tel Aviv-Jaffa, Israel: Archaeological Center Publication, 1999), 15.
60. Ibid.
61. Richard Pratt Jr., *He Gave Us Stories: The Bible Student's Guide to Interpreting Old Testament Narratives* (Brentwood, Tenn.: Wolgemuth and Hyatt, 1990), 220.
62. David A. Dorsey, *The Literary Structure of the Old Testament: A Commentary on Genesis–Malachi* (Grand Rapids: Baker, 1999), 31.

David Dorsey cites the body of the book of Judges (chapters 3–16) as an example. In the stories of seven major judges, the rule of Gideon stands at the center and functions as the story's turning point. "Until Gideon's rule, Israel did well under the judges; with Gideon's rule, however, things deteriorated, and from his time to the end of the period, Israel experienced a succession of bad rulers and civil wars" (see table A.12).[63]

Table A.12
The Chiastic Structure of Judges 3–16

a   Othniel and his <u>good wife</u> (3:7–11; cf. 1:11–15)
   b   Ehud and the victory <u>at the Jordan fords</u> (3:12–31)
     c   Deborah: <u>enemy's skull crushed by woman</u> (4:1–5:31)
       d   Gideon: turning point (6:1–8:32)
     c′   Abimelech: <u>judge's skull crushed by woman</u> (8:33–10:5)
   b′   Jephthah and the civil war <u>at the Jordan fords</u> (10:6–12:15)
a′   Samson and his <u>bad wives</u> (13:1–16:31)

One of the more obvious examples of chiasm appears in Genesis 11:1–9. J. P. Fokkelman has convincingly demonstrated that the chiastic structure consists of an "even six pairs, plus the turning-point flanked by them."[64] Verses 1–4 describe what the human beings do. Verses 4–9 then describe what God does. God's intervention in verse 5 forms the turning point of the story (see table A.13).[65]

Unfortunately, identifying chiastic structure is not a simple, objective task like identifying the main storyline, the use of repetition, the occurrence of a type scene, or the crisis in a story. Like trying to identify the sex and size of an elk by the track it leaves in the mud, identifying chiasm is a speculative venture.[66] For this reason, I recommend that most interpreters concentrate on the plot shape and storyline and leave chiasm to the experts. The more technical commentaries as well as David Dorsey's work *The Literary Structure of the Old Testament: A Commentary on Genesis–Malachi*, will identify the major symmetries or chiasms in a story.

63. Ibid., 31, 113–16.
64. J. P. Fokkelman, *Narrative Art in Genesis: Specimens of Stylistic and Structural Analysis* (Amsterdam: Van Gorcum, 1975), 22.
65. Ibid., 23. For an additional discussion of chiasm, see Sidney Greidanus, *The Modern Preacher and the Ancient Text* (Grand Rapids: Eerdmans, 1988), 209–11.
66. "Discussions on chiasmus in the Bible have offered an abundance of all sorts of writings in which there is chiastic repetition; but there is no one rule for all of them" (Avishur, *Studies in Biblical Narrative*, 15).

Table A.13
The Chiastic Structure of Genesis 11:1–9

A כָל הָאָרֶץ שָׂפָה אֶחָת
B שָׁם
C אִישׁ אֶל רֵעֵהוּ
D הָבָה נִלְבְּנָה לְבֵנִים
E נִבְנֶה לָּנוּ
F עִיר וּמִגְדָּל
X וַיֵּרֶד יְהוָה לִרְאֹת
F′ אֶת הָעִיר וְאֶת הַמִּגְדָּל
E′ אֲשֶׁר בָּנוּ בְּנֵי הָאָדָם
D′ הָבָה נָבְלָה
C′ אִישׁ שְׂפַת רֵעֵהוּ
B′ מִשָּׁם
A′ בָּלַל שְׂפַת כָל הָאָרֶץ

A   All the earth had one language (1)
  B   there (2)
    C   one to another (3)
      D   Come, let us make bricks (3)
        E   Let us build for ourselves (4)
          F   a city and a tower (4)
            X   And the Lord came down to see (5)
          F′   the city and the tower (5)
        E′   That the humans built (5)
      D′   Come, let us confuse (7)
    C′   everyone the language of his neighbor (7)
  B′   from there (8)
A′   (confused) the language of the whole earth (9)

Remember, if you possess enough Hebrew language skills to perform the steps described in this appendix, start with these steps. Then finish the process of plot analysis by going through the steps described in chapter 3. As noted in chapter 3, the culmination of plot analysis will be an exegetical outline that showcases the flow of the story.

Appendix B

✾✾✾✾✾

Commentaries on Old Testament Narrative Books

✾✾✾✾✾

Commentaries and studies of specific texts provide an important source of help for interpreters of Old Testament narrative literature. When it comes to selecting commentaries on Old Testament narrative books, Tremper Longman offers solid advice in his *Old Testament Commentary Survey*.[1] Articles on specific Old Testament narrative texts appear in evangelical scholarly journals such as *Bibliotheca Sacra*, *Journal of the Evangelical Theological Society*, and *Trinity Journal*, as well as in mainstream scholarly journals such as *Journal of Biblical Literature*, *Journal for the Study of the Old Testament*, *Vetus Testamentum*, and *Zeitschrift für die alttestamentliche Wissenschaft*. Using *Old Testament Abstracts* will help interpreters track down such articles. Of course, many of the journal articles make their way into full-length books or commentaries. Studies of specific texts also appear in *festschrift* volumes or collections of essays in honor of particular Old Testament scholars, both evangelical and mainstream.

The following list cites commentaries and studies of specific texts that seem to understand the art of Old Testament narrative. That is, these resources reflect an understanding of the literary dimension of narrative texts.

---

1. Tremper Longman III, *Old Testament Commentary Survey* (Grand Rapids: Baker, 1991), 55–95.

Although varied in their purpose and quality, they will all provide some help-ful exegetical insights, and many of them model how to do exegesis in Old Testament narrative texts.

Some comments are in order. First, suggestions appear for each Old Testament book from Genesis through Esther according to the English Bible's or-der of books. The list of suggestions includes Leviticus, Numbers, and Deu-teronomy, although these books consist primarily of legal literature. Even so, they contain some stories, and they make up part of the narrative about the origins of Israel as the people of God. Furthermore, the list of sources under each Old Testament book is preliminary and brief. Still, it will serve as a start-ing point for evangelical interpreters who want help in specific Old Testament narrative books and texts. For detailed publication information, consult the bibliography.

Genesis

John Sailhamer's commentary in volume 2 of *The Expositor's Bible Com-mentary* provides an excellent analysis from a textual approach. Allen Ross's volume *Creation and Blessing* builds on his conviction that "the biblical narra-tives . . . are far more than illustrative stories. They are highly developed and complex narratives that form theological treatises."[2] Ross provides an exposi-tory (central) idea and an expository outline for sixty-four preaching/teaching units in Genesis. These outlines consist of theological statements that are grounded in a sound literary analysis of the text. This is an excellent resource, although Ross's concern to derive the full exposition from the passage occa-sionally leads him to overdo his outlining. Sometimes it seems that he makes theological statements where the text is only relating background informa-tion. J. P. Fokkelman's *Narrative Art in Genesis* is worth consulting, even though it covers only two small units (11:1–9; 28:10–22) and three extended complexes of stories in the Jacob cycle (25–28, 29–31, and 32–35). Gordon Wenham's recent two volumes in the Word Biblical Commentary offer one of the finest evangelical treatments of Genesis. Writing before literary analysis of biblical texts was in vogue, Jewish scholar Umberto Cassuto offers some ex-cellent literary insights in his two volumes on Genesis. Although written from a more critical perspective, the commentaries by Walter Brueggemann and Gerhard von Rad also demonstrate a sensitivity to the literary aspects of the narratives in Genesis. Steven D. Mathewson's study of Genesis 38 in a 1989 issue of *Bibliotheca Sacra* offers an evangelical literary analysis of the Judah-Tamar story.[3]

2. Allen P. Ross, *Creation and Blessing: A Guide to the Study and Exposition of Genesis* (Grand Rapids: Baker, 1988), 13.

3. Steven D. Mathewson, "An Exegetical Study of Genesis 38," *Bibliotheca Sacra* 146 (October–December 1989): 373–92.

Exodus

A good starting point for studying Exodus is Brevard Childs's acclaimed volume in the Old Testament Library series. While Childs does not deny the presence of sources behind the text, he is most interested in the text in its final form and presents a literary analysis for each unit. From an evangelical perspective, Walter Kaiser's remarks in *The Expositor's Bible Commentary* reflect an awareness of how Old Testament narratives work. Umberto Cassuto's commentary on Exodus, like his work on Genesis, shows sensitivity to the literary artistry of the text.

Leviticus

John Sailhamer describes how Leviticus fits into the larger narrative of the Pentateuch in his book *The Pentateuch as Narrative*. For the handful of narrative sections (e.g., 10:1–20; 24:10–23), Gordon Wenham provides helpful insight in *The Book of Leviticus*, a volume in the New International Commentary on the Old Testament.

Numbers

Several works are available on Numbers, but many of them concentrate more on the historical issues than on the literary shape of the book and its narratives. There are a couple of exceptions. Ronald B. Allen demonstrates a good feel for Old Testament narrative in his commentary on Numbers in *The Expositor's Bible Commentary*. Gordon Wenham does the same in his brief volume on Numbers in the Tyndale Old Testament Commentary series.

Deuteronomy

While Deuteronomy possesses more narrative sections than Leviticus, legal materials dominate this final book in the Pentateuch. However, Peter Craigie handles the narrative sections well in *The Book of Deuteronomy*, a volume in the New International Commentary on the Old Testament series.

Joshua

Two evangelical scholars have produced recent commentaries that handle the narratives of Joshua superbly. Richard Hess authored the commentary on Joshua in the Tyndale Old Testament Commentary series, while David Howard has provided the volume on Joshua in the New American Commentary series. Both commentators incorporate some insights from a textlinguistic or discourse analysis approach to the text. Robert Polzin has offered an interesting literary study of Joshua in his volume *Moses and the Deuteronomist*.

Judges

Although his interests are mainly historical critical, Barnabas Lindars notices narrative art in his massive work on Judges 1–5. Unfortunately, his death prevented the completion of subsequent volumes on the remainder of Judges. An outstanding evangelical treatment of Judges appears in the volume on Judges and Ruth by Daniel Block in the New American Commentary series. Evangelical scholar John Stek contributes a model study of Judges 4 in *A Tribute to Gleason Archer*, a collection of essays that includes Stek's "The Bee and the Mountain Goat: A Literary Reading of Judges 4." For another helpful literary study of Judges, see Robert Polzin's volume *Moses and the Deuteronomist*.

Ruth

The leader in the field of commentaries on Ruth is the volume by Robert Hubbard in the New International Commentary on the Old Testament series. Daniel Block's treatment of Ruth is excellent in his volume on Judges and Ruth in The New American Commentary series. Another work worth consulting for its literary analysis is Frederic Bush's volume on Ruth–Esther in the Word Biblical Commentary series. Interpreters will find helpful insights in D. F. Rauber's brief essay on the book of Ruth in *Literary Interpretations of Biblical Narratives*.

Samuel

The price of J. P. Fokkelman's four-volume work *Narrative Art and Poetry in the Books of Samuel* may give you sticker shock. However, Fokkelman's brilliant literary analyses make it worth every dollar. Robert Bergen's work in the New American Commentary series is a fine contribution from an evangelical who has done extensive work in the field of discourse analysis. Ronald Youngblood's treatment of the books of Samuel in *The Expositor's Bible Commentary* deals extensively with historical and cultural issues, but it also offers some good literary insights. Walter Brueggemann's commentary on 1 and 2 Samuel is one of the more creative analyses that pays attention to the literature of the text. Also, Eugene Peterson's *Leap over a Wall: Earthy Spirituality for Everyday Christians*, while not a commentary, provides a superb retelling of and reflection on the David stories. Robert Polzin has offered an insightful literary study of the books of Samuel in his volumes *Samuel and the Deuteronomist* (1 Samuel) and *David and the Deuteronomist* (2 Samuel).

Kings

Writing in the Forms of Old Testament Literature series, B. O. Long holds a low view of the historicity of the text, but his literary analysis is excellent in

1 Kings with an Introduction to Historical Literature. For an evangelical treatment, interpreters can consult the volume by Paul House in the New American Commentary series. Alexander Rofe's volume, *The Prophetical Stories: The Narratives about the Prophets in the Hebrew Bible, Their Literary Types and History,* provides help with some of the prophetical stories involving Elijah and Elisha.

Chronicles

Roddy Braun and Raymond Dillard have provided helpful commentaries on 1 and 2 Chronicles in the Word Biblical Commentary series. J. A. Thompson's volume in the New American Commentary series offers, at times, some good literary insights.

Ezra-Nehemiah

The clear leader in commentaries on Ezra-Nehemiah is the volume in the Word Biblical Commentary series by H. G. M. Williamson, a specialist in postexilic literature.

Esther

Joyce Baldwin does an admirable job on the book of Esther in her commentary in the Tyndale Old Testament Commentary series. Also, William Lasor, David Hubbard, and Frederic Bush offer a helpful analysis of Esther in their *Old Testament Survey: The Message, Form, and Background of the Old Testament,* 2d edition. The analysis includes a detailed chart of the structure of the book. Frederic Bush's volume on Ruth-Esther in the Word Biblical Commentary series covers the same material in more detail.

BIBLIOGRAPHY

❀ ❀ ❀ ❀ ❀

Allen, Ronald B. "Numbers." In *The Expositor's Bible Commentary*, ed. Frank E. Gaebelein, vol. 2. Grand Rapids: Zondervan, 1990.

Alter, Robert. *The Art of Biblical Narrative*. New York: Basic, 1981.

————, and Frank Kermode, eds. *The Literary Guide to the Bible*. Cambridge: Harvard University Press, 1987.

Arthurs, Jeffrey D. "The Implications of the Plot Structure of Biblical Narrative For Homiletics." M.A. thesis, Western Conservative Baptist Seminary, 1987.

————. "Performing the Story." *Preaching* 12 (March-April 1997): 30–35.

Auerbach, Erich. *Mimesis*. Trans. Willard Trask. New York: Doubleday, 1953.

Aurandt, Paul. *Paul Harvey's The Rest of the Story*. New York: Bantam, 1977.

————. *More of Paul Harvey's The Rest of the Story*. New York: Bantam, 1980.

————. *Destiny*. New York: Bantam, 1983.

Avishur, Yitzhak. *Studies in Biblical Narrative: Style, Structure, and the Ancient Near Eastern Literary Background*. Tel Aviv-Jaffa, Israel: Archaeological Center Publication, 1999.

Bailey, Raymond, and James L. Blevins. *Dramatic Monologues: Making the Bible Live*. Nashville: Broadman, 1990.

Baldwin, Joyce G. *Esther: An Introduction and Commentary*. Tyndale Old Testament Commentaries, ed. D. J. Wiseman, vol. 12. Downers Grove, Ill.: InterVarsity, 1984.

Bar-Efrat, Shimon. *Narrative Art in the Bible*. Sheffield: Almond, 1989.

Bergen, Robert, ed. *Biblical Hebrew and Discourse Linguistics*. Dallas: Summer Institute of Linguistics; Winona Lake, Ind.: Eisenbrauns, 1994.

————. "Evil Spirits and Eccentric Grammar: A Study of the Relationship between Text and Meaning in Hebrew Narrative." In *Biblical Hebrew and Discourse Linguistics*, ed. Robert D. Bergen, 320–35. Dallas: Summer Institute of Linguistics; Winona Lake, Ind.: Eisenbrauns, 1994.

————. *1, 2 Samuel*. New American Commentary, ed. E. Ray Clendenen, vol. 7. Nashville: Broadman and Holman, 1996.

Berlin, Adele. *Poetics and Interpretation of Biblical Narrative.* Sheffield: Almond, 1983.

Block, Daniel I. *Judges, Ruth.* New American Commentary, ed. E. Ray Clendenen, vol. 6. Nashville: Broadman and Holman, 1999.

Bodine, Walter R., ed. *Linguistics and Biblical Hebrew.* Winona Lake, Ind.: Eisenbrauns, 1992.

———, ed. *Discourse Analysis of Biblical Literature: What It Is and What It Offers.* Society of Biblical Literature Semeia Studies. Atlanta: Scholars Press, 1995.

———. "Linguistics and Biblical Studies." In *The Anchor Bible Dictionary,* ed. David Noel Freedman, vol. 4, 327–33. New York: Doubleday, 1992.

Borden, Paul. "Preaching from Biblical Narratives." *Expositapes* 3. Denver: Denver Seminary, 1984. Audiocassette.

———. "Is There Really One Big Idea in That Story?" In *The Big Idea of Biblical Preaching,* ed. Keith Willhite and Scott M. Gibson, 67–80. Grand Rapids: Baker, 1998.

Braun, Roddy. *1 Chronicles.* Word Biblical Commentary, vol. 14. Waco: Word, 1986.

Brown, David M. *Dramatic Narrative in Preaching.* Valley Forge, Pa.: Judson, 1981.

Brueggemann, Walter. *Genesis.* Interpretation: A Bible Commentary for Teaching and Preaching, ed. James L. Mays. Louisville: John Knox, 1982.

———. *First and Second Samuel.* Interpretation: A Bible Commentary for Teaching and Preaching, ed. James L. Mays. Louisville: John Knox, 1990.

Buechner, Frederick. *Peculiar Treasures: A Biblical Who's Who.* New York: Harper and Row, 1979.

Busby, Douglas L., Terry A. Armstrong, and Cyril F. Carr. *A Reader's Hebrew-English Lexicon of the Old Testament.* Grand Rapids: Zondervan, 1989.

Bush, Frederic W. *Ruth-Esther.* Word Biblical Commentary, vol. 9. Waco: Word, 1996.

Buttrick, David. *Homiletic: Moves and Structures.* Philadelphia: Fortress, 1987.

Buttry, Daniel L. *First-Person Preaching: Bringing New Life to Biblical Stories.* Valley Forge, Pa.: Judson, 1998.

Campbell, Charles L. "Inductive Preaching." In *Concise Encyclopedia of Preaching,* ed. William H. Willimon and Richard Lischer, 270–72. Louisville: Westminster John Knox, 1995.

———. *Preaching Jesus: New Directions for Homiletics in Hans Frei's Postliberal Theology.* Grand Rapids: Eerdmans, 1997.

Carson, D. A. *The Gospel according to John.* Grand Rapids: Eerdmans, 1991.

———. *The Gagging of God: Christianity Confronts Pluralism.* Grand Rapids: Zondervan, 1996.

Cassuto, Umberto. *Commentary on Genesis,* 2 vols. Trans. Israel Abrahams. Jerusalem: Magnes Press, Hebrew University, 1964.

———. *Commentary on Exodus.* Trans. Israel Abrahams. Jerusalem: Magnes Press, Hebrew University, 1967.

Chapell, Bryan. *Christ-Centered Preaching: Redeeming the Expository Sermon.* Grand Rapids: Baker, 1994.

Childs, Brevard S. *The Book of Exodus.* Old Testament Library. Philadelphia: Fortress, 1974.

Chisholm, Robert B., Jr. *From Exegesis to Exposition: A Practical Guide to Using Biblical Hebrew.* Grand Rapids: Baker, 1998.

Clowney, Edmund P. *Preaching and Biblical Theology.* Grand Rapids: Eerdmans, 1961.

Coats, George W. *Genesis, with an Introduction to Narrative Literature.* The Forms of the Old Testament Literature, ed. Rolf Kneirim and Gene M. Tucker, vol. 1. Grand Rapids: Eerdmans, 1983.

Cobb, Stephen E. "Narrative Preaching: Communicating Biblical Truth through Story." D.Min. thesis, Gordon-Conwell Theological Seminary, 1997.

Coles, Robert. *The Call of Stories: Teaching and the Moral Imagination.* Boston: Houghton Mifflin, 1989.

Cotterell, Peter, and Max Turner. *Linguistics and Biblical Interpretation.* Downers Grove, Ill.: InterVarsity, 1989.

Craddock, Fred B. *As One without Authority.* Nashville: Abingdon, 1971.

———. *Overhearing the Gospel.* Nashville: Abingdon, 1978.

———. *Preaching.* Nashville: Abingdon, 1985.

Craigie, Peter C. *The Book of Deuteronomy.* New International Commentary on the Old Testament. Grand Rapids: Eerdmans, 1976.

Culley, Robert C. *Themes and Variations: A Study of Action in Biblical Narrative.* Society of Biblical Literature Semeia Studies, ed. Edward L. Greenstein. Atlanta: Scholars Press, 1992.

Davis, H. Grady. *Design for Preaching.* Philadelphia: Fortress, 1958.

Dawson, David Allen. *Text-Linguistics and Biblical Hebrew.* Sheffield: Sheffield Academic Press, 1994.

De Beaugrande, Robert, and Wolfgang U. Dressler. *Introduction to Text Linguistics.* London: Longman, 1981.

Den Exter Blokland, A. F. "Clause-Analysis in Biblical Hebrew Narrative—An Explanation and a Manual for Compilation." *Trinity Journal* 11 (spring 1990): 73–102.

Deuel, David C. "Expository Preaching from Old Testament Narrative." In *Rediscovering Expository Preaching,* ed. John MacArthur Jr., 273–87. Dallas: Word, 1992.

Dillard, Raymond B. *2 Chronicles.* Word Biblical Commentary, vol. 15. Waco: Word, 1987.

Dorsey, David A. *The Literary Structure of the Old Testament: A Commentary on Genesis–Malachi.* Grand Rapids: Baker, 1999.

Duduit, Michael. "Theology and Preaching in the 90s: An Interview with R. C. Sproul." *Preaching* 9 (March-April 1994): 19–23.

Ellingsen, Mark. *The Integrity of Biblical Narrative: Story in Theology and Proclamation.* Minneapolis: Fortress, 1990.

Eslinger, Richard L. *Pitfalls in Preaching.* Grand Rapids: Eerdmans, 1996.

Exum, J. Cheryl. *Tragedy and Biblical Narrative: Arrows of the Almighty.* Cambridge: Cambridge University Press, 1992.

Fant, Clyde E. "Memory." In *Concise Encyclopedia of Preaching,* ed. William H. Willimon and Richard Lischer, 330–32. Louisville: Westminster John Knox, 1995.

Fee, Gordon D., and Douglas Stuart. *How to Read the Bible for All Its Worth,* 2d ed. Grand Rapids: Zondervan, 1993.

Fields, Weston W. *Sodom and Gomorrah: History and Motif in Biblical Narrative.* Journal for the Study of the Old Testament Supplement Series, 231, ed. David J. A. Clines and Philip R. Davies. Sheffield: Sheffield Academic Press, 1997.

Fokkelman, J. P. *Narrative Art in Genesis: Specimens of Stylistic and Structural Analysis.* Amsterdam: Van Gorcum, 1975.

―――. *Narrative Art and Poetry in the Books of Samuel: A Full Interpretation Based on Stylistic and Structural Analyses.* Vol. 1, *King David (II Sam. 9–20 and I Kings 1–2).* Assen, The Netherlands: Van Gorcum, 1981.

―――. *Narrative Art and Poetry in the Books of Samuel: A Full Interpretation Based on Stylistic and Structural Analyses.* Vol. 2, *The Crossing Fates (I Sam. 13–31 and II Sam. 1).* Assen, The Netherlands: Van Gorcum, 1986.

―――. *Narrative Art and Poetry in the Books of Samuel: A Full Interpretation Based on Stylistic and Structural Analyses.* Vol. 3, *Throne and City (II Sam. 2–8 and 21–24).* Assen, The Netherlands: Van Gorcum, 1990.

―――. *Narrative Art and Poetry in the Books of Samuel: A Full Interpretation Based on Stylistic and Structural Analyses.* Vol. 4, *Vow and Desire (I Sam. 1–12).* Assen, The Netherlands: Van Gorcum, 1993.

―――. *Reading Biblical Narrative: An Introductory Guide.* Philadephia: Westminster, 1999.

Ford, Kevin Graham. *Jesus for a New Generation: Putting the Gospel in the Language of Xers.* Downers Grove, Ill.: InterVarsity, 1995.

Franklin, Jon. *Writing for Story: Craft Secrets of Dramatic Nonfiction by a Two-Time Pulitzer Prize Winner.* New York: Plume/Penguin, 1986.

Frei, Hans W. *The Eclipse of Biblical Narrative.* New Haven: Yale University Press, 1974.

Frye, Northrop. *The Great Code: The Bible and Literature.* New York: Harcourt Brace, 1982.

Fulgham, Robert. *All I Really Need to Know I Learned in Kindergarten.* New York: Ivy, 1986.

Galli, Mark, and Craig Brian Larson. *Preaching that Connects: Using the Techniques of Journalists to Add Impact to Your Sermons.* Grand Rapids: Zondervan, 1994.

Goldfajn, Tal. *Word Order and Time in Biblical Hebrew Narrative.* Oxford Theological Monographs. Oxford: Clarendon, 1998.

Goldsworthy, Graeme. *Gospel and Kingdom: A Christian's Guide to the Old Testament.* Minneapolis: Winston, 1981.

Grant, Reg, and John Reed. *Telling Stories to Touch the Heart.* Wheaton: Victor, 1990.

Greidanus, Sidney. *The Modern Preacher and the Ancient Text.* Grand Rapids: Eerdmans, 1988.

―――. *Preaching Christ from the Old Testament.* Grand Rapids: Eerdmans, 1999.

Gros Louis, Kenneth R. R., ed. *Literary Interpretations of Biblical Narratives.* Nashville: Abingdon, 1974.

Gunn, David M., and Danna Nolan Fewell. *Narrative in the Hebrew Bible.* Oxford: Oxford University Press, 1993.

Hall, Oakley. *The Art and Craft of Novel Writing.* Cincinnati: Story, 1989.

Harwell, Blake. "Why Story." *Preaching* 13 (March-April 1998): 43–44.

Hemingway, Ernest. *A Farewell to Arms.* New York: Charles Scribner's Sons, 1929.

Henderson, David W. *Culture Shift: Communicating God's Truth to Our Changing World.* Grand Rapids: Baker, 1998.

Herbert, Wray. "The Uses and Abuses of Cinderella." *U.S. News & World Report,* 29 November 1999, 62.

Hercus, John. *David,* 2d ed. Chicago: InterVarsity, 1968.

————. *God Is God: Samson and Other Case Histories from the Book of Judges.* London: Hodder and Stoughton, 1971.

Hess, Richard S. *Joshua: An Introduction and Commentary.* Tyndale Old Testament Commentaries, ed. D. J. Wiseman, vol. 6. Downers Grove, Ill.: InterVarsity, 1996.

Holbert, John C. *Preaching Old Testament: Proclamation and Narrative in the Hebrew Bible.* Nashville: Abingdon, 1991.

House, Paul R. *1, 2 Kings.* New American Commentary, ed. E. Ray Clendenen, vol. 8. Nashville: Broadman and Holman, 1995.

Howard, David M., Jr. *Joshua.* New American Commentary, ed. E. Ray Clendenen, vol. 5. Nashville: Broadman and Holman, 1998.

Hubbard, Robert L., Jr. *The Book of Ruth.* New International Commentary on the Old Testament. Grand Rapids: Eerdmans, 1988.

Jensen, Richard A. *Thinking in Story: Preaching in a Post-Literate Age.* Lima, Ohio: CSS, 1993.

Kaiser, Walter C., Jr. "Exodus." In *The Expositor's Bible Commentary,* ed. Frank E. Gaebelein, vol. 2. Grand Rapids: Zondervan, 1990.

————. "Narrative." In *Cracking Old Testament Codes: A Guide to Interpreting Old Testament Literary Forms,* ed. D. Brent Sandy and Ronald Giese Jr., 69–88. Nashville: Broadman and Holman, 1995.

Keillor, Garrison. *Lake Wobegon Days.* New York: Viking, 1985.

Kelley, Page H. *Biblical Hebrew: An Introductory Grammar.* Grand Rapids: Eerdmans, 1992.

Kitchen, K. A. *The Bible in its World: The Bible and Archaeology Today.* Downers Grove, Ill.: InterVarsity, 1977.

Klein, William W., Craig L. Blomberg, and Robert L. Hubbard Jr. *Introduction to Biblical Interpretation.* Dallas: Word, 1993.

Kort, Wesley A. *Story, Text, and Scripture: Literary Interests in Biblical Narrative.* University Park: Pennsylvania State University Press, 1988.

Kromminga, Carl G. "Remember Lot's Wife: Preaching Old Testament Narrative Texts." *Calvin Theological Journal* 13 (1983): 32–46.

Krondorfer, Bjorn, ed. *Body and Bible: Interpreting and Experiencing Biblical Narratives.* Philadelphia: Trinity, 1992.

Lambdin, Thomas O. *Introduction to Biblical Hebrew.* New York: Charles Scribner's Sons, 1971.

Larsen, David L. *Telling the Old, Old Story: The Art of Narrative Preaching.* Wheaton: Crossway, 1995.

Lasor, William S., David A. Hubbard, and Frederic W. Bush. *Old Testament Survey: The Message, Form, and Background of the Old Testament.* 2d. ed. Grand Rapids: Eerdmans, 1996.

Lewis, Ralph L., and Gregg Lewis. *Inductive Preaching: Helping People Listen.* Westchester, Ill.: Crossway, 1983.

Liefeld, Walter L. *New Testament Exposition: From Text to Sermon.* Grand Rapids: Zondervan, 1984.

Lindars, Barnabas. *Judges 1–5: A New Translation and Commentary.* Ed. A. D. H. Mayes. Edinburgh: Clark, 1997.

Lischer, Richard. "The Limits of Story." *Interpretation* 38 (January 1984): 26–38.

Long, Burke O. *1 Kings with an Introduction to Narrative Literature.* The Forms of the Old Testament Literature, ed. Rolf Kneirim and Gene M. Tucker, vol. 9. Grand Rapids: Eerdmans, 1984.

Long, Jesse C., Jr. "Text Story and Sermon Story in Dialogue: On Preaching Bible Narratives." *Preaching* 12 (January-February 1997): 19–23.

Long, Thomas G. *Preaching and the Literary Forms of the Bible.* Philadelphia: Fortress, 1989.

———. "Form." In *Concise Encyclopedia of Preaching,* ed. William H. Willimon and Richard Lischer, 144–51. Louisville: Westminster John Knox, 1995.

Long, V. Philips. "Toward a Better Theory and Understanding of Old Testament Narrative." *Presbyterian* 13 (1987): 102–9.

———. "The Art of Biblical History." In *Foundations of Contemporary Interpretation,* ed. Moisés Silva. Grand Rapids: Zondervan, 1996.

Longman, Tremper, III. *Literary Approaches to Biblical Interpretation.* Grand Rapids: Zondervan, 1987.

———. *Old Testament Commentary Survey.* Grand Rapids: Baker, 1991.

Lowry, Eugene L. *The Homiletical Plot: The Sermon As Narrative Art Form.* Atlanta: John Knox, 1980.

———. *Doing Time in the Pulpit: The Relationship between Narrative and Preaching.* Nashville: Abingdon, 1985.

———. *How to Preach a Parable: Designs for Narrative Sermons.* Nashville: Abingdon, 1989.

———. "Narrative Preaching." In *Concise Encyclopedia of Preaching,* ed. William H. Willimon and Richard Lischer, 342–44. Louisville: Westminster John Knox, 1995.

———. *The Sermon: Dancing the Edge of Mystery.* Nashville: Abingdon, 1997.

Lubeck, Ray. "'Talking Story': Narrative Thought, Worldviews, and Postmodernism." Paper presented at the national meetings of the Evangelical Theological Society, Orlando, Fla., 20 November 1998.

MacArthur, John, Jr. "Frequently Asked Questions about Expository Preaching." In *Rediscovering Expository Preaching,* ed. John MacArthur Jr., 334–49. Dallas: Word, 1992.

Mager, Robert F. *Preparing Instructional Objectives.* 3d ed. Atlanta: The Center for Effective Performance, 1997.

Maier, Paul L. *Pontius Pilate.* New York: Doubleday, 1968. Reprint, Wheaton: Living Books, 1983.

———. *The Flames of Rome.* New York: Doubleday, 1981. Reprint, New York: Signet, 1982.

Mansoor, Menahem. *Biblical Hebrew Step by Step.* 2d ed. Grand Rapids: Baker, 1980.

———. *Biblical Hebrew Step by Step.* Vol. 2, *Reading from the Book of Genesis.* 3d ed. Grand Rapids: Baker, 1984.

Marais, Jacobus. *Representation in Old Testament Narrative Texts.* Biblical Interpretation Series, ed. R. Alan Culpepper and Rolf Rendtorff, no. 36. Leiden: Brill, 1998.

Mathewson, Steven D. "An Exegetical Study of Genesis 38." *Bibliotheca Sacra* 146 (October–December 1989): 373–92.

———. "The Odd Couple of Sermon Preparation." *Leadership Journal* 15 (spring 1994): 91–93.

———. Review of *Telling The Old, Old Story: The Art of Narrative Preaching,* by David Larsen. *Leadership Journal* 17 (winter 1996): 95.

———. "Guidelines for Understanding and Proclaiming Old Testament Narratives." *Bibliotheca Sacra* 154 (October–December 1997): 410–35.

———. "From B.C. to 11 A.M.: How to Preach an Old Testament Narrative with Accuracy and Power." *Leadership Journal* 18 (fall 1997): 52–56.

Mattingly, Terry. "Star Wars—The Only Parable in Town." *Scripps Howard News Service.* 2 June 1999.

Mawhinney, Bruce. *Preaching with Freshness.* Eugene, Ore.: Harvest House, 1991.

Mayhue, Richard L. "Rediscovering Expository Preaching." In *Rediscovering Expository Preaching,* ed. John MacArthur Jr., 3–21. Dallas: Word, 1992.

McDill, Wayne. *The 12 Essential Skills for Great Preaching.* Nashville: Broadman and Holman, 1999.

McManus, Patrick F. *The Good Samaritan Strikes Again.* New York: Holt, 1992.

Michener, James. *The Source.* New York: Fawcett Crest, 1967.

Miller, Calvin, Paul D. Borden, and Mark Labberton. "Old Testament Narrative." *Preaching Today* 153 (1996). Audiocassette.

Miller, Cynthia L. *The Representation of Speech in Biblical Hebrew Narrative: A Linguistic Analysis.* Harvard Semitic Monographs, ed. Peter Machinist, no. 55. Atlanta: Scholars Press, 1996.

Miscall, Peter D. *The Workings of Old Testament Narrative.* Philadelphia: Fortress, 1983.

———. *1 Samuel: A Literary Reading.* Indiana Studies in Biblical Literature. Bloomington: Indiana University Press, 1986.

Osborne, Grant R. *The Hermeneutical Spiral: A Comprehensive Guide to Biblical Interpretation.* Downers Grove, Ill.: InterVarsity, 1991.

Parker, Simon B. *Stories in Scripture and Inscriptions: Comparative Studies on Narratives in Northwest Semitic Inscriptions and the Hebrew Bible.* Oxford: Oxford University Press, 1997.

Patrick, Dale, and Allen Scult. *Rhetoric and Biblical Interpretation.* Sheffield: Almond, 1990.

Peterson, Eugene. *Working the Angles: The Shape of Pastoral Integrity.* Grand Rapids: Eerdmans, 1987.

———. *Leap over a Wall: Earthy Spirituality for Everyday Christians.* New York: HarperCollins, 1997.

Polzin, Robert. *Moses and the Deuteronomist: A Literary Study of the Deuteronomic History, Part One.* Indiana Studies in Biblical Literature. New York: Seabury, 1980. Reprint, Bloomington: Indiana University Press, 1993.

———. *Samuel and the Deuteronomist: A Literary Study of the Deuteronomic History, Part Two.* Indiana Studies in Biblical Literature. San Francisco: Harper and Row, 1989. Reprint, Bloomington: Indiana University Press, 1993.

————. *David and the Deuteronomist: A Literary Study of the Deuteronomic History, Part Three.* Indiana Studies in Biblical Literature. Bloomington: Indiana University Press, 1993.

Postman, Neil. *Amusing Ourselves to Death.* New York: Penguin, 1985.

Powell, Mark Allan. *What Is Narrative Criticism?* Minneapolis: Fortress Press, 1990.

Pratt, Richard L., Jr. *He Gave Us Stories: The Bible Student's Guide to Interpreting Old Testament Narratives.* Brentwood, Tenn.: Wolgemuth and Hyatt, 1990.

Rad, Gerhard von. *Genesis.* Trans. John H. Marks. London: SCM, 1961.

Rauber, D. F. "The Book of Ruth." In *Literary Interpretations of Biblical Narratives,* ed. Kenneth R. R. Gros Louis, 163–76. Nashville: Abingdon, 1974.

Reed, Jeffrey T. "Discourse Analysis as a New Testament Hermeneutic: A Retrospective and Prospective Appraisal." *Journal of the Evangelical Theological Society* 39 (June 1996): 223–40.

Reigstad, Donald D. "A Narrative Nightmare." *Preaching* 13 (March-April 1998): 37–38.

Rhoads, David, and Donald Michie. *Mark As Story: An Introduction to the Narrative of a Gospel.* Philadelphia: Fortress, 1982.

Robinson, Haddon W. *Biblical Preaching: The Development and Delivery of Expository Messages.* 2d ed. Grand Rapids: Baker, 2001.

————. *Haddon Robinson: Great Preachers, Series 1.* Odyssey Productions Ltd., 1997. Distributed by Gateway Films/Vision Video. Videocassette.

————. "The Heresy of Application." *Leadership Journal* 18 (fall 1997): 20–27.

————. "Preaching Narrative." Unpublished class notes from Pr624, Gordon-Conwell Theological Seminary, 1998.

————, ed. *Biblical Sermons.* Grand Rapids: Baker, 1989.

Rocine, Bryan M. *Learning Biblical Hebrew: A New Approach Using Discourse Analysis.* Macon, Ga.: Smyth and Helwys, 2000.

Rofe, Alexander. *The Prophetical Stories: The Narratives about the Prophets in the Hebrew Bible, Their Literary Types and History.* Jerusalem: Magnes Press, Hebrew University, 1988.

Rose, James O. "The Big Valley." In *Biblical Sermons,* ed. Haddon W. Robinson, 51–67. Grand Rapids: Baker, 1989.

Rosenblatt, Jason P., and Joseph C. Sitterson Jr., eds. *"Not in Heaven": Coherence and Complexity in Biblical Narrative.* Indiana Studies in Biblical Literature. Bloomington: Indiana University Press, 1991.

Ross, Allen. *Creation and Blessing: A Guide to the Study and Exposition of Genesis.* Grand Rapids: Baker, 1988.

————. *Introducing Biblical Hebrew.* Grand Rapids: Baker, 2001.

Ryken, Leland. *The Literature of the Bible.* Grand Rapids: Zondervan, 1974.

————. *How to Read the Bible as Literature.* Grand Rapids: Zondervan, 1984.

————. *Words of Delight: A Literary Introduction to the Bible.* Grand Rapids: Baker, 1987.

Ryken, Leland, and Tremper Longman III. *A Complete Literary Guide to the Bible.* Grand Rapids: Zondervan, 1993.

Sailhamer, John H. "Genesis." In *The Expositor's Bible Commentary,* ed. Frank E. Gaebelein, vol. 2. Grand Rapids: Zondervan, 1990.

———. "A Database Approach to the Analysis of Hebrew Narrative." *MAARAV: A Journal for the Study of the Northwest Semitic Languages and Literatures* 5–6 (spring 1990): 319–35.

———. *The Pentateuch As Narrative.* Grand Rapids: Zondervan, 1992.

———. *Introduction to Old Testament Theology.* Grand Rapids: Zondervan, 1995.

———. "Reading the Bible as a Text." In *Narrative and Comment: Contributions to Discourse Grammar and Biblical Hebrew Presented to Wolfgang Schneider,* ed. Eep Talstra, 162–65. Amsterdam: Societas Hebraica Amstelodamensis, 1995.

Seow, Choon Leong. *A Grammar for Biblical Hebrew.* Nashville: Abingdon, 1987.

Sherwood, Stephen K. *"Had God Not Been on My Side": An Examination of the Narrative Technique of the Story of Jacob and Laban, Genesis 29.1—32.2,* European University Studies Series 23. Frankfurt: Lang, 1990.

Shields, Harry E. "From His Story to Our Story: A Skills Development Manual for Old Testament Narrative Exposition." D.Min. thesis, Trinity Evangelical Divinity School, 1996.

Silva, Moisés. *God, Language, and Scripture: Reading the Bible in the Light of General Linguistics.* Grand Rapids: Zondervan, 1990.

Simon, Ethelyn, Irene Resnikoff, and Linda Motzkin. *The First Hebrew Primer: The Adult Beginner's Path to Biblical Hebrew.* 3d ed., rev. Oakland, Calif.: EKS, 1992.

Sire, James W. *The Universe Next Door.* 3d ed. Downers Grove, Ill.: InterVarsity, 1997.

Ska, Jean Louis. *"Our Fathers Have Told Us": Introduction to the Analysis of Hebrew Narratives.* Roma: Editrice Pontificio Instituto Biblico, 1990.

Stek, John H. "The Bee and the Mountain Goat: A Literary Reading of Judges 4." In *A Tribute to Gleason Archer,* ed. Walter C. Kaiser Jr. and Ronald F. Youngblood, 53–86. Chicago: Moody, 1986.

Sternberg, Meir. *The Poetics of Biblical Narrative: Ideological Literature and the Drama of Reading.* Indiana Studies in Biblical Literature. Bloomington: Indiana University Press, 1985.

Sunukjian, Donald. "My Name Is Harbonah." *Preaching Today* 130 (n.d.) Audiocassette.

———. "A Night in Persia." In *Biblical Sermons,* ed. Haddon W. Robinson, 69–88. Grand Rapids: Baker, 1989.

Talmon, Shemaryahu. "The Presentation of Synchroneity and Simultaneity in Biblical Narrative." In *Studies in Hebrew Narrative Art Throughout the Ages,* Scripta Hierosolymitana, vol. 27, ed. Joseph Heinemann and Samuel Werses, 9–26. Jerusalem: Magnes Press, Hebrew University, 1978.

Taylor, Gardner. "Shaping Sermons by the Shape of Text and Preacher." In *Preaching Biblically: Creating Sermons in the Shape of Scripture.* Ed. Don M. Wardlaw, 137–52. Philadelphia: Westminster, 1983.

Thomas, Robert L. "Current Hermeneutical Trends: Toward Explanation or Obfuscation?" *Journal of the Evangelical Theological Society* 39 (June 1996): 241–56.

Thomas, T. L. "The OT 'Folk Canon' and Christian Education." *Asbury Theological Journal* 42 (1987): 45–62.

Thompson, J. A. *1, 2 Chronicles.* New American Commentary, ed. E. Ray Clendenen, vol. 9. Nashville: Broadman and Holman, 1994.

Thompson, Leonard L. *Introducing Biblical Literature: A More Fantastic Country.* Englewood Cliffs, N.J.: Prentice-Hall, 1978.

van der Merwe, Christo H. J. "Discourse Linguistics and Biblical Hebrew Grammar." In *Biblical Hebrew and Discourse Linguistics,* ed. Robert D. Bergen, 13–49. Dallas: Summer Institute of Linguistics; Winona Lake, Ind.: Eisenbrauns, 1994.

van der Merwe, Christo H. J., Jackie A. Naude, and Jan H. Kroeze. *A Biblical Hebrew Reference Grammar.* Sheffield: Sheffield Academic Press, 2000.

Vanhoozer, Kevin J. *Is There a Meaning in This Text?* Grand Rapids: Zondervan, 1998.

Waltke, Bruce, and M. O'Connor. *An Introduction to Biblical Hebrew Syntax.* Winona Lake, Ind.: Eisenbrauns, 1990.

Wangerin, Walter, Jr. *The Book of God.* Grand Rapids: Zondervan, 1996.

Wardlaw, Don M. "Introduction: The Need for New Shapes." In *Preaching Biblically,* ed. Don M. Wardlaw, 11–25. Philadelphia: Westminster, 1983.

Weingreen, Jacob. *A Practical Grammar for Classical Hebrew.* 2d ed. Oxford: Clarendon, 1959.

Weitzman, Steven. *Song and Story in Biblical Narrative: The History of a Literary Convention in Ancient Israel.* Indiana Studies in Biblical Literature. Bloomington: Indiana University Press, 1997.

Wenham, Gordon J. *The Book of Leviticus.* New International Commentary on the Old Testament. Grand Rapids: Eerdmans, 1979.

———. *Numbers: An Introduction and Commentary.* Tyndale Old Testament Commentaries, ed. D. J. Wiseman, vol. 4. Downers Grove, Ill.: InterVarsity, 1981.

———. *Genesis 1–15.* Word Biblical Commentary, vol. 1. Waco: Word, 1987.

———. *Genesis 16–50.* Word Biblical Commentary, vol. 2. Waco: Word, 1994.

White, Hugh C. *Narration and Discourse in the Book of Genesis.* Cambridge: Cambridge University Press, 1991.

Wiersbe, Warren W. *Preaching and Teaching with Imagination: The Quest for Biblical Ministry.* Wheaton: Victor, 1994.

Williamson, H. G. M. *Ezra, Nehemiah.* Word Biblical Commentary, vol. 16. Waco: Word, 1985.

Wolde, Ellen van, ed. *Narrative Syntax and the Hebrew Bible: Papers of the Tilburg Conference 1996.* Biblical Interpretation Series, ed. R. Alan Culpepper and Rolf Rendtorff, vol. 29. Leiden: Brill, 1997.

Wolf, Herbert M. "Implications of Form Criticism for Old Testament Studies." *Bibliotheca Sacra* 127 (October 1970): 303–6.

Wolterstorff, Nicholas. *Divine Discourse: Philosophical Reflections on the Claim That God Speaks.* Cambridge: Cambridge University Press, 1995.

Woodward, Kenneth L. "Heard Any Good Sermons Lately?" *Newsweek,* 4 March 1996, 50–52.

Woudstra, Martin H. *The Book of Joshua.* New International Commentary on the Old Testament. Grand Rapids: Eerdmans, 1981.

Wright, G. Ernest. *God Who Acts: Biblical Theology as Recital.* London: SCM, 1952.

Wright, N. T. *Christian Origins and the Question of God.* Vol. 1, *The New Testament and the People of God.* Minneapolis: Fortress, 1992.

Youngblood, Ronald F. "1, 2 Samuel." In *The Expositor's Bible Commentary,* ed. Frank E. Gaebelein, vol. 3. Grand Rapids: Zondervan, 1992.

Scripture Index

❀❀❀❀❀

SUBJECT INDEX

✿ ✿ ✿ ✿ ✿

❊ ❊ ❊   277

Steven D. Mathewson serves as senior pastor of Dry Creek Bible Church, Belgrade, Montana, and as an instructor in preaching and Old Testament studies at Montana Bible College, Bozeman, Montana.

Steve earned a bachelor's degree from Multnomah Bible College, a master's degree in Old Testament Language and Exegesis from Western Conservative Baptist Seminary, and a doctoral degree in preaching from Gordon-Conwell Theological Seminary.

Steve's articles have appeared in *Leadership Journal* and *Bibliotheca Sacra*. Also, his sermons have appeared in the *Preaching Today* tape series. He contributed the notes on Numbers 1–14 and Proverbs 21–31 in *The Quest Study Bible* (Zondervan). He also contributed to *Building Church Leaders* (Christianity Today), *Ninety Days in the Word for Business Professionals* (Broadman and Holman), and *101 Devotionals for Christian Leaders* (Tyndale House, forthcoming). *Christianity Today* featured him in the cover story article of its April 7, 1997 issue. The article was titled "Why Pastor Steve Loves His Job."

Steve and his wife, Priscilla, have four children, Erin, Anna, Benjamin, and Luke. When he's not attending his children's athletic events or music concerts, he coaches Little League baseball, roots for the St. Louis Cardinals, and likes to read about and explore sites associated with the Lewis and Clark expedition. He also enjoys fly-fishing, hunting, hiking, camping, reading, and traveling.